AUTONOMY AND INTERVENTION

Parentalism in the Caring Life

JOHN KULTGEN

New York   Oxford
OXFORD UNIVERSITY PRESS
1995

Oxford University Press

Oxford   New York
Athens   Auckland   Bangkok   Bombay
Calcutta   Cape Town   Dar es Salaam   Delhi
Florence   Hong Kong   Istanbul   Karachi
Kuala Lumpur   Madras   Madrid   Melbourne
Mexico City   Nairobi   Paris   Singapore
Taipei   Tokyo   Toronto

and associated companies in
Berlin   Ibadan

Published by Oxford University Press, Inc.,
200 Madison Avenue, New York, New York 10016

Library of Congress Cataloging-in-Publication Data
Kultgen, John H.
Autonomy and intervention: parentalism in the caring life /
John Kultgen.
p.   cm.
Includes bibliographical references and index.
ISBN 0-19-508531-0
1. Respect for persons.   2. Caring.   3. Paternalism—Moral and
ethical aspects.   4. Autonomy (Philosophy).   5. Community life.
6. Involuntary treatment—Moral and ethical aspects.   I. Title.
BJ1533.R42.K85   1995
177'.7—dc20   94-5588

987654321

Printed in the United States of America
on acid-free paper

Für Aline

Preface

While involved in a study of professional ethics some years ago, I found it necessary to investigate paternalism. I was struck not only by the quantity of the literature on the subject—what began as a trickle thirty-five years ago has become a stream and then a flood—but also by its inconclusiveness. Differences among the major camps of ethical theory—deontological, conventionalist, and consequentialist—were to be expected, but I was surprised to find so much disagreement within each camp. The quantity of the literature testifies to the prevalence of paternalistic practices. The disagreements testify to their moral ambiguity.

Paternalism is growing almost as rapidly as exploitation and, indeed, partially in an attempt to repair the ravages of exploitation. Moreover, paternalism and exploitation are becoming more subtle, with refinements in techniques of social control. Nevertheless, the point at which paternalism becomes as harmful as exploitation or neglect is uncertain. There is no consensus or even significant movement toward consensus. Age-old controversies persist about whether, when, and how people should intervene in one another's lives.

Exposure to current disputes over paternalism roused me to reflect on my own attitudes and practices. The ideas presented here very much reflect my personal experience. My analysis begins and ends with the way paternalism appears to me from my position in life, my commitments, and my debts for care received and resentments toward intrusions into my life. My conclusions are based on what I have learned from my achievements in human relations and, even more so, from my failures. Experiences reported by others give me reason to think that mine are representative and hence I am bold to make claims about human beings in general.

What inspires people to act paternalistically—properly and beneficially in some instances, improperly and harmfully in others? What makes the difference? What can be done to foster the desirable kind of paternalism and discourage the undesirable kind? I would be foolish to think that I could answer these questions in such compelling terms as to settled chronic disputes. In this book I do not provide hard and fast rules for how we should act; I do try to provide useful guidelines and pinpoint the places at which guidelines fall silent and the individual must rely on intuition or commitment in deciding what to do. Guidelines leave a great deal to the judgment of the agent contemplating an act. Their looseness inevitably leaves doubts and differences of opinion about specific cases, but they can help one steer a course through the shoals of moral quandary.

While this book proposes guidelines, this is not its sole or even primary purpose. It is designed to throw light on care—on the active life of caring for and taking care of others and oneself. The analysis of care throws light on paternalism, but, more important, the analysis of paternalism throws light on care.

The decision to act paternalistically confronts a person in two circumstances. In the first, an individual strives to take care of someone whom she knows and who she thinks is incapable or unequipped to take care of himself. She may face the option of engaging in what I will call "personal" paternalism if he resists her efforts. In the second, a group, organization, or institution has responsibility for an individual or a subordinate group. The immediate agent is acting as a representative of the custodial group and faces the option of engaging in what I will call "public" paternalism. I shall argue that the moral guidelines for paternalism should be somewhat different for its personal and public forms. Paternalism is treated in some of the literature in terms of moral rights and appropriate rules for the definition and protection of rights. I will argue that this approach tends to improperly apply conceptions appropriate for the public or political realm to the private or personal realm. If public practices are extended uncritically to the private sphere, they impoverish the very relationships they should enrich. Rights and rules have a central place in the efforts of officials to promote public welfare and justice; their role in interactions among individuals is more peripheral. They are indeed useful when mutual commitment and care have broken down or have failed to develop between individuals, but they are out of place where these flourish. Rigid insistence on "my rights" and "the rules" stunts the growth of such relations or chills them when they already exist. In the public sphere, on the other hand, people are unavoidably related more externally, and it is important to see that their rights are protected against one another, though even in this realm more intimate relationships are desirable to the extent that they can be cultivated.

The basic intuition on which this book was founded is that care lies at the core of ideal relationships between people. Rights and rules come into play when caring becomes inoperative or ineffectual when social structures must be erected to prevent illegitimate encroachments by people on one another's proper domain. Even these protective structures should be designed to sustain an environment in which care can flourish, however. It is care alone that binds autonomous agents together into a genuine community: no system of rules, rights, and duties can create a community without mutual caring.

The dynamics of care are involved in the process of self-realization of individuals as well as the creation of community. Every human being has a fundamental interest in becoming a complete person and living a rich life—that is, in self-actualization and self-fulfillment. At the same time, each must be aware of claims of others that impose boundaries on what he may do for and with himself. The strain between self-fulfillment and duty to others is resolved in the fact that the self is realized through relations with others—relations that are expressed, sustained, and nurtured through mutual care. Care requires that each party not only care for the other but open himself to care by the other. Independence, autonomy, and moral dignity, the fruits of self-care, are achieved through interdependence and reciprocity, the fruits of mutual care.

The notion of interdependence calls for an activist and interventionist conception of morality. It rejects the negative conception that moral responsibilities can be met by *not* intervening in the live of others, that doing right consists in *not* violating moral rules. The truly moral life consists in positive acts of care.

Caring acts carry their particular moral hazard: on occasion they require violation of rules which one should scrupulously honor in most of life, and the judgment that a particular occasion is such a one may be quite uncertain. Specifically, in relation to paternalism, one who actively takes care of another runs the risk of encroaching on his autonomy in an improper way or for inadequate reasons. However, the alternative also carries its hazard. One who shuns paternalism altogether may be obeying the rule of respect for autonomy so scrupulously as to neglect fundamental needs of the person in her care. The judgment that autonomy should be respected in a certain way at the sacrifice of other important values in a given case can be as uncertain as the judgment that it needs to be violated.

Since paternalism springs from the care the paternalist has for the recipient and involves taking care of him, Part I of the present study is devoted to an examination of care. It explores its personal dimension and then develops the notion of social structures that nourish personal care in the private sphere and compensate for its weakness in the public sphere by assigning care responsibilities to social roles. It is not my ambition to present a comprehensive argument in favor of care as a basic moral category. I wish rather to trace the implications of a basic existential commitment, to the life of caring, though I will try to place this commitment in common moral traditions and indicate ethical theories with which it is compatible.

In order to determine the place of paternalism in a caring life, it is necessary to be clear about the nature of paternalism as well as the nature of care. My concept, like any standard one, will be based on analogies between parent-child and other human relationships. In Part II I describe the care we expect from parents, propose a definition of paternalism, and develop guidelines that I believe the caring person should follow to ensure that her solicitude for those for whom she cares does not lead her into the wrong paths.

Most authors who write about paternalism condemn it in most of its forms. Their motif is antipaternalism. I agree that there is a prima facie objection to paternalistic actions because they encroach on the autonomy of recipients, but I will argue that the objection can be defeated. This leads me to reject or modify positions proposed by others. In Part III I try to justify my stand by examining the nature and value of autonomy, and in Part IV I argue for a limited antipaternalism based on the value of autonomy in competition with other values. One of the distinctive features of my view is the high value I assign to autonomy without allowing it to trump all other considerations.

The focus of my inquiry to this point will have been on relations between individuals. In the last portion of the work, Part V, I trace implications of my view for public acts, the actions of agents of the state and of professionals insofar as they occupy socially sanctioned roles in the care of other people.

A last remark, which is terminological but important: the paradigm for the human relationships under scrutiny is parenting rather than the more narrow one of fathering (or mothering, for that matter). Hence, I substitute the term *parentalism* for *paternalism* except when quoting others. One reason for this semantic move is that it helps eliminate patriarchal overtones from the concept. Another is that the new term sits more comfortably with the thesis of the key role of care as the foundation of interpersonal relationships and the deemphasis of rules, rights, and duties.

I will repeatedly discuss the relationship between the parentalist and the recipient of his or her care as a two party affair. It is convenient to speak in the singular and to use male or female pronouns for one party and the opposite for the other party. However, this runs the risk of reinforcing stereotypes. If I should refer to the parentalist throughout the book as "he" and the recipient as "she," it might enforce the stereotype that active parties in a relationship are always male and passive parties are always female. On the other hand, if I should refer to the parentalist throughout as "she" and the recipient as "he," it might reinforce the stereotype that caregivers are always female and care receivers male. To avoid gender bias, I adhere to one usage consistently throughout a given chapter (referring to the first party always as "he" and the second party as "she") and then I reverse the usage in the following chapter (referring to the first party always as "she" and the second party as "he").

I wish to thank members of of my graduate seminar in ethical theory, colleagues William Bondeson and especially Paul Weirich, and two anonymous reviewers for helpful comments. I also wish to acknowledge material support from the Graduate Research Council of the University of Missouri at Columbia and help with the mechanics of the manuscript by Mathew Chacko.

Columbia, Missouri   J.K.
June 1994

Contents

I

CARE

The human being is an entity for which its being is at issue in its being. . . . Being toward one's most own potentiality for being means that at any time the human being is always *ahead* of itself in its being. . . . The being of the human being, which is to be-there in the world, thus means to be ahead of itself already, in the way of being-alongside entities in the world. This kind of being fills in the meaning of care. Being alongside things that are ready at hand can be taken as concern and being with the being-with of other human beings, as solicitude.

Martin Heidegger, *Being and Time*

1

The Life of Care

In the middle of a school day, Martha, a widow, age 45, comes home unexpectedly to find her son Craig, 18, smoking marijuana. She already suspects that he has experimented with cocaine, LSD, and other hard drugs. Recently he returned from a party intoxicated and she thinks he has driven the family automobile while drinking.

Until recently, Craig has been a good student and responsive son. He plans to go to college and major in political science with a view to entering law, politics, or public administration. He has been accepted by a university with a strong academic reputation. Martha has some resources, but Craig will need financial aid—a scholarship, a job on campus, perhaps a student loan. Even so, Martha will have to sacrifice.

Martha is distraught that Craig may be into the drug culture and fears that he is losing his capacity and motivation for serious academic work. As she lies in bed at night, she imagines dire possibilities: he might be in an automobile accident; he might be arrested for drugs; he might drop out of school. She suspects he is already entangled in a sexual relationship with a young woman who has no interest in his academic and vocational ambitions.

Martha ponders her alternatives. What should she do? Ideally she would be able to ask Craig exactly how he is living and what he thinks without incurring his resentment. Ideally she could voice her fears, review the dangers of drug addiction and alcoholism, urge on him the importance of deferring commitments until he is ready for a career, discuss the challenges of growing up and how difficult life at college will be, and so on. Ideally Craig would be mature enough to face the facts, sort out his values, and follow her advice—or at least make decisions with full knowledge of the risks. Unfortunately, the reality of the situation falls short of the ideal. A barrier exists between mother and son.

Craig refuses to talk with Martha. She tries to imagine his state of mind. She knows he is aware that she drinks on occasion, has had liaisons with men since his father died, has even tried marijuana at parties a time or two. He may think she is hypocritical. He may feel she is using a double standard to control his life while living her own way. Still, he knows she loves him. Perhaps he thinks she just does not know what she is talking about. He may be telling himself that she grew up before kids knew the exhilaration of being high or stoned at parties and rock concerts, of sex without constraints, of the youth culture that stakes out a world

3

into which passé adults are not admitted. He must be saying, why can't I live my own life? I don't try to tell her what to do, why should she tell me?

Martha thinks about recruiting another adult, perhaps her brother or the school counselor, to speak with Craig. But she realizes she would have to pressure him into it and he might respond even more negatively. He would resent the older generation ganging up on him.

Martha's alternatives are to either let Craig sink or swim or employ punishments and threats. She might cut off his privileges until he shapes up. She might deny him the use of the car or ground him completely. She might withhold his allowance. She could insist that he get a job to keep him out of trouble after school. More drastically, she might threaten to deny him support for college; she might issue an ultimatum that he either get in line or leave home; she might refuse to have any more to do with him until he grows up.

Martha decides to reason with Craig rather than plunge into "tough love." However, her arguments are anything but cool and dispassionate. She pulls out all the emotional stops. She storms and cries. She enlists relatives to counsel and cajole. She lays down strict rules of acceptable behavior and imposes stern penalties to back them up. At the same time, she tries to be supportive in Craig's struggle to grow up—to be tolerant of his lapses and appreciative of his successes. She makes a special effort to make her love and respect for him visible. She hopes at least to keep him out of trouble until he matures. More, she may be able to break through his shell and cause him to weigh soberly all that he has to lose by the style of life with which he is experimenting.

Martha has no assurance that these measures will work, and she has no idea what she will do if they do not. But she cannot see how stronger measures have a better chance, and she cannot just let nature take its course. She can only pray that the basic values she has inculcated in Craig will take over in time.

Is Martha's approach justified? She steers a middle path between purely rational, that is, objective and nonemotional persuasion—a course that would express a total respect for Craig's autonomy—and the most severe coercion at her disposal, financial and emotional denial—an alternative that would largely disregard his autonomy for other goods. In choosing the middle path she encroaches on his autonomy to a limited degree to promote other aspects of his welfare. His autonomy remains a primary concern, but far from her only one.

Martha's choice of a middle path seems right. She is wise to show her emotions and expend such influence as she has over Craig without stint, but in ways that will not break connections and will have a chance of nurturing mature decisions on his part. She is making the best of a bad situation. Of course, she could well be mistaken. She is viewing Craig's life from the perspective of an aging adult for whom youthful experience and a fresh encounter with the world are faded memories. The insights of age may have displaced the insights of youth. Yet we must admire her approach. She takes Craig's thoughts and feelings seriously. She asks herself, do I really know that Craig is involved in all the things I suspect? Have I understood his attitude? She wonders whether she is sufficiently experienced in the world in which he lives to appreciate its satisfactions as well as its dangers: Does she really appreciate the release brought by intoxication, sexual freedom, and, yes, irresponsibility? In any case, can she really say that she knows better than he what is good for him?

In the end she must weigh her doubts against the danger of not intervening and try to do what seems best for Craig. She cannot be wrong in this.

Why 'Care'?

I have attributed Martha's intervention in Craig's affairs to care. She cares for him deeply and tries to take care of him. Let me begin the discussion by explaining why I choose to refer to her motive and that of parentalism in general by 'care' rather than a more traditional word such as 'love,' 'benevolence,' 'sympathy,' or 'compassion.'

'Love' has multiple meanings which interfere with one another and obstruct precise usage. Love can mean tender affection that does not involve action ("She loved him from afar") or practical dedication to another's welfare without affection ("She took care of him out of love, but she didn't like him very much"). If we hear the word used in one sense, we naturally assume the other. We presume, unless alerted otherwise, that a person who is striving to benefit another has affection for him and that tender feelings entail beneficence. Moreover, the two modes of love reinforce one another. If we want people to help each other, we cultivate affection among them. If we want to bind them together by ties of affection, we encourage them to help each other.

It is possible, of course, to make clear our meaning when we speak of love. Thus Kant takes pains to distinguish between "pathological" and "practical" love in order to maintain that only practical love has moral worth:

> It is in this way, undoubtedly, that we should understand those passages of Scripture which command us to love our neighbor and even our enemy, for love as an inclination cannot be commanded. But beneficence from duty, even when no inclination impels it or even when it is opposed by a natural and unconquerable aversion, is practical love, not pathological love; it resides in the will and not in the propensities of feeling, in principles of action and not in tender sympathy; and it alone can be commanded.[1]

Something of the same duality attends the term 'care.' To say that a person cares for another may mean either that she feels affection for him or that she is taking care of him. The latter is the sense that is central in the discussion of parentalism, for the effort to take care of another can spring from sources other than affection such as duty and habit. I will employ the term in this sense in the subsequent discussion. But if the objective is to see that people are taken care of, we should keep in mind that affection is a powerful motive for care and should be cultivated.

There are further difficulties with 'love.' The object of love may be human ("Martha loves Craig") or nonhuman, ranging from the trivial ("Buford loves fritters") to the sublime ("Iris loves philosophy," "Dietrich loves God"). The aim of the lover of a nonhuman object is seldom to benefit it, but rather to possess, consume, enjoy, or contemplate it. Of course the same can be true of love for a person. The lover may want to possess the beloved sexually ("Let's make love"), psychologically ("I want you all to myself"), or physically ("You belong to me; don't go playing around"; "These are *my* children; I will tell them what to do"). This possibility leads Christians to distinguish creative and giving agape from desiring and consuming eros. Scripture is referring to agapistic love when it proclaims, "Everyone who loves is a child of God, but the unloving know nothing of God. For God is love" and commands, "You must love the Lord your God with all your heart and soul and strength" and "You shall love your neighbor as a man like yourself."[2] As Socrates, a partisan of eros, insists, it is incoherent to ascribe to God erotic love with its needs and desires.[3] Hence, Christians conceive the divine love in which humans participate, whether directed toward God or other humans, to be agape.

Care is closer to agape than eros. However, as Diotima says to Socrates, the purpose of eros is "giving birth in beauty, whether in body or in soul."[4] The highest kind of care, like the highest kind of eros, inspires the caregiver to bring the person for whom she cares as close to a state of perfection as he is capable. Thus the case of Martha. Her care involves both agape and eros.

By pairing the second commandment (Love your neighbor) with the first (Love God),[5] Jesus implanted the idea that agapistic love for humans is a response to God's love for us.[6] I do not wish to tie my analysis to problematic, if inspiring, metaphysical claims such as this one, or to that of Plato's that love is a desire for everlasting possession of the Good.[7] However, I do want to appeal to the emotional resonance of these doctrines as reflections of the profound intuition that caring—specifically caring for human beings in a way that is helping, constructive, and creative rather than desirous, possessive, or domineering—is fundamental to being truly human. Moreover, I wish to describe a life that has space for agapistic love, including the mystical form in which the lover loves creatures because she sees what is divine in them and responds to the divine love which she thinks she has received. It is a phenomenon of care, and there must be a place for it in our philosophy. Likewise, I would make a place for people's desire for everlasting possession of the Good.

If the term 'love' is too rich in meaning, too laden with connotations and historical overtones, 'benevolence' is too impoverished. Its advantage is that it suggests practical love without a necessary connection with affection or liking. Like agape, it suggests giving rather than taking. But it is a tepid word. It carries no suggestion of sacrifice and toil. The benevolent person can wish the other well and yet do nothing. Care entails taking care of and becoming careworn. It has an essential dynamic that is missing from benevolence.

'Sympathy' and 'compassion' are also too narrow. They may exist without moving one to measures to relieve the condition that arouses them. Moreover, though in the more obvious cases of parentalism a person intervenes in the life of the other to prevent or rescue him from harm, in other cases the aim is to benefit the person. Compassion may be the motive for the first type of parentalism, but usually not for the second.

Through the story of Martha I have attempted to draw attention to the burdens imposed on a thoughtful and sensitive person by care. Martha agonized over her options in terms of a whole spectrum of considerations: Craig's autonomy, other values at stake for him, the magnitude of the threats to his immediate and long-term welfare, the reliability of her assessment of the threats, the depth of her understanding of what was good for him, her spontaneous feelings, the obligations which her role as mother imposed on her, and the consequences of courses of action for her relationship with him. In attempting to weigh these considerations, she had to survey all the means at her disposal: persuasion, threats, sanctions, and manipulation. Each had its risks and costs. None was easy. The middle way was preferable to the extremes of refraining from intervening out of exaggerated respect for Craig's autonomy and total disregard for it. Autonomy *is* a very important good. Martha held her encroachment on Craig's life to a minimum. By helping him avoid present dangers, she was protecting his future autonomy. But her way did not relieve her of grief and worry. 'Care' appears the best term to capture the motive that leads sincere people into parentalism in its many forms. It implies the will to benefit the other in an active way. The word evokes a network of related usages of the same and cognate terms that will help us explore what is involved in caring.[8]

Care is not only an essential structure of the way we exist, it is at the core of the way we should exist. We should care for and take care of ourselves. We should take care of certain others as we do ourselves. We admire caring and careful people, and we put ourselves into their care. We make self-reliant persons our models for self-care. To be human is to be able to care, to want to care, and to care deeply and widely. The companions of care are commitment, obligation, anxiety, and inevitably failure and guilt. If we really care and take care in our caring, we become careridden. When we endure a lifetime of care, we become careworn. But we also become human. The crow's-feet of care are marks of humanity.

Temptations as well as obligations reveal what we are. The burden of care arouses in us the urge to escape the human condition. We may resent the cost of being human. We become nostalgic for an idyllic state of youth in which we had no cares. We envy carefree people and allow ourselves to grow careless about important matters. But as we do, we sense that we are jeopardizing our humanity, that we are dehumanizing ourselves.

The burdens of care cause us to imagine that happiness consists in pleasure, ease, avoidance of suffering, serenity, contentment—that is, escape from care. But real contentment and lasting satisfaction are only blossoms on the sturdy plant of an existence that reaches maturity through caring and being cared for. They bloom in due season under favorable weather,[9] but happiness is not located in them or in things that make life easy or pleasant. Nor is happiness to be gained once and for all as a secure possession. It must be lived. To live it, we must act it out, and to act it out, we must enmesh ourselves in caring relationships.

Solicitude and the Objectivity of Values

We take care of both things and people. Let us refer to care for people as 'solicitude.' As Heidegger points out, solicitude takes two important forms in relation to the autonomy of the recipient. In the first form, the benefactor leaps in for him. This kind of solicitude takes over that with which he should concern himself and usurps his responsibilities, pushing him out of his position in the human world so that he must disburden himself of cares altogether or take them back as things that have been attended to. Such solicitude dominates the recipient and makes him dependent. If he is not dehumanized, it is because he stubbornly clings to his autonomy in other cares and erects a wall between himself and his would-be benefactor.

The second form of solicitude preserves the autonomy of the recipient:

> [It] does not so much leap in for the Other as *leap ahead* of him in his existentiell potentiality-for-Being, not in order to take away his "care" but rather to give it back to him authentically as such for the first time. This kind of solicitude pertains essentially to authentic care – that is, to the existence of the Other, not to a "*what*" with which he is concerned; it helps the Other to become transparent to himself *in* his care and to become *free for* it.[10]

This solicitude is constructive. It helps the recipient become an authentic human being by taking charge of his own becoming, choosing the cares that form his substance, and thereby creating an identity and meaning for his life. One person helps another achieve authenticity and persevere in being human when she frees him for autonomy by removing obstacles in the way of his effort to carry his burden of care and when she helps him carry that burden without relieving him of responsibility for it.

Here I am using the terms 'human' and 'authentic existence' normatively. I espouse an ethic of self-development and self-fulfillment according to which one of the central aims of life is to become fully human and live in a human way. Moreover, I do not suppose that authenticity is a rare or heroic achievement: it is within the reach of every human being.

If one cares for another and wants to benefit him, one should help him achieve and live an authentic existence even if this collides with his wishes. Some authors who write on parentalism think that respect for autonomy requires us to accede to the wishes of a person, to allow him to live as he chooses, as long as he observes minimal restrictions having to do with the well-being of others. In authentic solicitude, a person seeks to promote the true or objective well-being of the other. If she tries to preserve or enlarge his autonomy, it is because she judges that autonomy is good for him. This is true if she assumes (falsely) that respect for his autonomy requires her to honor what he wishes. It is also true if she forces him to make decisions when he desires irresponsibility.

One who cares for another should realize that autonomy is not the only objective good; other things are good, too. If it is true that the caretaker must respect autonomy, she must weigh it against other goods in deciding what is best for the other person. Therefore, if parentalism of any sort is justified, it must be parentalism that (intelligently and effectively) promotes the optimal balance between autonomy and other objective goods for the recipient. If other sorts of parentalism are not justified, it is because they diminish the sum of both autonomy and other objective goods, not merely because they diminish autonomy.

If a person does not necessarily desire what is objectively good for himself, how is good related to desire? Clearly, without the conative element in our nature—our feeling-desiring-choosing response to objects—not only would nothing *seem* good or bad, nothing would in fact *be* good or bad. I mean by "the good" that which an individual needs to live well. When he is aware that he needs it and has no countervailing desires that stand in the way, it elicits his effort to obtain it. The primary indices of living well are deep and lasting satisfactions with what one has and does. I take for granted that it is part of our nature to strive for such satisfactions and be discontented if we do not enjoy them, even if we get what we consciously want. As Plato says, we strive for what is truly good, not merely what seems good.[11] Appearances deceive. Yet appearances are what we go on in determining what is good just as they are what we have to go on in determining what is real. What we want is good only if we know its true characteristics and their relation to our true needs on the basis of its appearances. Therefore, the good is what we want only when our cognitive-emotive powers are functioning so as to make sense of what we experience.

Unfortunately, we cannot infer the converse. We cannot reason that, since if what we want is good, our powers must be functioning properly; therefore, if our powers are functioning properly, what we want is good. To know what is truly best for ourself might be beyond human ken or at least our own ken. Nevertheless, the fact that a person is rational, informed, balanced in his judgments, and in control of his feelings is clear evidence that what he wants is objectively good for him. Rational desires are the best indices that what is desired is good. Irrational desires are indices that what is desired is not good or not as good as the person thinks. This is true for judgments that an individual makes about himself, though in practice people seldom take evidence about their irrationality to heart and discount their wants on this ground. It is more obvious that irrational wants are for spurious goods in the case of another individual when one contemplates a parentalist act. The desires of the recipient carry greater weight as indices of what is best for him when he is rational, informed, and self-controlled.

Values are objective, and authentic solicitude is directed toward what is objectively good for the beneficiary. However, what is objectively good for an individual is not necessarily objectively good for another. To distinguish two important senses of the "objectivity" of values, let me state two conditional theses and discuss the extent to which their antecedents are true: (a) if a person has a settled makeup that determines which objects would bring him deep and lasting satisfaction and which objects would cause him serious distress and dissatisfaction, then the objects are good and bad for him regardless of what he thinks; (b) if objects bear the same relationships to several people because of similarities in their makeup, then what is good for them is shared even though they disagree because of differences in perceptions or reasoning capacity. The two senses of objectivity are these: (a) a good is objective in the *personal* or *private* sense when and only when, regardless of an individual's preferences, it really would bring her satisfaction by virtue of her makeup. It is an objective fact that the thing is related to her real needs by virtue of its real characteristics; (b) a good is objective in the *interpersonal* or *public* sense when it is really good for different subjects by virtue of commonalities in their makeup.

There are objective *human* goods in the interpersonal sense to the extent that human beings share a common hereditary nature which has been shaped into a common second nature by universal elements of culture. There are interpersonal goods in an intermediate sense when members of a group share hereditary or cultural characteristics that distinguish them from members of other groups.

Are the antecedents of the two conditional statements true? Some things do prove satisfying and others dissatisfying to individuals over the long haul. The predictability of satisfactions for a given person evinces a stability in his needs; the predictability of satisfactions for a group of people evinces commonality in their stable needs. We may conclude that these goods are objective in both senses. Stability and commonality are relative, however. The way in which particular needs are best met and hence the specific character of objective personal goods and their order of importance vary among individuals and shift over time for the individual. Everyone needs nourishment, and so food is an objective human good. But the kind of food best for a given person and whether he should take nourishment at a given time, defer it for another pursuit, or perhaps refuse to eat altogether to serve some cause are variables for individuals and between individuals. Goods are interpersonally objective, but only in respect to their general lineaments in relation to generic human needs. Their modes of realization in the concrete are diverse in the extreme.

The objective relativity of values—the notion that values are relative to the needs of the individual and groups, but objectively so—will be critical when we turn to the forms of parentalism. The parentalist should promote what is objectively good for the subject under her care. What he wants and what is good for other persons are no more than clues to what this is.

Solicitude and Being Human

My solicitude can help or hinder you from existing authentically, depending on whether I recognize that autonomy, cares, and other ingredients of authenticity are important for your objective well-being. But what do my solicitude and its character have to do with *my* authenticity and humanity? If I leap in for you and take your cares from you—if I dehumanize you by transforming you into my dependent, pet, tool, or artifact—I may contribute to your ease and contentment and I may provide you the things you want, but I close the door to the deeper human relationships. I deny myself the companionship of a genuinely human being. If, on the other hand, I extend the proper kind of solicitude, we will interact as authentic human beings and an authentic companionate relationship may emerge. Companionship is as essential to authentic human existence as are autonomy and care. How so?

Each of us is a center of consciousness from which rays of attention radiate to transcendent objects in the world. When we turn away from the world and our involvement in it to reflect on ourselves, we become aware of our otherness from other beings. We become conscious of our existential isolation. We realize that we must rely on ourselves to find meaning and value for our existence. No one can be with us in the intimate way that we are with ourselves. No one can do for us what we must do for ourselves: decide the course of our being. This is a truth that is known in solitude.

If it were the only truth, we would be so separated from the other pools of consciousness in which humans are centered that we would not even be aware of their existence. Yet we *are* aware of it, and this is the poignancy of our isolation. Loneliness is the apprehension of what it is to be human in terms of absence, the absence of other humans. Escape from loneliness and self-transcendence is possible only by truly caring for particular others.

Breaking out of our confinement at the center of our world of phenomena through care, however, does not mean that we are able to assume the position of others in the world or experience their experiences. What it does do is enable us to interact with them, know of their existence, and nourish and be nourished by them. By caring we see others beyond the limits of our thoughts – others who are also afloat in the ocean of being and hear their voices through the noise of our interminable conversation with ourselves. We offer our aid and enlist theirs to find purpose and direction for our journey through life.

Encounters with other persons as persons decenters our world.[12] It provides avenues through which we can enter the worlds of others within the inexhaustible horizon of the common world. This is a world of endless possibilities, for it is by the changes that we work in it that we exercise some control over the future world in which we will be situated. Entry into the realm of possibilities thus provides the context in which we discover potentialities for our own being and the things around us for carrying forward our projects. It emancipates us from our existing self and empowers us to determine our future one. To be human is to be always becoming human. It is to be coming into being in a human way. In this becoming we run ahead in thought of what we are. Hence our existence is a process whose issue is always at issue. We actively participate in the process: we anticipate the future and strive to make it ours. We become what we are by how we choose to act and what happens to us as a consequence.

We choose the future in terms of our understanding of our own potentialities and, since we live in a world of entities whose possibilities are interconnected with our own, we choose in terms of our understanding of the potentialities of those we encounter. In this way our projects imbue every object in our situation with meaning, with values we strive to reach or evade, as ends and means or instruments and obstacles, as opportunities or threats. Life is an unremitting challenge to make something of ourselves and to perfect the things around us as a means to making our lives and our selves what we want them to be.

Because it is always possible to turn attention back from the decisions before us upon our existence and ask ourselves what we are making of life, the meaning of our life as a whole is always at issue. When we take thought, we lay out a plan of life that becomes the horizon for every particular choice. Since our conduct and its consequences may alter the significance of our past and we may adopt new plans of life along the way, the meaning of life as a totality remains at issue until the very end.

'Care' is the name I have chosen to use to designate the structure of human existence insofar as it incorporates this forward-looking and problematic involvement in one's own becoming and that of other beings. To explore the worlds of others and "the" world of intersubjectivity, we must communicate with particular others. We must relate to them as subjects; we cannot just hold them before us as objects or elicit behavior from them as things alongside us in the world. To do so, they must *be* subjects. They must achieve something like authentic self-consciousness. They must shoulder their own burdens of care. To the extent that we rob them of their cares, their eyes become unavailable for us to look at the world from a perspective other than our own. An essential dimension of being human is to be with other humans who are in the world in the same way as we. To exist as humans we must be with others like ourselves, not just alongside them. We must penetrate their consciousness and concern ourselves with what concerns them. We must live in a community based on this kind of communion and communication.

We are social animals and were brought together into groups by our organic needs. But animals held together by instinct and interacting only through animal signs do not compose communities. In communion we discover that we are more than animals, and our modes of interaction become more than devices to satisfy biological needs. True humans compose communities of self-directing persons pursuing together the will-o'-the-wisp of happiness. Such communities are possible only if its members communicate and interact with each other as subjects, and this requires mutual solicitude. To break out of our circle of solitude, we must not merely live among other human beings, we must communicate with individuals who live authentically. Once we locate them, they must make themselves accessible. We must not treat them in a way that takes their humanity from them or causes them to close the door to their subjective life. We must not ignore or manipulate or destroy them in pursuit of our interests. Equally, we must not treat them with the destructive solicitude that leaps in to rob them of their cares. We must treat them with the constructive solicitude that leaps ahead to free them for their cares and nurtures an authentic human existence.

In sum, to become authentic we must contribute to the authenticity of others. Moreover, we need to receive care from them. If we were omniscient, omnipotent, and in total control of our destiny—if we were gods—we would need no help. But we are beset by ignorance, error, and doubt. We are thrown into the world among things that resist our efforts to get what we want and entice us to want what we should not have. Personal identity and self-mastery are goals for lifelong pursuit, not natural endowments or the spoils of a decisive victory. In pursuing them, we need the care of other people. It is as important to open ourselves to the constructive solicitude of others as it is to bestow it upon them.

Social Atomism

Lurking behind many treatments of parentalism is a conception of human nature at odds with the organic conception just advanced. Social atomism pictures moral agents as completely human apart from social relationships. In metaphysical terms, it conceives their relations as external rather than internal to their being: they would be essentially what they are without relationships.

Alasdair MacIntyre maintains that the atomic conception—what he variously calls "the emotive self," "the democratized self," and "the individual" of liberal individualism—has dominated the thought of moralists since the Enlightenment. It depicts moral agency in the following way:

> Everything may be criticized from whatever standpoint the self has adopted, including the self's choice of standpoint to adopt. It is in this capacity of the self to evade any necessary identification with any particular contingent state of affairs that some modern philosophers, both analytical and existentialist, have seen the essence of moral agent. To be a moral agent is, on this view, precisely to be able to stand back from any and every situation in which one is involved, from any and every characteristic that one may possess, and to pass judgment on it from a purely universal and abstract point of view that is totally detached from all social particularity. Anyone and everyone can thus be a moral agent, since it is in the self and not in social roles or practices that moral agency has to be located.[13]

The atomist does not deny the obvious—that human beings are born into relationships and shaped by them—but for him true agents are fully formed, self-conscious, rational, and self-interested beings who freely choose their relationships and hence transcend the ones in which they find themselves and that which their relationships have made of them.

According to the atomist, moral agents define what is right in terms of rules of contract that allow them to pursue their ends without interference to the maximum extent possible for all. These are the rules that rationally self-interested agents would negotiate in a state of nature to make cooperation possible and protect them against those who would interfere. Restrictions on liberty are accepted to make the rules work. The purpose is to enable each person to achieve his own ends, not the ends of those with whom they cooperate, though the observance of the rules by each incidentally benefits the others. The atomist takes no particular wants to be normative, nor does he view particular needs to be so basic that rational people would turn every stone to see that they were filled for themselves and those for whom they care. Thus, crucially, he assigns no conceptual or practical priority to the need to receive and give care.

It is reasonable to imagine that parties to an agreement under the contractarian model would reserve as much autonomy for themselves as would be compatible with having an agreement at all. They would agree not to encroach on the autonomy of others, but they would retain absolute autonomy over actions that affect only themselves. This neat and simple model might work for a society of fully formed, fully rational, and fully self-sufficient social atoms, each knowledgeable about his own needs and so egoistic that his happiness did not lie in the flourishing of any others. The model requires qualifications without end to be useful to real people who find themselves in a network of caring relations in which their interests and powers are intertwined. The precise mixture of norms that would provide real people effective guidance in caring for themselves and others for whom they care must be worked out context by context, not imagined in the abstract, as we will see when we address the issue of parentalism. Social atomism provides the foundation for an absolutist position which resolves the issue by a simple prohibition based on a single right. No parentalism is justified because parentalism by definition encroaches on autonomy in self-regarding matters and such autonomy is an absolute right.

Atomists do not preach indifference or hostility toward one's fellow human beings. They envision a society in which people actively engage in cooperative enterprises and may help those who ask to be helped. But a society cut to their specifications would be inhospitable to energetic solicitude. Let us imagine a society dominated by their ideology. Its members would condemn intervention in one another's lives in the name of autonomy. They would think it their right, even their duty as self-reliant beings, to pursue personal goals independent of care for and care from others. Contractual arrangements would enable them to use and be used by one another, but only to promote their own life plans. Such arrangements would inhibit desirable as well as undesirable solicitude. Its institutions would harden individuals toward one another and encourage each to pursue his own interests with no more than an incidental glance at the needs of others.

Dogmatic condemnation of intervention in the lives of people invites not just indifference and neglect, but mean satisfaction at their misfortunes: "What joy it is, when out at sea the stormwinds are lashing the waters, to gaze from the shore at the heavy stress some other man is enduring! . . . What joy, again, to watch opposing hosts marshalled on the field of battle when you have yourself no part in their peril!"[14] The frigid Epicurean spectator is more offensive than the warm-hearted busybody. Voyeurism of misfortune is the last step to misanthropy and the willful infliction of harm.

Care and Parentalism

The abstract conception of a person as a social atom is directly opposed to the organic conception that recognizes the authentic human being is never fully formed or socially self-contained, but always engaged in a cooperative struggle to become and stay human. The human being is *essentially* enmeshed in concrete caring relationships. The individual's relationships and hence her character as a moral agent are *essentially* historical; they result from her particular process of becoming. No attempt to conceive what she should be or want to have or do, or the rules and institutions she would support if she were fully rational, can be valid if we abstract from these features of her existence.

Recognizing that solicitude is essential to human relationships, we must view the efforts of parentalists sympathetically. If they did not care for those in their care or feel responsibilities toward them, they would not be moved to intervene in their lives. At the same time, they may take cares from them which they should carry and thereby dehumanize them. We must therefore view parentalistic efforts critically. We must maintain an alert ambivalence and be both critically sympathetic and sympathetically critical. We know that the parentalist cares, but we must see whether she is sapping the humanity of the person for whom she cares. We must look closely at the kind of solicitude that is driving her efforts.

More globally, we should be repelled by the prospect of a world of do-gooders and busybodies prying into the affairs of their neighbors and badgering them for their own good. Yet we must sense that a rigid refusal to take the initiative in entering the lives of others, a stern inhibition of all warm impulses to press our wisdom and strength on those for whom we care, freezes care itself. Without active solicitude, society would indeed fulfill the fantasy of the atomist. It would dissolve into a congerie of solitary, self-absorbed individuals plodding toward meaningless ends with scarcely a sidelong glance at the anguish of their fellow travelers.

If we are caring people interested in building a caring society, our stance toward parentalism must be complex. The issues are intricate and subtle. We need guidelines that will not inhibit solicitude, but that will make it constructive. The guidelines I propose in this book sanction a good deal of parentalism, certainly more than that sanctioned by those who imagine people can attain an authentic and satisfying existence without active solicitude from and for others. But the danger that the parentalist will succumb to the kind of solicitude that dominates its recipient demands that we draw boundaries around the forms of justified parentalism carefully and erect strong barriers of conviction to prevent these boundaries from being overstepped.

2

Care and Moral Intuition

Ambivalence toward parentalism may reflect personal experience. Being treated parentalistically inclines us to condemn it. We resent incursions on our autonomy. Enough restrictions are imposed for the protection of others besides ones for our own good. Privacy is precious in a crowded world. We know how much damage people can do who try to help without being attuned to our true needs. We are acutely aware of how "for your own good" can rationalize exploitation and self-interest. No thank you. I'd rather do it myself!

Yet we recall some occasions when we were grateful for unsolicited help and others when we shunted it aside only to rue our stubbornness. We grieve over the self-inflicted harm of friends and bitterly regret that we did not insist on helping. We are proud of occasions when we intervened, though it was not welcome or appreciated at the time. Therefore, we cannot honestly say that aid should be given to others only when they ask for it. Sometimes it should be urged on them.

My feelings beat against one another. I am restive when parentalistic care is directed toward me, but not always. I am uneasy about acting parentalistically toward others, but I do not always refrain. My reactions sanction neither free indulgence, nor total abstinence. But how seriously should they be taken in a rational analysis of this issue?

Parentalism and Moral Experience

Many moralists appeal to what they call "intuition" or "considered judgment" in evaluating norms. They use their intuitions to identify cases as morally prohibited, permitted, or obligatory. They claim that principles which sort cases into the categories in which they intuitively belong are confirmed. They claim that principles which assign cases to categories in which they do not intuitively belong are disconfirmed. They call the confirming cases "examples" of the principles and the disconfirming cases "counterexamples." Confirmed principles are "intuitive" and disconfirmed principles are "counterintuitive." Appeal to intuition is thus presented as an inductivist source and test for principles. Intuitions provide the experiential base from which principles are generalized or tested in a hypothetical and deductive fashion.

16

In science, the objectivity of judgments rests on the ability of competent observers to agree on what is being observed. Disagreements about the way moral intuitions sort out examples and counterexamples of specific principles show that the inductivist approach does not work so well here. Consider Joel Feinberg's basis for dissatisfaction with two extreme positions on legal parentalism (paternalism) and Alan Soble's challenge of it. Feinberg observes:

> Legal paternalism seems to imply that since the state often can know the interests of individual citizens better than the citizens know them themselves, it stands as a permanent guardian of those interests *in loco parentis*. Put in this blunt way, paternalism seems a preposterous doctrine. . . . Yet if we reject paternalism entirely, and deny that a person's own good is *ever* a valid ground for coercing him, we seem to fly in the face both of common sense and our long established customs and laws.

Feinberg rejects the two extremes on the basis of "our intuitions": "The problem is to reconcile somehow our general repugnance for paternalism with the apparent necessity, or at least reasonableness, of some paternalistic regulations. My method of dealing with this problem will not be particularly ideological. Rather, I will try to organize our elementary intuitions by finding a principle that will render them consistent."[1]

This inductive approach works only to the extent that Feinberg's intuitions are accepted as reliable observations of objective facts. Soble questions them: "What Feinberg is proposing here is to formulate a mediating maxim which would qualify paternalism so that the resulting principle will prohibit what he (preanalytically) wants to prohibit—the activities of the sale and use of heroin—and will not prohibit what he does not want to prohibit—the activities of the sale and use of whiskey, cigarettes and fried food."[2] Thus what are "intuitions" (objective insights) for Feinberg are "preanalytical wants" (poorly considered judgments or prejudices) for Soble. The difference is critical: it is reasonable to generalize from concrete insights; it is not reasonable to generalize from prejudices.

Authors who appeal to intuitions typically do not treat them as private possessions. Like Feinberg they assume that normal moral agents intuit things the same way and correctly. Now, no doubt intuitions on which normal, insightful, and mature observers agree are more reliable than those on which they differ among themselves and those of prejudiced people. The literature on parentalism shows that what one intelligent and informed author takes to be common intuitions often seem to another to be shared prejudices. A partisan of a particular moral principle can always dismiss alleged counterexamples as abnormal, uninsightful, or immature.

Despite the disagreements about intuitions, few authors on parentalism explore their logic. One who does is Tom Beauchamp. He points out two obvious difficulties with the appeal to them: we lack clear intuitions about some cases, and the intuitions we do have conflict with those of other people. In "hard-core cases" strong intuitions speak to everyone's satisfaction. In "hard cases" people have conflicting intuitions or no intuitions. Hard cases challenge us to harmonize our intuitions rather than merely devising a rationale for them. Beauchamp's term "harmonize" is misleading: to obtain a harmonious set of intuitions from conflicting ones, some must be altered and with them the principles derived from them; it is not possible to harmonize them as they stand. However, Beauchamp draws the appropriate methodological implication:

> I share the skepticism of those contemporary philosophers who believe that the reliance upon intuition and upon quasi-legal notions such as the "outweighing" of one right or principle by another may ultimately fail to resolve important issues. Also, I am prepared to agree that ethical argument by analysis of examples is not purely descriptive of our common ethical beliefs, and hence is not simply a matter of systematically bringing general intuitions into harmony. Often such argument is revisionary of our ethical beliefs. Examples shock intuition and alter belief.[3]

The harmony of shared intutions may be due to prejudices that have evolved and been transmitted over generations. When this is the case, appealing to "our intuitions" about "core cases" only shows how a principle fits our cultural prejudices. Even consensual intuitions are not the last word in testing principles.

The Nature of Moral Intuition

Despite their unreliability, intuitions are indispensable in the search for moral principles. I shall analyze what they amount to as a first step toward assessing their evidentiary value and in turn explaining how they should be used in evaluating parentalism.

   Moral intuitions do not involve problematic faculties of the human mind, nor are the properties of objects or actions which they disclose non-natural, if we accept that "nature" includes the properties that things possess in relation to our consciousness, desires, volitions, and satisfactions. Accordingly, moral intuitions are not rare occurrences or the province of special persons. However, they can be improved by practice, reflection, and criticism. Hence there is reason to assign greater weight to the intuitions of people who meet certain criteria— people whom we recognize as practically wise—when their intuitions conflict with the intuitions of others.[4]

   Moral intuitions are preanalytic cognitive-emotive responses to concrete actions, qualities of persons, and social arrangements that affect the interests of persons for whom the person with the intuitions cares and toward whom he feels obligations. Thus there is a specifically normative dimension to them, and this dimension is a function of the central role of care in human relations.

   An intuitive response to an action, personal quality, or social arrangement may be either identificational or normative. That is, it may be either a recognition of the object as an instance of a morally relevant category (for example, that an act is sufficiently like parental acts in relevant respects to be parentalistic) or a spontaneous sense of its rightness or wrongness (for example, that the act is unjustified parentalism). These two sorts of intuition function in the concrete as phases of a single mental act. That is, we normally identify an object as an instance of a category and evaluate it according to norms for that category in one seamless response.

When our minds generate intuitions, they function as self-conscious computers. The brain-computer is distinctive in that it is partially conscious of its inputs (the experience or imagination of cases) and outputs (the identification and evaluation of those cases and a disposition to act accordingly). However, it is unaware of the program that generates the outputs from the inputs. The task of the philosopher is to reconstruct programs under the charge "Know thyself"—that is, to formulate the definitions by which her computer identifies cases and the principles by which it sorts them into right and wrong. The two parts of the programs are connected. Definitions specify the variables that trigger valuative responses, and principles specify the values of the variables that determine whether cases are approved or disapproved. Our brains are unique computers in their ability to rewrite their programs to accommodate new considerations—that is, it can reconcile them with principles of an ethical theory or cause them to generate the output that will make the machinery the computer controls (the human body) do as its owner wants upon the input of particular stimuli.

Let me set aside the metaphor of the computer and say directly what must be occurring in moral intuitions if they are to be accepted as evidence for moral principles. In order to identify an action as, for example, parentalistic, we must perceive or imagine empirical properties of the behavior by virtue of which it resembles something that parents typically do. We must also grasp the intention behind the behavior, namely, parental solicitude. In the identificational intuition, we see the act as appropriate to the parental role. Thus we utilize norms even at this stage, including norms for the parent-child relation. Moreover, specific similarities and differences between the parental and parentalistic acts bear on evaluation of the latter. Hence, in moral intuitions of parentalist acts, we sense the applicability of particular norms to the acts by virtue of empirical characteristics they share with the particular parental acts that we single out.

If our intuition not only identifies the act as parentalistic but evaluates it, we must be applying the norm to the act. We must be seeing not only that the norm is applicable, but also what the application reveals about the act. At this point our emotions come into play. Intuitions present acts as attractive or repugnant, as praiseworthy or blameworthy, as things that ought to be enjoined or forbidden. In these guises, the acts attract or repel us, and our conative response is expressed in feelings of approval, toleration, or repugnance. The feelings also express our disposition to perform or shun the acts.

The reference to "norms" in the foregoing characterization of intuitions is overly intellectualistic. To apprehend objects as good or bad, it is not necessary to hold general principles before the mind as abstract templates. Concrete actions, consequences, traits of character, and social structures are intuited as *themselves* good or bad, as possibilities to-be-sought or to-be-done or to-be-evaded or to-be-eschewed. Goodness and badness are phenomenal properties of the object, albeit relational ones. It is a pragmatic question whether and under what circumstances critical consciousness of norms causes one to make better decisions and behave in a better way. Sometimes spontaneous responses are more satisfactory. For example, overanalysis and intellection may be harmful to intimate relationships with those for whom one cares.

When desires are shared, the same things seem good (bad) to different subjects and hence become objects of shared intuitions. This is not to say that the objects are actually good (bad) or that the intuitions are correct. As we have noted, intuitions may be due to the common acculturation of the experiencing subjects and matters of prejudice rather than insight. To explore the notion of critical intuitions, let us consider an example provided by Lansing Pollock.[5] A young man aspires to become an attorney and applies for admission to law school. His father, an influential politician, fears that his grades and LSAT scores will not be adequate. He knows his son vehemently rejects special favors and so secretly uses his connections to ensure the son's admission. The son never learns of this, does well in law school, secures a good position, and prospers in his career. He is happy. His father is happy. Where's the harm?

We sense that there is something wrong about the father's action over and above the injustice done to the person with better credentials who has been bumped from admission. We feel that the son has been betrayed in some way. On reflection we see that the father has violated his autonomy just as surely as if he had browbeat him into accepting help. Our intuition that this is wrong leads us to reflect on the moral equivalence between deception and coercion. We see that the father interfered in the life of another adult in an offensive way. We recognize a significant difference between the action of this father toward his adult son and a good father toward a small child. We would not blame a father for moving to a neighborhood with superior schools to provide educational opportunities for his 5-year-old, nor for asking a friend to provide a summer job for his 11-year-old, but we see that it is wrong to treat a grown son in a similar fashion.

It is our prereflective uneasiness about the case that provokes us to analyze what is wrong. This we do by appealing to general principles. We see that the father undermines the son's autonomy at a decisive moment of his life. We see that the web of deception is as harmful as intimidation; it corrupts what should be one of the most rewarding relationships in life — a son has only one father, and the wrong relation with his father may prevent him from enjoying a filial relationship with other older men. We see that opportunities to enter relationships of mutual respect in which both parties accept each other as masters of their own destiny while still caring for each other are rare. The father is willing to abort a relationship of mutual respect to gain something for his son which *he* has decided is in the son's best interest — and that is wrong.

The example suggests the role intuitions should play in both life decisions and ethical analysis: they should be taken seriously. We always know more than we can say. Our feelings about concrete situations reflect the tacit knowledge at our disposal — factual information, general principles that have served us well in the past, our understanding of the possibilities immanent in the situation. This is knowledge we may not be able to spell out, but that we must not uncouple from our judgments and actions. Our feelings challenge us to reflect on principles, and they provide a check on the results of reflection. We cannot rest in the reflective process until our principles harmonize with our intuitions and our intuitions harmonize with our principles.

Though intuitions are indispensable, they involve fallible mental processes and so cannot be the last word in practical reasoning. Saying this, we should not conclude with MacIntyre that "the introduction of the word 'intuition' by a moral philosopher is always a signal that something has gone badly wrong with an argument."[6] But we should keep in mind that our emotional reactions may reflect mistakes about the facts of a situation or the implications of norms, and the norms that shape our reactions may be ill-considered or products of biased acculturation.

Many intuitions fade when we analyze what they are about. Bernard Gert and Charles Culver imagine a case in which a physician orders a blood transfusion for an unconscious accident victim without regard for his religious convictions.[7] Our initial feelings about the case may be quick and strong, but surely confidence will ebb when we reflect on the issues: the importance of religion to certain individuals and the doctor's commitment to preserve life. Our intuitions may shift as we analyze the case. We may form new ones or not be left with any at all after we have tried out different analytical frameworks.

The vagaries of intuition prove that alone they are not a reliable guide for judgment, action, or reflection. Nevertheless, we cannot do without them. Intuitions that survive reflection and criticism ("postcritical" or simply "critical" intuitions) are a rock-bottom basis for principles. They function much in the way that the educated observations of the skilled investigator function as a basis for scientific generalizations and hypotheses. Just as no observation is sacrosanct in science and yet observations furnish the ultimate ground for knowledge, so no intuition is sacrosanct in moral theory, yet the intuitions of sensitive, reflective, and critical agents are the rock-bottom foundation for principles.

The Dialectic of Intuitions and Ideas

To provide an empirical base for reliable judgments and principles, our intuitions must be extensive and critical. Unfortunately, the stock of personal intuitions available to any human being is limited and unreliable. What can be done to expand and improve the stock?

We have at our disposal our emotive-conative responses both to events in our own lives and to events that we imagine or hear about from others. First-hand experiences are more illuminating because they bring to mind more details of situations that trigger intuitive responses. They engage our entire cognitive, emotive, conative, and behavioral makeup. Our emotional reactions are likely to be representative of our future reactions to similar events.

Unfortunately, the personal experience of people with even the richest of lives is circumscribed. To gain a sense of the variety of human options, moralists supplement their own experience with experiences reported by others and further ones which they conjure up in their imaginations (what Husserl called the "method of imaginative variation" and current philosophers "thought experiments"). Unfortunately the schemata provided by hearsay and imagination engage only part of our makeup, and our responses to them may not be representative of the way we would respond to real events in our own lives. By learning from others and elaborating on what we learn in our imagination, we can expand the range of examples that are the inductive base for our principles, but the price is to make the items in this base more questionable.

The distinction between actual and imaginative intuitions is not sharp. Since we do not reflect on general principles while we are acting, we must dredge up cases from memory. As experiences recede into the past, memories become like imaginings, and feelings about the cases become more like imagined intuitions than actual ones. Furthermore, when we are actually interacting with other people, we are directly acquainted with only one side of the situation, our own. We can only imagine how the other experiences it. If I treat you parentalistically, I experience what it is to perform the parentalist act, but not how it is to receive it. The reverse is the case when you act parentalistically toward me. In both cases I can only imagine what you think and feel.

What precisely must I intuit to judge the goods and harms which my actions will produce for someone for whom I care? I can react intuitively to a total transaction, identify what is going on both sides, and evaluate it in terms of the values of the recipient only if I supplement what I observe with what I imagine. My judgment is determined by my framework of concepts for understanding what I observe and hypothesize. Especially relevant are my conceptions of human nature and the human condition and my beliefs about the particular individual and the particular situation in which I am acting. The reliability of my intuitions, therefore, is a function of the soundness of my settled ideas about the world. This is what opens the door for the possibility of justified parentalism. One who has sounder ideas about the world may be in a position to intuit and know what is best for another with less sound ideas.

Most of the intuitions to which the moralist appeals as examples of his principles or counterexamples of competing principles are imaginative. This is most certainly the case with the examples in this work. To mention a few: I cannot claim to have given blood transfusions to people with strong religious objections; enforced contracts of bondage; educated my children at home in order not to expose them to the secular influence of the public schools; covertly used my influence to gain a place for my child in law school; intervened to prevent a friend from committing suicide or voted to enact protective legislation—nor have I been on the receiving end of these acts. To be sure, I have performed and been subjected to actions that are similar to some of them, but I am forced to extrapolate from personal experience if I am to use the examples to evaluate the many varieties of parentalism. Reliance on the imagination weakens the authority of intuition. It is one thing to argue for a principle by reminding ourselves of personal reactions to real-life situations. It is another to appeal to how we would react to imaginary ones. Still, thought experiments are not without weight because good imaginary cases resemble actual cases which a wide range of people experience. Reasoning by analogy is, after all, our only recourse if we want to generalize to rules and principles.

Let me tie these thoughts together into a summary assessment of the role of intuition in moral reasoning. Intuitions provide the experiential ground on which value questions arise and in terms of which they must be decided. They are the data for moral judgments. An intuition consists of an emotive-conative response to presumed (perceived, imagined, or inferred) features of a concrete action, quality of a person, or social arrangement. There are two phases to the response. The first identifies features of the object as ones that affect the interests of the intuiter or of others in whom he has an interest. Thus the person recognizes the object as an instance of a moral category, that is, something to be valued positively or negatively. The second phase of the intuition is a favorable or unfavorable feeling about the object and disposition to pursue or shun it. The second phase thus consists in the actual assessment of the object as good or bad within its category. The intuitive response is a function of apparent features of the object in relation to apparent interests of persons. It is a function of real features and interests if appearances are veridical. The preconceptions and psychological set of the intuiter can make features seem what they are not, so a person may respond appropriately or inappropriately: he may desire what is good and shun what is bad or desire what is bad and shun what is good. Intuitions, while indispensable for action and reflection, are fallible. The ultimate test of the verity of a person's intuitions is whether they lead him to a satisfying existence, directly through the actions they trigger and indirectly through the beliefs and habits he receives from society and works out for himself by reflecting on moral experience. There are procedures by which one can make intuitions more critical and hence reliable. He must follow these procedures in making concrete decisions if he is to grow morally. He also must follow them if he is to generalize successfully about how he and others should live. An indispensable procedure for moral reflection is to test one's own intuitions against those of others, since one's first-hand experience is limited. To the extent that others share a nature and hence values *and* reflect on their experience critically, analyze it, and communicate the results, he can learn about himself by comparing notes with them. No one achieves much in the way of self-understanding without utilizing the experiences of others. Shared critical intuitions are more likely to be reliable than personal or precritical ones. They are essential to ethical inquiry. However, people share prejudices and misconceptions as well as insights and truths. An imperfect culture instills defective attitudes, harmful habits, and false doctrines. Hence, consensual intuitions no more provide an infallible avenue to truth than do private intuitions. Still, though fallible, they are corrigible by further experience and criticism. We are cursed (or blessed) with singularity. What seems good, what *is* good for each of us, varies considerably from what is good for others. Moreover, as moral agents we must act on our own judgments, not on those of others, even when it is our judgment to adopt the judgment of another or conversely to make a judgment for her. In the last analysis, then, the individual who aspires to the highest level of moral life must be true to his own intuitions once he has reflected on them, compared them with those of others, and rendered them as critical as possible.

Level C Moral Experience

I will turn now to a body of critical intuitions reported by others which confirms my own belief that care informs the higher forms of moral conduct and proper caring involves a concern for both the autonomy of the beneficiary and other objective goods. Lawrence Kohlberg has developed a theory of stages of moral development and an instrument for assessing the stage at which a given individual makes judgments. The theory is relevant to the present discussion in that it projects a conception of the way ethical theory is related to moral experience. Moreover, the studies of Kohlberg and his colleagues record intuitions of the broad range of people.

According to Kohlberg people develop through six stages of moral formation.[8] The highest, Level C, "the postconventional, autonomous or principled level," consists of Stage 5, "the social-contract legalistic orientation," and Stage 6, "the universal-ethical-principle orientation." One is not morally mature until reaching Level C, and only at this level are his intuitions valid. Formal ethical theories reflect the philosopher's intuitions and hence his level of moral development. Stage-5 thinking produces social contract, rule utilitarian, and natural rights theories. Stage-6 thinking produces deontological theories. Kohlberg, in accordance with his own Kantian predelictions, finds Stage-6 thinking more valid than that of Stage 5.

Both stages of Level C involve "a clear effort to define moral values and principles that have validity and application apart from the authority of the groups or persons holding these principles and apart from the individual's own identification with these groups."[9] There is no place provided at either stage for the sensitive, caring attitude I have described. Kohlberg relegates concern for consequences in situ to lower stages of thinking, where they take a crude, physicalistic, and fundamentally egoistic form. The only form of consequentialism at higher levels of thought is abstract rule-utilitarianism. Thus Kohlberg has no place for a Martha agonizing over the consequences of her son's behavior and her intervention in his life. A Kohlbergian test administrator would relegate her concerns to a sub-C level or perhaps find no place at all for them on his developmental map.

Kohlberg claims that people are led to the higher stages of thinking by "processing moral experience" so that movement through the sequence is "not derivative from particular teachings or particular moral ideologies or theories."[10] He attributes moral development to interaction of the (human) organism with the environment in which it learns how to think more effectively. He thus discounts the possibility that the shared intuitions of Level-C persons are the result of acculturation in modes of thought into which modern ethical theories have seeped. (This is a possibility we cannot disregard. Level-C people may intuit cases the way they do because they have been taught to do so by moral training based on Level-C moral theory.)

One of the most searching criticisms of Kohlberg's theory and hence of his test instruments and empirical data comes from his own camp of developmental psychology. It was launched by Carol Gilligan[11] and her mini-school of (mostly) female psychologists. They charge Kohlbergians with systematic gender bias reflecting the patriarchal culture. Gilligan points out that the great majority of subjects studied by Kohlberg and his predecessor Jean Piaget were male. (The centerpiece of Kohlberg's personal research is a study of seventy-five boys every

3 years over a span of 15 years.) Kohlberg, Piaget, and their forebears were males shaped by a male-dominated culture. As a result, their theories and psychological instruments are not attuned to female experience. They interpret the responses of both males and females with the male course of life in mind. They do not provide a place for distinctively female conceptions or, relevant to our purposes, for the intuitions of morally mature women: "Implicitly adopting the male life as the norm, [psychologists] have tried to fashion women out of masculine cloth." Failing to do so, they treat women as deviant, mysterious and in the end inferior. Since as empirical scientists they speak with authority, they contribute to making women "question the normality of their feelings and to alter their judgments in deference to the feelings of others."[12]

The charge is that cultural bias infects not only psychological theory but also the intuitions taken to be foundational for ethical theory. Bias gains entry because of the difficulty of objectivity. Kohlberg bases his "cognitive-structural" approach on "the assumption of phenomenalism,"[13] which takes descriptions of ethical situations in ordinary language by experimental subjects to be an accurate representation of their moral orientation and requires a sympathetic interpretive act on the part of the psychologist to understand what they are saying. The psychologist treats these and other responses of subjects as texts. He must have engaged in the same forms of moral reasoning as they to read the texts correctly. But this means that he may read his own meanings into what they say rather than reading from it what they have in mind.

The subject himself must engage in a hermeneutic act to articulate his own intuitions for the psychologist. He must read the meaning of the things he observes and responds to intuitively, including his own behavior. This presupposition of communication reflects an important logical point: evidential relationships hold between statements, not between raw experience and statements. Strictly speaking, intuitions are not evidence for generalizations; reports of intuitions are. Hence, the subject must articulate to himself how a moral situation appears in order to tell the psychologist—that is, he must read his situation and report what he sees in appropriate language. The language, unfortunately, is borrowed from others and so comes laden with normative judgments.

Gilligan points out that the problem with utilizing the experience of both men and women is that they speak in different voices:

> My research suggests that men and women may speak different languages that they assume are the same, using similar words to encode disparate experiences of self and social relationships. Because these languages share an overlapping moral vocabulary, they contain a propensity for systematic mistranslation, creating misunderstandings which impede communication and limit the potential for cooperation and care in relationships.[14]

A more adequate language incorporating both voices would not only reduce misunderstanding and enable psychologists and moralists to profit from the experiences of both sexes, but also alleviate the confusions which beset women when their meanings are systematically distorted by authority figures such as psychological and philosophical "experts."

Androgynous Moral Intuitions

Let me now describe the content of mature female moral experience as Gilligan reports it. I should say at the outset that I find that experience to resonate with my own. This suggests that, while it is appropriate in some circumstances to view the world through Kohlberg's Stage-5 and Stage-6 glasses, it is a mark of moral development to transcend them. The mature person has moved not only from the child's unthinking conformity to external commands to rules of his own devising, but beyond this to a sensitivity to values that demotes rules to mere guidelines or pointers. This is the case for care. In its higher forms it takes into consideration all of the values at stake for the recipient and seeks creative ways to cultivate them; it does not discharge responsibilities by rule.

Surely Gilligan is right that much of the testimony for this basic truth comes to men from women: mothers and grandmothers, friends and lovers, wives and daughters, female psychologists and philosophers. If the moralist is a man, he should supplement his intuitions with those of women, not just check them against those of other men. The reverse, of course, applies when the moralist is a woman.

Gilligan compares women's and men's experience in two areas: their responses to moral dilemmas and their views of themselves. Subjects' responses to dilemmas involve both judgments about what actors in the cases should do and rationales for these judgments. This means that they involve interpretations which are incipient generalizations. When presented a dilemma, male subjects typically choose one of the actions presented in the description of the case. The most mature subjects justify their choice in terms of the rights of the parties involved, whom they conceive as independent, autonomous, and equal moral agents. In Kohlberg's Heinz dilemma, the options proposed are either to steal or not steal a drug needed by Heinz's wife. If he steals, he disobeys the law and violates the property rights of the druggist. If he refuses to steal, he violates the obligation to help his wife. For many male subjects, the wife's right to life dictates the first choice, regardless of the harm to the druggist and Heinz. For others, doubts about whether the wife has a claim on Heinz under her right to life dictate the second choice. But almost all male subjects choose one or the other option.

Many female subjects simply refuse to accept the options as defined in the dilemma. They search for an alternative that would enable the actor to avoid hurting anyone while meeting the needs of all in a caring way, an alternative that would protect and deepen the social relationships between those involved— Heinz, his wife, the druggist, and perhaps the judge who hears charges against Heinz.

Gilligan generalizes from the intuitive responses of male subjects that their judgments tend to be deontological: a man must do his duty and respect rights, regardless of the consequences. The judgments of females are consequentialist: a woman must avoid hurting others and fortify relationships even if she has to violate rules of justice. Males tend to treat rules as absolute and deduce judgments about cases from them. The judgments of females tend to be contextual; they are prone to bend the rules to deal with the case. "Maturity" for males comes when they adopt rules that seem to them to be universal and impartial rather than self-serving or merely conventional. "Maturity" for females comes with the realization that no rules are absolute.

The typical self-descriptions of males and females, like notions of morality, reflect the positions of the two sexes in society. The traditional demand on men to win a place for themselves in the economic sphere and on women to nurture in the private sphere suggest different concepts of personal responsibility. Gilligan detects two meanings for the term 'responsibility.' Citing the intuitive responses of a male and a female subject, Jake and Amy, she reports:

> Proceeding from a premise of separation but recognizing "you have to live with other people," [Jake] seeks rules to limit interference and thus to minimize hurt. Responsibility in his construction pertains to limitation of action, a restraint of aggression, guided by the recognition that his actions can have effects on others, just as theirs can interfere with him. Thus rules, by limiting interference, make life in community safe, protecting autonomy through reciprocity, extending the same consideration to others and self. . . . To [Amy], responsibility signifies response, an extension rather than a limitation of action. Thus it connotes an act of care rather than the restraint of aggression.

Gilligan observes, "The interplay between these responses is clear in that [Amy], assuming connection, begins to explore the parameters of separation, while [Jake], assuming separation, begins to explore the parameters of connection. But the primacy of separation or connection leads to different images of self and of relationships."[15] Males describe themselves in terms of traits that enable them to hold their own in the world of competition and confrontation. They are threatened by intimacy because relationships make them vulnerable and jeopardize their position in the social hierarchy of ability, the pyramid of accomplishment. Maturity comes when they realize that others have abilities similar to their own and hence deserve respect. Females describe themselves in terms of relationships with others which assure them a place in a web of care and protection. They are threatened by their own achievements, which may separate and isolate them. Maturity comes when they realize both that they are nevertheless responsible for what they do and deserve to receive as well as give care and that morality is not to be equated with self-sacrifice and self-abnegation. Gilligan summarizes her findings in a study of female and male self-images:

> in response to the request to describe themselves, all of the women describe a relationship, depicting their identity *in* the connection of future mother, present wife, adopted child, or past lover. Similarly, the standard of moral judgment that informs their assessment of self is a standard of relationship, an ethic of nurturance, responsibility and care. . . . Although the world of the self that men describe at times includes "people" and "deep attachments," no particular person or relationship is mentioned, nor is the activity of relationship portrayed in the context of self-description. Replacing the women's verbs of attachment are adjectives of separation—"intelligent," "logical," "imaginative," "honest," sometimes even "arrogant" and "cocky." . . . These different perspectives [on

the self] are reflected in two different moral ideologies, since separation is justified by an ethic of rights while attachment is supported by an ethic of care.[16]

Gilligan's message is that women's moral experience is as valid as men's. This, of course, implies that men's experience is also valid and, since the experiences differ, there are limits to the scope of both. Recognition of the complementarity of the two views suggests a higher stage of ethical thinking than either Stage 5 or Stage 6, an androgynous one:

> Development in both sexes would therefore seem to entail an integration of rights and responsibilities through the discovery of the complementarity of these disparate views. For women, the integration of rights and responsibilities takes place through an understanding of the psychological logic of relationships. This understanding tempers the self-destructive potential of a self-critical morality by asserting the need of all persons for care. For men, the recognition through experience of the need for more active responsibility in taking care corrects the potential indifference of a morality of noninterference and turns attention from the logic to the consequences of choice. . . . In the development of a postconventional ethical understanding women come to see the violence inherent in inequality, while men come to see the limitations of a conception of justice blinded to the differences in human life.[17]

As far as content goes, the androgynous point of view involves seeing (contrary to the male bias) that autonomy is achieved and expressed through caring interdependence with other people. It also involves seeing (contrary to the female bias) that caring interdependence is nurtured and realized by autonomous beings who insist on their own right to receive care as well as an obligation to give it. It thus involves a reconciliation of the two truths: "[W]e know ourselves as separate only insofar as we live in connection with others, and . . . we experience relationship only insofar as we differentiate other from self."[18]

To achieve a synthesis in either concrete thinking or an abstract ethical theory, one must be able to assume the point of view of the opposite sex, as well as that of one's own. The difficulty of achieving the higher, androgynous level of moral maturity may be easing as women enter the public world of economic and political life and men assume traditional caring responsibilities. This should enrich the life experiences of both sexes and make it easier for each to enter the perspective of the other. And of course both sexes have experience in caring for others and in adjudicating conflicting rights—notably men as caretakers in the role of father, and women as adjudicators in the role of mother. Thus, none of us is totally unfamiliar with intuitions that reflect either the morality of care or the morality of justice, though we often need to be reminded of one or the other by comparing notes with other sensitive moral agents. Particularly important to overcome gender bias is for men to talk to women and women to talk to men. When they do so, I believe that the importance of caring will come to the fore. It is possible to ignore the subjective life of others when treating them justly and respecting their rights, but one must enter into their subjective experience to communicate with them and one must care for them to enter into their experience in any adequate way.

The obstacles to the project suggested here are formidable. One is Gilligan's "different voice" phenomenon, the tendency of men to lose sight of care when viewing moral matters in terms of justice and women to lose sight of justice when viewing them in terms of care. How then can one keep the intuitive data of both sorts in mind when seeking a synthesis of the lessons to be learned from both? The resolution, I believe, is to be found in guidelines that instruct us what to focus on in particular contexts. The guidelines must be developed on the basis of the concept of care rather than justice. Enlightened care tells us when to focus on the needs of those immediately before us and the relationships we should nurture with them and when to focus on rules and rights without regard for immediate consequences. Concern for rights does not tell us when to forget about rules and rights and seek only to take care of the other. Caring, on the other hand, instructs us to pay proper attention to rules and rights where they are needed to implement care.

3

Care and Morality

Care is too important to be left to the vicissitudes of family affiliation and friendship. For there to be genuine community among any sizable group of people, solicitude must be a routine feature of daily intercourse. Since natural bonds of affection do not suffice, the group must cultivate caring relationships in a systematic way. Though no large society has ever aroused a *wholehearted* commitment to taking care of one another among *all* of its members, lesser groups—well-favored communes, brotherhoods and sisterhoods, families—have approximated the ideal. Such triumphs of care throw into relief the central place of social forms in developing solicitude.

No one has the wisdom or power to create a comprehensive set of caring institutions for a society *ab ovo*; progress comes through piecemeal changes in practices and customary norms. But a utopian vision of the caring society can precipitate parameters for realistic efforts to improve them—to promote caring attitudes of the proper sort, discipline attitudes that cause people to care improperly, and discourage those that cause them not to care at all.

The Infrastructure of Care

By *infrastructure* I will mean the complex of institutions, organizations, practices, and shared beliefs by which a society nurtures and guides mutual care among its members. It encourages solicitude, teaches people how to implement it, and provides outlets for doing so.

In a good society the infrastructure is coherent, permeates all social relationships, and creates something like a true community. Attitudes from each sphere of life tend to spill over into other spheres. Care that a person experiences at home makes her more solicitous in dealing with people at work. Hostility, abuse, indifference, or callousness outside of the home makes her less responsive to those near and dear. It is important, therefore, that institutions of society be coordinated. The infrastructure of care incorporates all institutions, not just those in which care is a focus of concern, such as home, school, church, and medical facility. Economic, political, and recreational organizations and practices also have a role to play. Each has mechanisms to socialize its members to discharge institutional roles, and these are not neutral to moral values. They encourage either solicitude or indifference or abuse as a feature of role performance. It is vital that socialization into every institution encourage solicitude if the ties of community are to be sustained in the larger society.

Morality is the glue that holds the infrastructure together. By *morality* I will mean the functional mores of a society, the shared beliefs about how individuals should live their lives and especially how people should treat one another. We may say that morality is the moral code that has currency in a community,[1] but "code" and "currency" should not be taken to mean that morality must be codified, uncontroverted in its particulars, or universally followed. Moralities are loose collections of ideas and maxims in terms of which people think about the purpose of their existence and the good of their community and the best way to achieve these. To the extent that a morality has currency, it defines the art and guides the practice of the good life by members of the community. To the extent that it is sound, it equips its disciples with beliefs and skills to become authentically human through freely chosen actions and enjoy the satisfactions that bring happiness to the extent that fortune allows.

Morality *simpliciter* must be distinguished from *rational morality*, the norms at which one would arrive were he to completely understand human nature and the human condition and determine how humans should live to fulfill their nature in the circumstances in which they find themselves. It is the body of beliefs which the philosophical moralist seeks to articulate. If he finds rational norms already incorporated in the mores of his society, his tasks is to analyze ordinary morality. If ordinary morality misses the mark, his task is to devise a better alternative.[2] In practice, these enterprises prove to be complementary. To analyze is to make explicit, expose to criticism, and invite defense or reform. To conceive an ideal alternative is to provide a template for determining what should be preserved and what changed. This book aspires to do something of both. To the extent that my intuitions are shaped by my culture and moral traditions, it is analytic and apologetic. To the extent that I transcend inherited prejudices on the basis of my life experience, critical thought, and the testimony of others, it is constructive— conservative in some particulars and reformist in others.

I shall refer to the beliefs of the individual (whether shared or idiosyncratic and whether the product of impulse, unthinking habit, or critical reflection) as one's *personal morality*. It is shaped by the morality of the community and, to the extent the person is reflective, by considerations of rational morality. One of the basic moral decisions is whether to follow the norms of common morality and support its practices by encouragement and example. Within my scheme, a person should do this to the extent that common morality and its infrastructure nourish care, but not if they induce hostile and destructive attitudes. Solicitous for the welfare of others, the moral person will support social arrangements that secure care for them when she is unable to provide it herself and vigorously oppose them when they pit people against one another. Social action, in other words, is an integral part of the life of care and is guided by the same objectives.

What I shall refer to as the *institution of morality* embraces not only common mores, but the practices of special organizations, associations, and affiliations insofar as these inculcate moral values and provide outlets for moral action. The influence of the institution of morality is pervasive: a sound morality creates caring persons who discharge their cares intelligently and sensitively. A defective morality produces defective persons. Ordinary morality produces ordinary persons—people such as you, me, and our neighbors, who have virtues but are not perfect.

Since happiness presupposes wholeness achieved through mutual care of the sort that respects autonomy, the institution of morality in a caring society engenders efforts on the part of all to promote the happiness of each without imposing any individual's form or conception of happiness on the rest. To be whole and happy, each has to carry his burdens his own way. At the same time, he must be sustained by the solicitude of others mobilized, focused, and made effective by moral institutions.

Among the ways in which the completely caring society would be ideal is that it would be a completely voluntary one. The satisfactions that its members enjoy would give each a reason to accept the way others intervene in their lives. Not being omnipotent, its members would not be able to win the struggles of life without help. Not being omniscient, they would not always understand the help they received. But they would be patient with the caring mistakes of others and self-forgiving toward their own. Enlightened as to the true meaning of care, they would be grateful for the environment of mutual involvement and solicitude which their institutions provide. They would not just accept its constraints as a necessary price for its protection; they would be intensely loyal to it and they would do everything they could to make it work and perfect its institutions. They would look on its norms as their own, as extensions of their will, even when it denied them things they wanted.

In sum, the authentic life is not lived in solitude; the authentic person is actively engaged in the affairs of the community. She must not only practice solicitude toward those with whom she deals personally, she must also support institutions that affect the lives of a multitude of strangers. This imposes two fundamental social obligations on her: she must follow her personal morality in discharging institutional responsibilities, and she must help perfect the institutional structure of society to ensure that the expectations it imposes on her and others are as supportive of caring as possible.

The Pragmatics of Norms

This book is written from the abstract moral point of view according to which all members of the community are given equal consideration, as opposed to the points of view of prudence and special loyalties that give priority to the interests of the agent or members of groups with whom the agent has special affiliations. Conscience speaks in the guise of moral intuitions, as described in the preceding Chapter. Normally it reflects commitments dictated by the moral point of view, which in some sense should be the same for everyone, in some blend with those dictated by prudence and loyalty, which necessarily vary from person to person. This book is designed to formulate moral guidelines which the individual can incorporate into her conscience in such a form as to allow due attention to prudence and loyalty.

Moral norms take many forms, including ideals, goals, rules, and guidelines. *Rules* are formulas prescribing what one should do in particular situations. An ideal system or perfect code would divide all situations into exclusive categories and leave no doubt what one should do in each situation. The advantages of consensual rules are several. They provide the individual an objective basis to determine what is "right." They provide a common court of appeal by which the group can resolve disputes and assign praise or blame. They enable the individual to anticipate whether her conduct will meet with general approval.

Rules cannot be the last word for conduct. To see this we need only reflect on ordinary experience. When we have lively solicitude for one another, we do not follow rules or even reflect on what the rules may be, neither those of common morality conveyed by custom nor those codified by institutions nor any that we devise for ourselves. Care has different sources. Solicitude springs spontaneously from the heart, that is, from character, moral intuitions, and sentiments. The ways we implement solicitude are governed by habits and practices which speak as good sense and conscience. Concepts of right and wrong and formal rules usually come into play when something is amiss or deficient in human relationships. When authentic interaction and communal spirit falter or fail to evolve, actions that should flow spontaneously must be enjoined and directed. Rules and sanctions must be brought into play. While these are second-best measures, they tend to become permanent features of the social environment and stand ready for use. We find ourselves falling back on them all too frequently. They attest to the chronic failure of human beings to realize their nature and society to realize its essence as a true community.

Real societies are not composed of fully developed and completely caring people. People who do care must deal with many who do not. Solicitude competes with avarice, jealousy, and cruelty. The part of the infrastructure that nurtures mutual solicitude in a positive way must be complemented with and balanced against another part that restrains wrongdoers. Rules prohibiting wrongful behavior with a certain rigor and strictness are particularly in place in this context. Only by imposing and following them is it possible for people of ordinary good will to clear a space in which they can take care of one another without heroic virtue and undue sacrifice.

Guidelines, in contrast to rules, do not specify exactly what one must do in a given situation. Rather, they indicate the factors the agent must take into consideration. They formulate the variables the values of which must be assessed in making a decision. They therefore leave much to the judgment of the agent. They are less likely than strict rules to lead to agreement on what to do, even among those who accept them; by the same token, they lack the rigidity of rules and allow a more flexible response to the exigencies of the situation. They have the further, and critical, advantage that there can be guidelines telling agents when to follow a rule and when to disregard it for other rules or norms of other sorts.

What all of this amounts to is that moral norms are pragmatic instrumentalities rather than absolute commands. Their utility lies in cultivating solicitude and compensating for its failures. They must not themselves be allowed to interfere with solicitude. They do so when they are absolutized, when the superstition arises that some norms have authority in themselves or because of their source in tradition, revelation, or pure reason. They do so when people assume that there is nobility in following principles in exceptional circumstances just because they hold in ordinary ones, in particular, that it is a measure of strength to adhere to them stubbornly at the cost of caring relationships.

The ordinary morality of the community is accepted in different ways by different people. For the wise, it is a repository of flexible guidelines ("When X, take Y into account"). For the moralistic, it is an oracle that issues absolute commands without reference to context ("Thou shalt do A"). Philosophical apologists for absolutism seek to capture the essential content of morality in categorical imperatives.[3] Such imperatives of necessity would have to be negative ("Never . . .", "Act only in such a way that . . .") since one cannot always be *doing* particular things, one can only *not* be doing them.

Absolute rules simply do not work for a being who is striving to live authentically. Life is always subject to positive exigencies of care. The individual finds herself thrown into existence at a particular place and time in a particular network of relationships with people and things. She does not choose the world in which she must live; she can only choose how to act in it and what to modify from the present moment on. What is right for her is a function of her situation here and now and cannot be specified exhaustively by a set of rules. Concrete circumstances bestow on her becoming a unique historical and biographical character which devolves on the particular norms and strategies for living which she adopts.

However, since there is a great deal of commonality in the worlds of different people, as discussed in Chapter 1, it is possible to formulate standards for the guidance of life in general terms. Certain things are basic to human nature and the human condition—notably care and what is necessary for care. It is useful to formulate ultimate or first principles to direct attention to those basics, and it is useful to derive guidelines from principles for typical situations in life, as long as we remember that principles and guidelines are signposts or reminders. They help us take into account what must be taken into account in the pursuit of a good life; they in no way relieve us of the burden of careful judgment that sometimes forces us to transcend the whole fabric of general truths to fulfill special demands of care in the flux of concrete relations with particular things and people.

In view of these considerations, the norms for parentalism that I will propose in the following chapters are flexible. They are guidelines, not rules, though incidentally they help us determine when it is desirable to formulate strict rules and when to codify and adhere to them. Since there is a place in life for rules, let us now turn to the kind of rules that are relevant to parentalism.

Rules for Rights

Personal morality should provide us guidelines about how to act in recurrent situations, and these guidelines should be flexible enough to sanction exceptions on intuitive grounds when this is demanded by sensitive caring. On the other hand, guidelines should tell us when strict adherence to rules have a point. Specifically, they are valuable in institutions that regulate external and routinized relations among people. One important kind of rule assigns rights. Since many forms of antiparentalism in the philosophical literature appeal to the right to autonomy, we need to consider when and how rules for rights should be incorporated into the institution of morality. The contextual concept of rights advanced here is inspired by Mill, but it is developed in terms of distinctions drawn from current literature.

Rights[4] are claims sanctioned by rules to performances by others which affect the claimant's interests. The claims are directed toward either specific persons or groups or all the members of the community. Performances can be actions (required by positive rights) or forbearances (negative rights). In the case of forbearances, the purpose can be to allow the claimant to act (active rights) or to exempt him from being acted upon (passive rights). In strict rules for rights, claims of specific individuals are matched with correlative duties toward them for other individuals: A has a right to R if and only if some B has the duty either to perform an action which helps provide R for A or to refrain from interfering with A's pursuit of R.

This correlativity is absent from ideological declarations of natural and human rights. They do not prescribe specific conduct for individuals or even policies for governments because they are not intended to regulate the relations of people but to express general aims and standards of achievement to which governments should commit themselves. We are not concerned with manifestos, but I will espouse the notion that humans have valid claims to the satisfaction of basic needs even when no institutions have assigned specific duties to individuals. If our obligations are grounded in care – that is, if they comprise intelligent ways of taking care of those for whom we should care – it is everyone's obligation to see that all human beings are cared for to the extent practicable. Hence, in structuring society we must concern ourselves with the well-being of all, not just those under our particular care. Since as individuals we seldom have the opportunity to contribute to the general welfare in any direct way, we must seek ways to act in concert with other caring people. Collectively, we must support, seek, and invent institutions that afford the means of happiness to as many people in as fair a way as possible. That is, we must devise ways to *impose* obligations on individuals, including ourselves, which will help meet the basic needs of all. And this means that we will create or support an appropriate system of social rights. Our recognition of human rights is an expression of our acknowledgment that we cannot be content until the claims are secured through social rights which impose obligations on specific individuals, though such rights do not yet exist.

In the rules conception, rights are moral or legal, depending on whether the rules that define them are moral or statutory. Moral rules are principles that are valid on some objective ground, not merely mores, though the mores in a good society incorporate valid principles. Rules are valid when they are moral canons obtained by reasoned criticism (Benn and Peters) and principles of an enlightened conscience (Feinberg).[5] They are backed by the force of conscience and enlightened public opinion. Legal rights are created by positive laws, and their sanctions are imposed by the authority of the state. They are claims not merely against individuals and the members of the community but against the state to enforce claims against individuals.

To respect rights is to obey the rules that define them; to violate rights is to break the rules. This is uncontroversially true of legal rights. Extending the notion of rights to the moral context commits the moral theorist to treating moral questions in terms of rule-governed activities. It imposes the obligation on the moral agent to know the rules and it requires her to follow them on most occasions rather than moral sentiment, intuition, judgment, or cultivated conscience, except to the extent that these are involved in telling her what a rule implies. This last exception is a major one. No system of rules is so complete as to eliminate judgment in determining which and how rules apply to the given case. Good rules can reduce the role of intuition and invoke it where it is least likely to be irrational or purely subjective, but they cannot eliminate its role altogether. Utilitarians rely on intuition for the assessment of utilities when quantitative measures are unavailable. Rights theorists rely on it to weigh rights when they conflict.

Some moral rights are too important to be left to the conscience of individuals, so society institutes them as legal rights. Legal rights are enacted by legitimate authorities and are enforced by state sanctions. This gives people a triple motive to honor them: the obligation to obey the moral rule embodied in them, the obligation to obey laws because they are laws, and the prudent desire to avoid punishment. On the other hand, it is undesirable to squander enforcement powers on some moral rights because they are unimportant or too hard to enforce or will be honored more conscientiously if left to the individual. Conscience and public criticism are the only sanctions for such rights. Finally, society enforces some morally neutral claims in order to install orderly social processes and other utilitarian purposes. Such claims become legal rights, but they are backed only by the duty to obey the law and a desire to avoid punishment, not by any moral force in their content.

At present, we are concerned with moral rights, in particular the right to autonomy. Are there absolute moral rights, and is this one of them? First, what would an absolute right look like? To elucidate the concept, Feinberg draws the distinction between making claims and having rights.[6] Rights are valid claims. To be valid, a claim does not have to be expressed or defended, nor does it have to be recognized or respected. Nor are all of the claims people make or honor valid. Rights can exist without being recognized and without the right-holder being able to demonstrate their validity, and many "rights" (claims that are made and honored) are spurious.

Though to have and to make claims are distinct, it is very important to make them. What is valuable is not the possession of a right, but its exercise. What is important is to do or have what one has a right to, not to have a valid claim to the doing or having. But others cannot be expected to honor a claim if it is not made public. Moreover, spurious rights are used as rationalizations for trampling on genuine rights, and they need to be exposed: making claims is an essential step toward testing them for validity. Thus it is important for the right-holder or someone qualified to speak for him to make a case for his right. He must do everything within reason to make the claim known and show its validity. Moreover, one can have a case for a right without having the right. A person may make a claim in good faith and present reasons to justify it. Exploration of the reasons may strengthen his case or refute it, depending on whether the claim falls under recognized rules and the rules are valid. But he must make his case before this can happen.

Feinberg calls a claim for which a case has been made, but which is less than a decisive one, a "presumptive" right. Presumptive rights may conflict. Those should not be exercised or honored which require the sacrifice of more important rights or interests. Therefore, Feinberg notes, if one is to maintain a belief in absolute rights, one must find a way to deal with "the apparent impossibility in a world full of conflict of treating any right as an unconditional guarantee."[7]

One practice is to treat presumptive rights as prima facie. This implies, however, that on the occasions when they are overruled by other considerations, they are not genuine rights, and when they are genuine, they are never overruled and hence are absolute. Feinberg rejects this proposal because he wants to hold on to the notion that rights are grounded *claims*. They exist as such even when it would be wrong to exercise or honor them because of stronger claims.

Feinberg's conception has problems of its own. Rights are valid claims and validity is determined by a system of rules. What kind of rules bestow valid claims but are nevertheless sometimes not right to honor? In respect to immunity from parentalistic acts, we may say that a person has right, R, where R is a form of action, if he has a valid claim on another for a performance, P, where P is an abstention from interference with R. The maximum logical scope for R would be all of those occasions on which P or its opposite could be performed. Thus, if R is the right to autonomy and it has maximum scope, it extends to all of those occasions on which others have the power to intervene. If a right has that scope, Feinberg points out, "the limits of the right would correspond with the limit of the form of conduct specified, and once these wide boundaries had been defined, no further boundary adjustments, incursions or encumbrances, legislative restrictions, or conditions for emergency suspensions would be permitted." A right defined by a rule of this scope would be absolute in the strongest sense: "For a right to have this character it would have to be such that no conflicts with other human rights, either of the same type or another type, would be possible."[8]

What is at issue for our discussion is whether there is an absolute right on which parentalism infringes per se, that is, whether the abstention from parentalistic acts is unconditionally enjoined by moral rules. An ideal system of rules is that which would be reached after exhaustive reflection and would cover all cases and incorporate all exceptions. Its rules would be absolute in a sense weaker than unconditional or categorical rules, that is, the rules would hold only in cases other than those spelled out in exceptive clauses. But the rights they defined would be equally nonconflictive. Thus, Feinberg notes, all rights as valid claims under perfect rules are "unconditionally incumbent within the limits of their well-defined scope" whether the scope extends to all conditions in which the regulated action is possible or is confined to defined conditions.

There are a number of difficulties with the notion of ideal rules and consequently with absolute ones. For whom are they ideal—ideal or actual persons? In an ideal or the actual social environment? It is hard to imagine how one would determine what would be ideal for ideal persons or an ideal society, but this may not be necessary. The issue here is what sorts of rules a caring person would support for the actual persons in his actual society, rules that have a chance of becoming mores and would function well if they did. The notion is akin to but slightly different from Brandt's when he defines right actions in terms of conformity to learnable rules which, were they to gain currency, would maximize value for the community.[9] The difference from my view is that I see no reason to follow rules when it diminishes the welfare of persons in the particular situation, contributes nothing to gaining currency for the rules, and is not critical for the integrity of the agent. The guidelines I propose would sanction violation of even the best rules in such circumstances.

Under these concepts, are there any absolute moral rights? Feinberg observes that manifesto writers are able to proclaim rights as absolute by expressing them in glittering generalities. This is the case with the right to autonomy, as well as the related rights to be treated as a human being and as a person rather than a thing, popular notions among those who would prohibit parentalism absolutely on the basis of the right to autonomy. When pushed to specify exactly what respect for autonomy requires in the way of performance, most rights theorists would concede that there are exceptions to any rule that might be proposed; for example, they say that one may interfere with a person's autonomy if he threatens to inflict grave and irreversible harm on himself. Until all exceptive clauses are spelled out, rules merely assert prima facie rights and may be overruled. Since it is impossible to spell out all possible exceptions to a given rule, no system of rules eliminates indeterminacy and the need to rely on judgment or intuition in determining what rights to honor when they conflict. If any right is absolute, it is too indeterminate to know what is entailed in honoring it. Any right that is determinate enough to impose definite obligations on others proves not to be absolute.

To put this a somewhat different way, an ideal system of rights would rank them in lexical or linear order (R must never be sacrificed for R', R' for R", etc.). It is impossible to do this for the complex and shifting circumstances of the actual world. In practice, systems of rights provide individuals with indications of how to act unless they have overriding reasons not to. Such reasons are always possible because no right is absolute, though the reasons will be rare, and a heavy burden of justification will rest on those who violate the rights of others if the system is well designed. To repeat, it is impossible to devise perfect rules. Any set of rules must leave scope for discretion by those who would conscientiously follow them. Genuine solicitude may require—that is, morally demand—disobedience to any given rule and hence violation of a genuine right. No right is absolute in the strong sense that violations of it are always wrong.

The Utility and Disutility of Rights

Some moralists place the concept of rights at the center of their ethical system. Rejection of this move does not commit one to denying that rights have a place in the institution of morality. A socially promulgated battery of rights and duties is a useful tool, perhaps an indispensable one, for maintaining conditions under which care can flourish. Now, where care does flourish, mutual solicitude generates a strong urge to parentalism. Ill-considered solicitude becomes the source of illegitimate forms of parentalism, and self-interest masquerades as solicitude in exploitative pseudo-parentalism. Therefore, even in—indeed, especially in—a caring society the parentalistic impulse must be scrutinized and disciplined under the guidance of a firm schedule of rights.

But what kind of restrictions can be imposed without dampening genuine care? In particular, does it help to recognize a moral right to autonomy and codify strict rules against encroachments on it? What is the utility or disutility of doing so?

The utility of a rule can only be demonstrated in the empirical circumstances in which it must operate, not deduced from self-evident truths. Hence, any schedule of rights should be contextual and conditional. This means three things. First, there must be a general understanding of the circumstances under which it is appropriate to appeal to rights and those under which it is beneficial to make moral decisions in other terms. The sphere of rights and rules must be delimited for each society, according to its peculiar circumstances. Second, the specific system of rights must be appropriate for the concrete conditions. Definition and enforcement of a particular set of rights are justified by their tendency to maximize and distribute the conditions of happiness fairly in those conditions. It should be expected that different schedules of rights, though with similar elements due to common features in human nature and the human condition, will work in different concrete circumstances. Third, specific rights must be spelled out in detail as appropriate for circumstances in which individuals find themselves in an actual society with its particular environment.

Since the contextual character of rights robs moral rules of simplicity, permanence, and cross-cultural invariance, one may well wonder whether there is any utility at all in recognizing them. If a duty is mandated for every right, why not deal with morality entirely in terms of duties? After all, this seems only to be a matter of the direction from which we look at the same normative relation. The reply is that society is not interested in rules in the abstract, but in their observance. Public recognition of a right brings to bear on the goods and duties which it entails favorable attitudes that have accumulated through a long tradition dating from the rebellion against the parentalistic structure of feudalism. The mobilization of these attitudes helps motivate people to carry out their moral obligations. Given the potency of rights rhetoric in Western societies and its growing impact on non-Western societies, the moralist would be foolish to ignore it as a social tool.

The way in which rules are formulated and promulgated affects their efficacy. Couching rules in terms of rights and cultivating a lively concern for rights among the members of society focuses attention on the harm done by violations of rules. Transgressors are reminded not only of their guilt but also of the harm they inflict. Disinterested parties—judges, legislators, fellow citizens, and passers-by—are directed to the injury to the victim, as well as the venality of the offender. The victim is challenged to stand up for his interests and to demand protection and reparation. As Feinberg observes:

> A claim-right . . . can be urged, pressed, or rightfully demanded against other persons. In appropriate circumstances the right-holder can "urgently, peremptorily, or insistently" call for his rights, or assert them authoritatively, confidently, unabashedly. Rights are not mere gifts or favors, motivated by love or pity, for which gratitude is the sole fitting response. A right is something a man can *stand* on, something that can be demanded or insisted upon without embarrassment or shame.[10]

In an uncaring society and in a caring society where solicitude is ignorant or insensitive, it is important for people to be able to demand their rights.

To preserve their efficacy, rights should be confined to interests so basic and widely shared as to warrant public definition and protection. Rights are claims to specific forms of treatment by others. In keeping with the notion of objectivity of values advanced in Chapter 1, interests are defined by genuine goods; the individual cannot and should not be guaranteed whatever she wants or others want for her. Still, society can guarantee rights only on the basis of some estimate of what is good for its members. In view of this, the protection and enforcement of rights should be treated as a fallible enterprise, and those charged with defining rights and affording protection for them must avoid fanaticism. Enforcement must be no less vigorous for that.

Without further qualifications, the conception of rights explicated to this point would require claims that even trivially affect basic interests to be labeled rights. To conserve the rhetorical force of the term, it is better to restrict *rights* to claims that seriously affect the vital interests of the right-holder. Among such claims, the most important may be called *basic rights* and the remainder *secondary rights*. The basic rights particularly relevant to parentalism are minimal autonomy and minimal welfare (in the narrow sense of possession of fundamental physical and social goods exclusive of autonomy). Both autonomy and welfare are important ingredients of happiness and conditions for the pursuit of other goods.

Not the least benefit of a correctly designed system of rights is the instruction which it provides the individual about her interests. Thus, the value of autonomy and the various resources and liberties necessary for its practice would not be widely appreciated if our moral and political traditions did not emphasize them. Declaring autonomy as a right and establishing practices to educate people in their right to it helps them appreciate its value. Such practices are especially important when infringements on autonomy are unconscious and well-intentioned, as is the case in misguided parentalism.

Every social practice with utility unfortunately also tends to carry certain disutilities. One who would design or reform practices should explore ways to maximize their utility while minimizing their disutility. We have reviewed the utility of incorporating guarantees of rights in the moral institutions of modern society. What is the disutility? Recall that rights are indeterminate without rules assigning specific duties to specific persons. In contexts in which rules get in the way of desirable forms of human interaction, rights are out of place. For example, an individual's welfare may be better promoted if his caregiver is guided by ideals or affection or noble traits of character rather than the desire to live up to a code of conduct or the resolution to do her duty in the face of contrary inclinations. For the recipient of care to appeal to rules or demand his rights might alter the whole gestalt for the person who cares for him, freeze her generous impulses, and encourage her to do strictly, and no more than, what the rules require. The individual would then be worse off for the bargain.

Public recognition of rights calls the right-holder to action. Rights are things to demand. The rules guaranteeing them are a platform to stand on in demanding them. By the same token, however, standing on rights places rightholders in an adversarial relation with supposed violators. If a person in whose life another intervenes merely questions the wisdom of the other's conduct—if he argues, "I know you are trying to help, but don't you see, I will be better off doing it myself even if I make mistakes?"—attention is centered on what is being done. If he charges, "See here, I have the right to run my own life as I see fit!" he adopts the accusatory mode and puts his benefactor on the defensive. This is counterproductive in many circumstances.

Readiness to stand up for one's rights is important. Unless it is widespread, there will be plenty of people prepared to exploit others and not a few prone to misguided parentalism. But one should be aware of the price of constantly harping on rules and rights. It distances people from one another. It brings their relationships under a judicial or quasi-judicial framework. It puts the parties in the posture of justifying disputed behavior before disengaged third parties and thus publicize and externalize it. Rigid insistence on one's rights or "the rules" when they are not needed stunts the growth of such relations or chills them where they do exist.

It would seem that the primary reason to maintain a system of moral and legal rights is to ensure at least that people do not harm one another. For this reason, it is important to school ourselves to respect the rights of others in our effort to take care of them. Respect for rights is important to sustain a moral order in which more positive obligations can take hold. It is why a policy that goes beyond rules and rights such as that toward paternalism must be fitted into a system that contains rules and rights.

The Private and Public Spheres

Distancing and impartial adjudication have their place, and they do not damage anything important if the parties are already at a distance from one another. The less people are involved in one another's lives and the more external their relations, the more desirable it is to formalize those relations—that is, the more useful it is to govern their interactions by formal rules that specify what, and no more than what, is required of each person and what, and no more than what, can be demanded by the other. Rules are a useful mechanism when personal relationships falter. They are therefore for exceptional rather than ordinary circumstances and should be used with discretion.

The more intimately people are involved in each other's lives and the more personal solicitude they feel for each other, the less use and more harm there is in formalizing relationships. Standing on rights may create a distance where none exists and none is desirable. This is not to say that intimate interaction can always be left to impulse and feeling. Solicitude can be misdirected; it easily overflows its bounds into conduct that hurts the recipient; it may eventually degenerate into exploitation masquerading as care. Even in the context of genuine solicitude, guidelines are important. The solicitous agent needs to remind himself of the ways he can go wrong.

These reflections suggest a crude distinction between contexts in which rights-concepts are useful and those in which they are counterproductive. This dichotomy corresponds, though not perfectly, to the divisions between the public and private spheres of a person's life and between the spheres of positive laws and informal mores in society. Generally, but not universally, rules and a fortiori rights are relevant to human interaction when people stand in public, impersonal, and limited relationships with one another, for example, citizen to bureaucrat, customer to supplier, client to professional. What each demands and has a right to expect can be reduced to rules that can be promulgated and enforced. This reduction is appropriate not only for the agencies of the state with its laws but also for other institutions and organizations with their operational procedures and codes of conduct. It is useful to define rights in terms of claims to quite specific treatment by specific others by virtue of their positions in the institutions.

Also generally, but not universally, rules and rights are impediments to interactions on a personal level. Intimate relationships and open-ended responsibilities are not to be captured in strict definitions or induced by rigid rules. In these relationships, it is not sufficient for each to refrain from violating the other's rights. Mutual solicitude must carry them beyond rights to the other's needs, beyond what is expected to what they demand of themselves, beyond what they feel they ought to do to what the caring heart wants to do.

To generalize, recognition of basic interests as rights promotes fairly shared general happiness. But rights must not be so emphasized as to bring all interaction under formal rules of rights and duties. The disutility of rights is magnified when the schema for rules and rights appropriate to the public sphere of positive law is applied uncritically to the private sphere of intimate relationships. The mistake is to generalize the legal model to all of life. Laws with their case histories and coterie of advocates and adjudicators are essential to making recurrent interactions in society reliable and fair, but only interactions that fall easily into predetermined grooves because they are limited and external. Public rules are also indispensable for reducing and resolving public disputes by providing objective grounds for their resolution. But the very virtues that make public rules and rights useful in regulating external relationships make them impediments for human relationships that do and should overflow narrow grooves. The most vital and intimate human relationships fall into this category, and it debilitates them to incite their participants to preoccupation with rules and rights.

The mores that govern interaction in society in areas where it is harmful to impose laws are necessarily general and vague. They are not formally inscribed in authoritative documents but exist in the informal expectations which people have for themselves and each other. Hence, they leave wide discretion for the conscientious individual as to how to carry out their imperatives. They do not impose exact forms of conduct. Thus, for example, rational morality demands that spouses be concerned for one another's welfare down to trivial details of daily life. At the same time, it demands that they respect each other's privacy and autonomy. Neither partner should dominate the other for his or her own gratification or the other's presumed welfare. Exactly how the balance between mutual solicitude and mutual respect is concretized is a matter for daily concern and continual negotiation between them. In this ongoing process, it seldom helps for the parties to stand on their rights or to be overly concerned about the rights of the other rather than his or her needs.

Instead of the legalistic model of a society of self-interested individuals following rules whose purpose is to protect rights, I propose the caring model of people so involved in each other's lives that they go beyond rights and duties in caring for those in their care. In such a society, rights are recognized because they discipline the desire to help, as well as block the temptation to exploit. They are not, however, constantly brought into play; in most relationships most of the time they lie unused and unnoticed in the background of caring interactions.

II

PARENTALISM

4

The Parental Analogy

The concepts of paternalism and parentalism are based on analogies between paternal or parental and other forms of care. The analogies are relational: they point out similarities between the relation of parent to child and other common human relationships. These similarities, and differences which reflection brings to light, help us sort out our intuitions about the desirability of some forms of parentalistic care and the repugnancy of others. In each case it is necessary to ask whether the relation between parentalist and beneficiary is sufficiently like that of parent to child to justify the treatment of the beneficiary like a child.

Fixing the Analogy

At the outset, let us reflect on why the analogy is inviting. Personal experience and popular wisdom teach that a parent's solicitude is the most unflagging that one can enjoy. If there is a paradigm of care, this is clearly it. The question is, What are we to do with it? It is elusive. Fathers in a particular culture enter a great many relationships with their children and the expectations for fathering vary from culture to culture. The same is true of mothering, as well as parenting in general. As one or another aspect of the parent-child relationship is highlighted, different aspects of relationships compared with it are thrown into relief. Differences of opinion about which parental concerns are desirable lead to different evaluations of parentalism. Moreover, as the parental analogy is applied to new relationships beyond those for which it was first drawn, it illuminates, by reflection as it were, additional facets of parenting, thus enriching the analogical base and causing us to reevaluate parenting itself.

With such fluidity in usage, it is difficult to pin down what a given author means by 'paternalism,' as N. Fotion points out.[1] No one would claim a strict identity between the parental and other relations (the king as "father" to his subjects does not beget them). An author who discusses parentalism may disclaim the relevance of some similarities and the context may neutralize others; but, contrary to Fotion's suggestion, these are usually not sufficient to set determinate limits on the analogy. The extent of the analogy is open in both everyday speech and formal philosophical discourse. What is intended, to the extent that this is definite at all, shifts, contracts, expands from one context to another. For clarity it is necessary to stipulate the precise analogies one has in mind.

Perhaps stereotypes of parents and children provide a shortcut. After all, cannot an author assume that his audience is familiar with those he has in mind? Does not common understanding of stereotypes in the speech community provide the linguistic context required to make the intentions of particular speakers clear? Unfortunately, even stereotypes vary with the audience and even with members of a given audience. The stereotypes of a pluralistic and shifting culture do not provide a reliable semantic background for intracultural communication, not to mention cross-cultural. Furthermore, when cases come under critical scrutiny, stereotypical thinking tends to slip back and forth between the ideal and the usual. The stereotyper confuses what fathers ought to do with what they actually do and degrades the ideal, and confuses what they do with what they ought to do and idealizes the actual — in both cases blurring the distinction between actual and ideal.

Despite the uncertainties, we ignore stereotypes at our peril. They lurk in our minds and in the minds of those with whom we talk as barriers to reasoned inquiry. For example, our parental stereotypes reflect patriarchal and patrynomic customs. I do not know how far this has penetrated the literature on parentalism; but it is significant that authors, almost all males, use fathers rather than mothers as models for evaluating the efforts of people to care for one another and typically refer to the child as a "son." Jack Douglas and John Kleinig are two exceptions, but neither considers the matter sufficiently important to suggest a substitute for the term paternalism.[2]

I wish to neutralize the assumptions that the male is or should be the principal actor in the world and that the male role in the family is or should be the model for action in the larger world. Hence the substitution of 'parentalism' for 'paternalism' in my work. Moreover, 'parentalism' is more appropriate for the broad range of activities that are considered paternalistic. If we were interested in multiplying types, we might posit paternalism and maternalism as species under the genus parentalism. Significantly, this suggestion has received attention in nursing, a profession that is both caring in its self-conception and predominately female. Parentalism takes two forms in health care: the "paternalism" of physicians (mostly men) and the "maternalism" of nurses (mostly women). The implication is that maternalism is less offensive and thus that the forms of parentalism traditionally identified with the narrower category of paternalism have a different and lower moral status than the forms appropriate for nursing.[3] Without pursuing this, I will utilize parentalism as a broad category that covers forms of care analogous to both mothering and fathering. This tactic is more than terminological. It brings a wide range of cases together for comparison and enlarges the empirical footing of the analysis.

Fromm on Mothers and Fathers

Turning to the parental analogy, I will begin with some thoughts of Erich Fromm. There would be little to say for parentalism if the parentalist were not trying to emulate the *loving* parent. The parental analogy therefore takes its departure from instances of parental love. Fromm provides stereotypes of mother and father love, but he renders them both realistic on the basis of his observations as a psychologist and idealized on the basis of his judgments as a moralist. He presents both the prevailing kinds of parenting and the ideal as ideal-typifications or models. Typifications are abstractions, so it is possible for women to exemplify fatherly love and men motherly love, but the fatherly forms predominate among men and the motherly among women. Significantly, Fromm's typifications of the ideal forms of parental love converge: the relations of good mothers and good fathers with older children are very much alike. When he describes this convergence, Fromm breaks free from the patriarchal bias in his earlier analysis.

Fromm begins with mother love because this is what the child first encounters and is the foil against which it experiences fatherly care. In recognition of this, when people speak of men "fathering" children, they have only biological insemination in mind, but when they speak of a women "mothering" them, they think of caring and nurturing. The mother's social parenting begins with conception. The father's begins in a serious way only when the child leaves the womb and then less vigorously.

Fromm observes that the child's self-consciousness develops concurrently with consciousness of its mother as its first significant other. Essential to the child's normal development is its awareness of being loved in a special way:

> To put it in a more general formula: *I am loved for what I am*, or perhaps more accurately, *I am loved because I am*. This experience of being loved by mother is a passive one. There is nothing I have to do in order to be loved—mother's love is unconditional. All I have to do is *to be*—to be her child. Mother's love is bliss, is peace, it need not be acquired, it need not be deserved.

As Fromm sees it, the son's relationship to his father (he chronically refers to the child as "the son") becomes more important as he grows older. This is due to the son's destiny to pass into the larger world of affairs:

> The relationship to father is quite different. Mother is the home we come from, she is nature, soil, the ocean; father does not represent any such natural home. . . . [H]e represents the other pole of human existence; the world of thought, of man-made things, of law and order, of discipline, of travel and adventure. Father is the one who teaches the child, who shows him the road into the world. . . . Fatherly love is conditional love. Its principle is, "I love you *because* you fulfill my expectations, because you do your duty, because you are like me."

An integral part of ideal care for both parents is the child's training to care for itself:

> In the ideal case, mother's love does not try to prevent the child from growing up, does not try to put a premium on helplessness. . . . Part of her life should be the wish that the child become independent and eventually separate from her. Father's love should be guided by principles and expectations; it should be patient and tolerant, rather than threatening and authoritarian. It should give the growing child an increasing sense of competence and eventually permit him to become his own authority and to dispense with that of his father.[4]

Thus father and mother provide the two ingredients of full-bodied love: uncondi-tional acceptance and demanding standards. The aim is to empower the child both to accept and expect much of itself. It is also to teach it to treat others in like manner. That is, parents must not only practice the art of loving on their children, but teach them the art. Children must master it for a full life in their relations with others and to play the role of parent in their turn.

Douglas makes this point with vigor. First, he observes that parents promote their children's lifetime interests at some cost to their short term pleasures, and he notes, "one of their primary goals in doing this is to teach the child to be a competent adult, and . . . a large, but culturally variable, degree of independence from paternalistic (and maternalistic) control is a vital part of the competence training parents provide. Genetic paternalism is, on average, sincerely aimed at helping the child over the long run to become largely independent of paternalism." Parents are promoting the interests not only of their children, but of themselves and society. This is why Douglas labels the higher type of parentalism "cooperative." Thus he catalogs a great range of benefits which are realized when parents assume the responsibility of making their children independent:

> The biological reason for this is that independence is in fact central to children's best survival interests, to the best interests of those who sincerely feel caring love for them (because their interests, while not identical with children's, largely overlap theirs), to the best economic interests of parents who are supporting them, and to the best biological interest of anyone who shares their genes. . . . Parental love, genetic interest (in the child's producing grandchildren), and economic interest are powerful motives for parents to teach children to become independent.[5]

Douglas notes that parents also have a personal interest in teaching their children the art of parentalism for the time when they themselves age and become dependent.

To put the thoughts of Douglas and Fromm in the language of care: society exploits the natural basis of emotions generated by the biological relationship of parents to children to assure the care of its youngest members. It entrusts children to their natural parents and expects the parents to watch over every aspect of their lives carefully. Both mother and father take care of their children because they care for them deeply, doing things for them that they cannot do for themselves, protecting them from dangers, and eventually teaching them how to care for themselves. The goal is to equip children both for self-care and for assuming the burden of care for others, that is, for adult existence. In the process, parents become careworn, but more human, because caring is essential to humanity and obligations and sentiments of care grow in the children to ensure that the parents in turn are cared for when they need to be.

Meeting the Needs of Children

Adults, whether parents, guardians, mentors, or merely members of the commu-nity, are obligated to take care of children's basic needs. The following are some forms of care that are relevant for the parental analogy. In connection with each I will mention some forms of parentalism addressed to similar needs. I do not mean to suggest that all of the latter are legitimate; issues in connection with each will be discussed later.

1. *Sustenance*. Parents see that their children are fed, clothed, and sheltered and their medical needs met. For this, parents must do many things before the children can know they are necessary, are ready to ask for them, or are equipped to appreciate them. Analogously, society provides custodial care for the incapacitated and assistance for the indigent. Since many of these groups do not participate in public decisions, their treatment is parentalistic. Similarly, landowners and corporate employers in some societies see that their employees have shelter, food, and medical care. Physicians may administer treatment without the fully informed consent of patients and other professionals do likewise with other services.

2. *Protection*. At the outset of life children are helpless. They must be protected from all manner of injuries, including ones they inflict on themselves. Sometimes they must be physically restrained. They often must be coerced and conditioned to avoid danger. Society taxes tobacco and alcohol to deter people from using them. It mandates seat belts and helmets as a condition for operating cars and motorcycles. The government and employers require employees to use safety devices at work. The national defense is in the hands of a security establishment that makes decisions "in the national interest" in secret, independent of the public will. Friends and relatives intervene to prevent individuals from committing suicide, and society places them in institutions for their own protection.

3. *Psychic health*. Parents must protect children from psychic injury and take care not to inflict it themselves by abuse, overprotectiveness, or denying affection. According to current theory, it is necessary to provide infants an absolute sense of security and make them aware of dangers only gradually within a context of basic safety. Parents should move as rapidly as they can from coercion, beneficent myths, and psychological manipulation to rational persuasion to help their children develop the capability for protecting themselves. Analogously, some government agencies try to administer welfare in such a way as to prevent the recipient from becoming dependent. In the area of mental health, some public funds are spent to enable people to help themselves, but some are committed involuntarily for treatment of psychoses and addictions.

4. *Skill*. Parents must see that children learn the skills to deal with people and things in a complex society. Even after they are able to take care of their own physical needs, they need support and direction to master advanced skills. Parents have to exercise their authority and exert pressure for some period after children become restive at their juvenile status. Here it is difficult to find analogous forms of parentalism. A certain level of education is forced on individuals for the enrichment of their lives as well as to make them useful members of society, but by and large society relies on pressure to contribute to the economic and political life of the community to provide individuals an incentive to acquire necessary skills. The skills may enable their possessor to enjoy a satisfying life, but this is not the primary aim of the pressure.

5. *Morality*. Sustenance, security, mental health, and skill are preconditions for a good life. Practical wisdom is necessary to utilize these resources for worthy and satisfying ends. Freedom from external control is worth little — indeed, it is positively bad — for those who lack the character and insight to govern themselves. Parents must help their children develop serviceable habits, a rationally informed and efficacious conscience, and an adequate ego ideal. The domain of autonomous action for individuals is the cares they take upon themselves, including self-care and the care of particular others. To exercise those cares in a careful way, they need both self-regarding virtues (of prudence) and other-regarding virtues (of practical love). Moral training equips children to care both for themselves and others and to take care in their caring. Society tries to protect and improve the morals of its citizens by training in schools and indoctrination through the media of propaganda and entertainment, and negatively by screening out unwholesome influences. More subtly, it supports religion in indirect ways on the assumption that religion makes people better morally and spiritually. While one aim of morality is to make people more cooperative and less dangerous to one another, another is to improve the quality of their lives by helping them live in a satisfying way.

6. *Reflection*. A truly human existence requires consciousness of what is involved in one's life. What one does and suffers must be *for* something; it must have some point or purpose. Life is, among many other things, a search for meaning. To be human is to ask ourselves, What is it all (our efforts, skill, character, security, very being) for? And to be able to give a cogent answer. Parents play a critical role in the process that leads to this end by shaping its beginning. They provide the first and the most important model which their children have of what it is to be human. They share their philosophies by word and example. They ought to nurture the spirit of inquiry so that the children will be equipped to find their own way when they are on their own since their declaration of emotional and philosophical independence is the capstone of parental care.

In relation to parentalism I can think of few practices in which adults try to get others to reflect on their lives when they are not inclined to do so. Individuals may provoke friends, spouses, and colleagues to think about what they are doing, how they are living, and what they are making of their lives, but this is prone to be viewed as intrusive. The clergyman who challenges his flock is viewed as meddlesome. More typical are efforts of true believers to convert others to their faith or ideology, to share with them the good news about the universe that they think they have, and this not always by the route of rational persuasion. Here is indeed parentalistic moralism, but of an offensive sort.

Meeting the Needs of Adults

Parents have the right and the responsibility to exercise the power entrusted to them to carry out the above tasks of parenting. While they work toward the day when their children will make wise choices for themselves, in the meantime they must act for and on them without their consent. In doing this they sometimes resort to coercion and deception. Nature provides them the means and society the authority to do so. The kinds and extent of control which they legitimately exert, however, are strictly limited by the ultimate objective—to prepare their children for autonomy—and they must stand ready to step aside as soon as their children can use autonomy responsibly. Ideal parenting exercises a temporary and strictly circumscribed power over the child for its own good, and it relinquishes it just as soon as the child can take it on itself.

The primary reason to stand in loco parentis toward people who are not our children must be something that resembles parental love. It cannot be identical with it, for it is not possible to feel that powerful affection toward the large number of others who need our care. Nor would it be desirable. We owe our strongest feelings to those with whom we are intimate, who care for us as we do for them. What is required for genuine parentalism is therefore a pragmatic equivalent of parental love. What is required is genuine caring, active benevolence, or practical love, not sentiment or affection. If there is an art of loving, as Fromm preaches, it does not come automatically. The father may nurture his children in order to realize a frustrated ambition, enhance his own ego, enjoy the pleasures of possession, or extend the range of his will. In like manner, affection in other areas of life can generate pseudo-care in which the person takes care of others for his own gratification and basks in self-congratulation for the services he renders or expects to be repaid with reciprocal service or gratitude.

Given needs in adults that parallel those of children, what kinds of objectives should the parentalist pursue in meeting them? Here I will bring to bear Fromm's insights regarding the care of children. What can the art of loving children tell us about the art of caring for adults?

Here I want to make a point that will be basic for the subsequent analysis. The same practical love that requires the parent to intervene in the life of the child in some circumstances requires her to abstain from intervention in others. Children may learn to enjoy helplessness and dependency. They may welcome irresponsibility. They may accept as their due having their needs met without the burden of care or responsibility. In like manner, adults may not cherish autonomy. Its exercise is not always pleasant, and it is seldom easy. The adult can luxuriate in irresponsible subservience to others. Since, nevertheless, autonomy is a basic value, care for a person may require one to thrust it upon him for his own good. It is sometimes our duty to resist the impulse of compassion and refuse to do for fellow human beings what they will not do for themselves, just as it is sometimes our parental obligation to withhold help and challenge our children to stand on their own feet even though our feelings cry out otherwise. The parental analogy, together with the parent's obligation to prepare children for independence, teaches us that we sometimes have the obligation to refrain from helping, to challenge others to independence, and to respect their potential autonomy by resisting their impulse to abandon it.

Fromm's stereotypes suggest what goes into the nurture of independence. Mother wishes her child to become self-sufficient, but her role is passive: "[M]other's love does not try to prevent the child from growing up, does not try to put a premium on helplessness." Father's role is active; his expectations force the child to grow up and point out the directions for growth: "Father is the one who teaches the child, who shows him the road into the world."[6] While I wish to avoid patriarchal concepts, I want to emphasize the centrality of the "fatherly" function in the care of children and the importance of incorporating it in the right kind of parentalistic care. Some authors, notably Gerald Dworkin, make it a necessary condition for the justification of parentalism: encroachment on autonomy is warranted *only* if it contributes to the subject's future autonomy.[7] While this goes too far, it highlights an important prima facie obligation of the parentalist: to reduce the need for her care by pressing its recipients to take care of themselves as soon as possible. We do not promote the real good of others by reinforcing their dependence, just as parents do not discharge the duties of their role if they fail to make their acts of caring lessons for self-care.

Fromm's "motherly" function likewise has its place in both parenting and parentalism. The mother cares for the child just because it is her child: "*I am loved for what I am. . . . I am loved because I am. . . .* All I have to do is *to be* — to be her child." Analogously, parentalism may be motivated by practical love toward the other just because he is a human being, a person, or (as it is sometimes put) a member of the human family. It is because we have a generic obligation to promote the welfare of others just because they are (humans) that we are obligated to care for particular people in particular ways by virtue of our concrete relationships with them — as public functionaries, physicians, counselors, custodians, friends, or indeed as parents. And it is because of the generic obligation and the fact that autonomy is a primary good that we are required at times to refrain from intervention in people's lives even though other important values are at stake for them.

Fromm rhapsodizes over the infant's bliss at basking in mother's love. Ideally, we continue to enjoy unconditional acceptance from our parents after we have grown restive at their control and left to be on our own. Parallel if not equivalent in our lives may be the knowledge that *someone* in the world accepts us, which is brought home by parentalistic acts. The assurance that we are valued by someone who is committed to our welfare, that we are not aliens in the human community, can compensate for the chagrin of being under parentalistic care.

It is not enough to be unconditionally accepted by one's parents to enjoy the bliss that Fromm describes; one must be conscious of that acceptance. It is not enough for parents to care; they must communicate their solicitude. The purpose should not be to extort gratitude, but to teach the child the meaning of care. In like manner, the recipient of parentalistic care sooner or later must be informed of the reason. Otherwise there is no way to assuage the humiliation of dependency or challenge him to self-care.

Herbert Morris points out that this is the parentalistic element in punishment. Parents punish their children because they are responsible for their moral development. To inculcate values such as respect and responsibility toward members of the family and prepare them for relationships in the outside world, they must use coercion and impose deprivations. For these to constitute punishment and do their job, the child must see that they are imposed because he has violated legitimate norms. The communicative component is essential because the aim is to teach the nature of wrongdoing, the damage it does, and the entitlement of others to inflict pain on the wrongdoer, and the parent must convey the depth of her attachment to the values that the child has flaunted.

Morris asserts that communication of the reason for the penalty is critical for any legitimate form of punishment. Punishment is *essentially* a communicative act. Its purpose is to allow the culprit to discharge his guilt and reenter normal relations with others. For this he must know why the deprivation is imposed on him. He must understand that the reason is his transgression, not the benefit that the punishment may bring him. Similarly the parent must say, "You have to stay in your room because you did not come home when you promised," not "I'm only doing this for your own good." The latter ignores the child's unhappiness and imposes the additional burden of being grateful for what is making him unhappy. It shifts attention away from the wrongness of the act and the propriety of the punishment.[8]

To generalize this point, both parents and parentalists are obligated to make those under their care aware of what is being done to and for them, not only in punishing but also in nurturing and protecting them. They are obligated to do so in a way that will challenge their charges to act responsibly in the future. Moreover, the parents' role is socially sanctioned and sustained. They owe an accounting to appropriate others, including their children, for how they discharge it. Good parents must stand ready to submit their motives, methods, and actions to review. Making their care known not incidentally puts it on the table for critical scrutiny. So also parentalism is occasioned by social roles such as professional, trustee, and caretaker. It must be evaluated in terms of the functions of those roles in society. Parentalists owe an account of their performance to society and especially to the subjects upon whose autonomy they encroach.

The foregoing reflections on the responsibility of the parent and parentalist to cultivate autonomy while taking care of their charges in other ways give force to Douglas's typology of paternalism. *Sincerely cooperative paternalism* is "any form of paternalism (doing good for others in the name of 'what is good for them') in which those acting paternally are sincerely acting to help the other person become more independent over the long run, and the other person sincerely believes that this is the case." In *minimally cooperative paternalism* one acts "for the dependent's best interest, but *not* to make the dependent independent over the long run." *Conflictful paternalism* "is not aimed at the long-run independent competence and equality of the submissive member of the relation. . . . [In it] individuals may or may not exploit submissive persons materially, but they necessarily exploit them in terms of power and pride."[9] (Conflictful parentalism is actually pseudo-parentalism since genuine parentalism entails the intention to benefit the subject, but here it is only pretended.)

The importance of cooperative parentalism is attested by the fact that it is used by the pseudo-parentalist as a pretense to justify domination. The exploiter takes advantage of the high esteem in which parents and parentalistic friends are held to mask abuse of the victim. As Douglas observes:

Exploitive power-seekers have almost always tried to appear cooperatively paternalistic, in the same way they have tried to appear wise, magically powerful (in control of the power of God, etc.), and everything else that is appealing. . . . Those who would exploit human beings by dominating them, by keeping them in dependent submission, have always recognized that they will be the heir of this high esteem, and thus more apt to be dominant, if the potentially submissive people see them as parent-like.[10]

Douglas notes that the reason both genuine and pretended care are characterized as parentalistic is that parent-child relations are the bedrock of human society. They are the most intimate and important relations in the child's life and prepare it for participation in the larger society. No society could endure without parenting by either natural parents or surrogates because otherwise it would find itself composed of adults who had not learned the rudiments of social competence. Parenting thus has a critical social function.

Routine and Reflective Care

Douglas observes that society chooses natural parentage to assign the parenting role because biology assures the necessary solicitude.[11] He goes on to argue that the sincerely cooperative parentalism of parents is also found in friendship and certain teacher-student relationships where close personal contact over long periods nurtures caring feelings. In the absence of this kind of intimacy, he feels that generalized benevolence or love of humanity as such is inadequate to sustain care. As relationships become more impersonal, sincerely cooperative parentalism devolves into the degenerate forms, first minimally cooperative and then conflictful parentalism. Douglas doubts not only the efficacy of generalized benevolence, but even its occurrence. He thinks that relations with people other than family and close friends is almost always predicated on self-interest. Whenever anyone professes to act altruistically, we must suspect a desire to dominate.

Even if this sour thesis is rejected, care is obviously harder to arouse and easier to pervert into exploitation as we move along the continuum of human relations from the intimate to the external and impersonal. I have tried to come to terms with this fact by distinguishing between personal and public acts and acknowledging the importance of rules and sanctions to assure beneficial interactions among people in the public sphere.

Parenting is a socially defined act and parentalistic acts are performed by virtue of social roles. These facts call attention to the need to evaluate not only individual acts but also practices and the institutions that reinforce them. The analysis of parentalism begins with the very personal and intimate relation between parent and child and moves naturally to other personal relationships. However, it must also take into consideration the social structure that provides the background of these relationships. What is legitimate on the individual level may not be so as a general practice, and vice versa; in addition, the justification of particular actions is affected by that of the practices to which they contribute, and vice versa.

The observation that the parental role is founded in both nature and custom brings to mind another feature of the parent-child relationship relevant to parentalism: the relationship is unchosen. It is absolutely so for children—they are simply dropped into existence and abandoned to parents they happen to have. They must accept the relationship as a given until they acquire the power to reshape it. Parents have more options but, while they may have chosen to have children, they have not chosen the children they have. They must accept who is delivered and negotiate a relationship with the stranger. Moreover, once the relationship between parents and children exists, neither party can fully control the emotions and obligations entailed. Being a parent and being a child are caring states into which individuals are thrown, statuses in which they find themselves, realities to which they must adjust in giving and receiving the most important form of care in life. Adults likewise find their responsibilities of care defined for them in relationships that call for some measure of parentalism—as professional, legislator, or accidental Samaritan. Even when they freely choose their role, its responsibilities come with it independent of their will.

The complex relationship of parent to child is socially conditioned. Both parent and child are subject to societal expectations that have evolved over centuries. Their reactions to the expectations and their own initiatives build up the family relationship by unconscious increments. The importance of the relationship and its many dimensions means that it has a profound influence on the way its participants act in every other area of life, parents no less than children.

In view of the difficulty in finding one's way through the intricate maze of parenting, it is no wonder that its analog, parentalism, is hard to puzzle out. No more than a small portion of the network of relationships between parent and child comes under conscious scrutiny in the course of their living together. Usually the network is a taken-for-granted matrix for individual acts of care, only gradually evolving through constant negotiation of details. Thus, while the association between parents and children is voluntary in the sense that those involved can break it off once children are older, and the parties negotiate its particular features as it goes on, for the most part both parents and children take it as given. It is acted out without constant referendums. The result of all of this is that parents' care is routinely parentalistic, being motivated by loving care and discharged with little consultation with those who receive it.

Children eventually become solicitous for their parents. From the example of their parents' care, they learn the art of loving. Well-cared-for children learn to be considerate of their parents and try to make them happy. In due time, this care too takes on a parentalistic cast as parents decline into the infirmity and confusion of old age. Thus there is a mutuality in parent/child care that deepens if parental care is successful. In other relationships in life, parentalism is seldom reciprocal in just this way. We are not treated parentalistically by precisely those whom we have so treated. But almost everyone who treats some others parentalistically is treated in like manner by different others.

Parental care is based largely on tacit assumptions about the child's welfare. Parents take for granted that they know what is best, that they have been given the authority to tend to their children's welfare by routines they choose. While this is right and proper, their parenting should be assessed from time to time by moral standards. As in every area of life, the best intentioned actions may be ineptly performed, and apparently good intentions may conceal self-interested ones.

Moral review typically comes after mistakes are made in particular acts or when characteristic evils of a practice are noticed—for example, illegitimate infringements on the recipients' right to autonomy or their incapacitation for making responsible choices. In their moments of reflection, good parents check the direction in which their control is taking their child and assure themselves that they are achieving their goal, the child's true welfare. Welfare in the broadest sense includes not only physical health and comfort but also mental health, moral development, skills for dealing with life, and the strength to exercise autonomy responsibly. The routines of care should not lead parents or parentalists to neglect these more subtle values. The moment of moral reflection is the opportunity to determine whether adequate attention is being given to *all* of the needs of the child.

The point of these commonplaces is to raise the question of the extent to which other human relations dictate behavior similar to that which is appropriate for parents toward their children. People find themselves in a given network of relationships and commitments, just as parents find themselves endowed with the children under their care. While moral agents choose to enter many of the social interactions that structure their lives and have the freedom to break off most, the relationships seldom resemble voluntary agreements entered with a clear-eyed understanding of the details, much less contracts whose provisions are spelled out formally. At any point in our lives we *find* ourselves in immensely complicated relationships of mutual involvement with others in which first one of us and then the other takes the initiative in caring, frequently on the basis of a judgment about what the other needs rather than the other's own judgment. This resembles the interaction between parents and children, except that care is not as unidirectional. Members of a caring society stand in relations of mutual parentalism.

Just as parental practices need to be reviewed periodically for aims and efficacy, so do parentalistic practices. Some routine parentalism is desirable in ordinary social life and integral to the caring society, but this very fact means that more caring mistakes are to be expected than in a society of hostile competitors. Vigilance to prevent or correct them are that much more important.

To sum up these reflections on the parental analogy: parental love is a natural sentiment, but it is supported, channeled, and implemented by society to ensure that children will be nurtured until they are able to care for themselves. True parents love their children unconditionally just because they are their children. This does not deter them from holding the children to high standards; indeed, it obligates them to do so. To prepare children for adult life and show them "the road into the world," parents make their expectations known. They inculcate the skills necessary to survive on the road and travel it to worthy destinations. They discipline their children to ensure that they will use their skills prudently to further their own interests and morally to further the interests of those who fall under their care. And parents provide their children the necessaries—food, protection, affection, and so on—for survival and satisfaction as they set out on their journey.

Analogously, the motive of the parentalist is practical love. It may assume a form dictated by the moral point of view, helping the other just because he is a person and member of the human community, or it may spring from loyalty to the group with which the parentalist identifies, or it may be due to her commitment to individuals. The recipient of help may be under the parentalist's care due to his particular role in society or come under it due to chance circumstances. In any case, the aim of the parentalist, like that of the parent, is to meet the subject's needs in such a way as to equip him to do without her help in the future and see that he survives and prospers physically and psychologically in the interim. Therefore, parentalism ought to incorporate unqualified acceptance of the other as a person. It should be designed to promote not only well-being but autonomy.

Neither parental nor parentalistic acts can be evaluated in isolation of the framework of social norms for specific roles: those for the parent in relation to child and those for parentalists in various capacities toward the recipients of their care. These norms have been more clearly drawn for parents over the long history of the family as a stable institution than for many sorts of parentalists, who occupy shifting roles in a constantly changing culture. This is one reason why it is useful to compare expectations for these roles with those for the parent. The comparison proves to be illuminating in the opposite direction as well: as goods and evils are detected in parentalistic practices, there is a new basis for assessing the practices of parents.

Of course, more, much more, can be said about parenting, but I will utilize the functions I have singled out as the basis for the analogy in terms of which I will define parentalism and as a clue to some principles of justification for evaluating it. We act parentalistically when we undertake to perform some of these functions for persons who are not our children and without their full consent. Whether we are justified in doing so often turns on whether or not the conditions that cause children to need the help of their parents obtain for that person. Parentalism is unjustified when the relationship between the parentalist and the subject differ from that of the parent to child in significant respects due to differences in the nature or circumstances of one or both parties. The parental analogy thus is the key to determining what is wrong with some forms of parentalism as well as what is right about other forms.

5

Parentalism Defined

The impulse to rush to a neighbor's aid engages some of the best and worst elements of human nature; hence, the urge to help must be both encouraged and disciplined. A caring society promotes parentalism where it is needed and blocks it where it is repugnant. To do this it must sort out the forms and develop guidelines for its members. This is what we will now try to do.

The Need for a Definition

Parentalistic practices and institutions far antedate the writings of social philosophers. When the latter did begin to reflect on society, they did not assess practices and institutions under this description. A few discussed the parental analogy, notably Locke, who was anxious to show that it does not justify despotic powers for the king, but none exploited it as a basic analytic category. This is of recent vintage, as is reflected by the late appearance of the word 'paternalism' in the English language.[1] Widespread use of it by Anglo-American philosophers began with influential articles by Gerald Dworkin and Joel Feinberg, who in turn were picking up on ideas of John Stuart Mill and H.L.A. Hart. A steady flow of discussions has now swelled to a flood in response to developments such as strains in the welfare state, the exponential growth of technology and professionalism, and a variety of "liberation movements" that demand freedom from parentalism as well as from exploitation.

Despite the discussion, practical disputes over parentalism are chronic. No policy for handling cases is generally accepted, and moralists do not even agree on the weight that should be given to various factors involved in them. The disarray of moral theory is reflected in the lack even of an accepted definition of the phenomenon. On reflection, this is not surprising. The primary issue is justification. Authors categorize cases in ways that anticipate the normative judgments they make. Hence, in their definitions they single out the variables relevant to their evaluations. Insofar as contrary approaches to evaluation are represented, different conceptions of parentalism are employed.

State parentalism exercised through legislation was the first form to receive attention. Feinberg attests to its importance when he lists two forms of legal parentalism among the six major kinds of restrictions imposed on individuals by the modern state.[2] Later the focus shifted to less public spheres of action such as professional practice, especially medicine, treatment of children and the handicapped, and prevention of suicide. In the process a number of abstract issues relating to parentalism as such were raised. This sequence of topics is significant. One cause of the inappropriate application of the idea of rigid rules to the evaluation of parentalism seems to be an uncritical transfer of concepts from the public to the personal sphere.

Everyday usage and the philosophical literature have saddled us with the term 'paternalism' but they have failed to tie it down to a single meaning. It is fruitless, therefore, to attempt a reportive definition. We must stipulate our meaning for the term or a substitute. Stipulative definitions are to be judged by their utility. A good definition of paternalism (or parentalism) must be formulated in terms of variables the values of which determine whether instances are justified. To close in on a useful definition, we must specify parameters for evaluation. I take the following into account.

1. The analysis must retain a strong connection with the parental analogy. Though the analogy is open and flexible enough to develop in ways that we wish, we should not label relationships parentalistic that do not resemble significant and loving relations between parents and children. It is the genuine care of parents for their children that raises the question of whether parentalism is justified.

2. Some continuity with the popular usages of 'paternalism' should be maintained in assigning a technical meaning to the term or its substitute. The reason is to minimize conceptual confusion and help maintain existing social and psychological barriers to practices that are clearly offensive and which are now effectively condemned by labeling them paternalistic. The technical term should retain some of the pejorative force of the word in everyday life. However, we should not incorporate a negative evaluation in its very definition. The term 'parentalism' is preferable to 'paternalism' not only because it is androgynous, but because its negative odor is not so powerful as to bias judgment of actual cases. The mildly pejorative tone ("Why, that's parentalistic!") only alerts one to the need to provide a justification ("Whatever you call it, I must do it because he really needs help").

3. The definition of parentalism should be true to firmly established, widely shared, critical intuitions that suggest the range of actions to be evaluated according to similar considerations; that is, the definition must be true to what I called "identificatory intuitions" in Chapter 2. Such intuitions distinguish subsets of core cases of clearly right and clearly wrong actions, the rationale of which helps settle hard cases whose morality is problematic.

4. My intuitions suggest that parentalism should be conceived broadly because common features of a wide range of interventions in the lives of people for their own good are relevant to their evaluation.

5. The definition and principles of justification based on it must be coherent with some general ethical theory. Intuitions must be adjusted to principles as well as principles to intuitions. The ethical tradition that provides the background for my definition is consequentialist. My version assumes a liberal view of the

"consequences" of an act. They include the quality of the act itself as experienced by the agent and the fairness of the distribution of the values which it generates. The version also incorporates the concept of objective basic goods shared in general outline by all humans, and it recognizes autonomy as an important good of this sort, though not the only one or an absolute one.

6. The dialectical interplay between intuitions and concepts and between the way issues look to me and the way they look to other reasonable people closes the door to any finality for the analysis. It will have succeeded if its criticisms of other views of parentalism are cogent, if it incorporates their insights and brings these into some kind of coherence, if it advances a defensible position on disputed questions, and if it pushes forward our understanding of the place of parentalism in human affairs.

The Definition

I will now propose a definition of parentalism that fits the parameters listed above and captures my intuition of the relevant similarities of actions to desirable parental behavior. Though the definition is normatively neutral, many of the actions that it delimits are intuitively objectionable, which ensures that some of the negative force of 'paternalism' will adhere to the term.

For convenience, I will refer to the parentalistic agent as P, the subject acted on as S, and the parentalistic act as A. A definition must specify the properties of P and the relationship of P to S which make A parentalistic. It must refer to P's intentions and the measures which P may employ, since these are points of comparison between parentalists and parents. Moreover, P's relation to S, his intentions toward S, and the measures he uses entail certain properties for S, which may be included in the definition or specified in the accompanying text. Thus, some characterizations of paternalism refer to the institutional settings of A and to other persons involved in A such as those upon whom P acts in intervening in S's life.

The definition: *Action A is parentalistic if and only if (a) P believes that A is an intervention in S's life; (b) P decides to perform A independently of whether S authorizes A at the time of the performance; (c) P believes that A will contribute to S's welfare; and (d) P performs A for this reason.* We may say briefly that an action is parentalistic if it is an intervention in a subject's life for his benefit without regard to his consent.

The ultimate justification of this definition lies in its utility for the evaluation of cases. Here let me explain some of the features in which it differs from other definitions in the literature. Note first that it focuses on P's state of mind. P's view of A makes it parentalistic, not the qualities of A itself. This repairs a deficiency in early characterizations, for example, when Hart speaks of protection of people against themselves.[3] One may protect another against herself for a nonparentalistic reason—for example, a master may prevent a slave from killing or disfiguring herself in order to use her as a prostitute. One may attempt to protect and fail—for example, a person may try to prevent a clumsy friend from injuring himself by refusing to lend him skiing equipment, but the friend departs in a huff and promptly breaks his leg in his bathtub.

Donald VanDeVeer's definition requires that A be contrary to S's "operative preference, intention, or disposition."[4] Mine only requires A to be performed independent of S's preferences. P may have no idea of S's preferences. He might believe that S endorses his course of action but act without regard to that fact. What matters is that P not act as S's agent. This point renders unnecessary VanDeVeer's distinction between S's preferences at the time of A and those which he may have at the time when he is affected by A, which may be later (for example, P writes into his will a provision to subsidize S's education at Harvard when S is still an infant). What is critical is that P disregard S's preferences, if S has any, at the time P chooses to perform A. If S later approves of the deed, this does not make it retroactively nonparentalistic.

Gert and Culver require that P believe that he is violating a moral rule in helping S before an act is parentalistic.[5] This builds into the definition the prima facie objection that should be raised against any action when it is identified as parentalistic. It seems preferable for the definition to be value-neutral, though mild negative connotations hover over the term. VanDeVeer cites cases of interference in the lives of others that are similar to acknowledged cases of parentalism, but which do not violate generally accepted moral rules.[6]

Parentalistic Agents and Subjects

I have characterized parentalism as intervention in another's life for his benefit without regard to his consent. Let us turn to complexities which this simple definition covers. The great variety of actions that can be fruitfully classified as parentalistic is determined by the values that can be assigned to the variables in the definition, notably, (a) the kinds of agents who can fill the role of parentalist, (b) subjects who can be recipients, (c) relationships of the one to the other which allow the parentalist to act, (d) aims that make the action parentalistic, and (e) measures available to pursue these aims.

We may appeal to Mill's authority to justify a broad concept of parentalism. 'Paternalism' is not Mill's word[7] nor is his position on the practice a refined product ready for use, but it is a rich lode to be mined and a source to which discussions of parentalism continue to return.

The primary aim of *On Liberty* is to erect barriers to interference with the liberties of individuals by society, and so most of Mill's discussion is devoted to public parentalism, but he couches his principle in broad enough terms to cover personal parentalism. Thus he says that it applies to interferences by mankind "individually or collectively" with the liberty of any of its number.[8]

The considerations that lead Mill to condemn parentalistic measures employed by society apply to the actions of lesser collectivities (for example, classes, organizations, and sex and age groups) and individual agents. The same generality is found in the subjects whose liberty must be respected, but with critical exceptions: "We are not speaking of children, or of young persons below the age which the law may fix as that of manhood or womanhood" nor of "those backward states of society in which the race itself may be considered as in its nonage." Mill's failure to discuss these exceptions leaves unclear the exact line he would draw between those whose liberties should be respected and those whose liberties may be abridged. The boundary problem plagues later authors whose theories recognize that such things as maturity, rationality, being informed, and having civilized values are preconditions for the fruitful use of liberty.

Other than the exceptions, Mill opposes parentalistic treatment of any individual or group. The subject of parentalism may be an individual who chances into a transient relationship with the agent or a whole group of individuals who share a property that allows a dependent relationship to develop, such as age, infirmity, or subjection to the state. The subject group may include the entire society (indicated by Mill's fatuous congratulation of barbarians fortunate enough to be ruled by a benevolent despot), a minority (implied by his condemnation of the tyranny of the majority), or any other definable aggregate or set (exemplified by his concern for women trapped in indissoluble marriages).[9] Following Mill's example, I will stretch the conceptions of the parentalistic agent, subject, relationship, aim, and measure to their natural limits. That is, I will conceive parentalism as broadly as possible in order to compare the greatest possible range of relevantly similar acts.

The early contemporary papers focus on legal parentalism, in which the agent is the state acting in the person of legislators and the executors and enforcers of the law. A spate of subsequent papers broaden the discussion of individuals acting in private capacities, moving from state to personal parentalism.[10] This inaugurates a search for principles common to both levels of analysis on the assumption that there are such, despite the ontological differences among kinds of agents and kinds of subjects. When we turn to the issue of justification, we will find that there are different reasons for and objections against parentalistic acts at the two levels because of differences in the relata of the relationships there. It is important not to transfer concepts uncritically from one level to another. The interests, liberties, rights, and modes of consent of groups differ from those of individuals and affect the justification of parentalism in different ways. Uncritical generalization from state to personal parentalism leads to misconceptions such as Gert and Culver attribute to Gerald Dworkin. They charge that he thinks of parentalism entirely in turns of coercion because of his preoccupation with the legal form: "Paternalism in law doubtless does involve interference with liberty most of the time, but this is due to the nature of the law, not to the nature of paternalism."[11] With this caution in mind, it is fruitful to examine legal parentalism for insights into personal forms. Legal parentalism reminds us, for example, to take into account the effect of parentalistic actions on third parties, since laws affect many people besides those for whose benefit they are enacted.

Again, many treatments of personal parentalism are couched in terms of direct action on neighbors, associates, or contemporaries. The analysis of legal parentalism calls our attention to the way in which actions affect people who are remote from the agent, whom she may not even know, through intermediaries or the effects of general rules and practices. Indeed, one can serve future or past generations, for example, by protecting the environment or honoring ancestors, only in this indirect way.

What relationship must exist between agent and subject to make parentalism possible? It is useful to begin with notions embedded in the definition of 'paternalism' found in *Webster's Third New International Dictionary*: "The care or control of subordinates (as by a government or employer) in a fatherly manner; esp. the principles or practices of a government that undertake to supply needs or regulate conduct of the governed in matters affecting them as individuals as well as in their relations to the state and to each other." Note that this focuses on state parentalism, but its reference to employers invites us to consider parentalism in other hierarchical relationships—of sovereign to subjects, general to troops, teacher to students, warden to prisoners, and so on. Moreover, the definition refers not only to regulating conduct but to supplying needs. This suggests that the parentalist must have power over the subject and over features of the world that can be controlled to do things for the subject.

This broad approach to parentalistic relationships is found in the recent philosophical literature. Forms of subordination that have drawn attention include the following.

1. *Citizens to the state*. The sovereign is empowered by force, tradition, or constitution to issue decrees and laws that require or prohibit behavior or control the resources necessary for the actions of inhabitants of a territory. Agents of the state are mandated to implement the laws and are given latitude in the way they do so. With the growth of state power and functions, the opportunity for parentalism is found in every nook and cranny of government. The literature has dealt with legislators, judges, police, and regulatory commissions among the agents who have been able and willing to utilize this opportunity.

2. *Charges to those assigned to watch over them*. Society delegates power to individuals by law and custom to care for specific others. The growing complexity of life, specialization of functions, and interdependence of people expand this sort of parentalism. Attention in the literature has been given to school officials, physicians, and psychiatrists, as well as to guardians of children, the incapacitated, and the mentally deficient. A natural extension of this approach is to generalize to all kinds of professionals and fiduciaries.

3. *The individual to the public*. Those who chance to interact with an individual have the power to influence him insofar as they bring popular expectations to bear and he desires approval and acceptance. The wishes of the agent is backed by the weight of numbers and force of custom. Some people can be coerced by merely pointing out that certain actions are expected or "the thing to do."

4. *"Incompetents" to those with de facto influence over them*. Many people have power over the lives of others by virtue of ties of nature, law and affection. Men, parents, guardians, "normal" individuals, "elite" classes, and races and nations assume responsibility, respectively, for "the weaker sex," children, deviants, "inferior" races, and "underdeveloped" countries. Kleinig even speaks of parentalism toward animals on the ground that they "have a good that is

susceptible to frustration and . . . may sometimes be more effectively preserved or furthered by means of some imposition."[12]

For parentalism to be possible, a person or group must have the power to control another or act upon or for it. This puts the latter in a de facto subordinate position, but it does not entail that the parentalist is superior in any normative sense. The conception that the subject must be treated as inferior for an act to be parentalistic, together with the ethical principle that persons should be treated as moral equals, biases the case against any form of parentalism. Discarding the conception, we can retain the principle and observe that there are many situations in which people should act for others without their consent simply because they have the power to benefit them. They need not be superior or even presume to be. In other cases, parentalists may indeed be superior to their beneficiaries in respects relevant to the action while inferior to them in other respects. The moral superiority (or lack of it) of the parentalist has nothing to do with whether the action is parentalistic or whether it is justified. What is relevant is that the parentalist believes that she has the power to benefit the subject and chooses to try to do so.

Parentalistic Aims

Parentalism is characterized loosely as an attempt to benefit a subject without consent. Since "to benefit" includes both provision of positive goods and protection from harms, two forms of parentalism have come to be distinguished. They are labeled "promotive" and "preservative" by Michael Bayles and "positive" and "negative" by Kleinig. I will call them beneficent and protective parentalism.

Early papers concentrated on protective parentalism. Perhaps the authors assume that parentalism is hard to justify in any event but protective parentalism is easier to justify than beneficent; hence, whenever protective parentalism is unjustified, a fortiori beneficent parentalism is too. Also, these same authors are preoccupied with the coercive means typical of legal parentalism, and coercion is more often used to prevent people from harming themselves than to force them to pursue their welfare. In the concentration on protective parentalism, the conception may also be at work that all moral obligations can be subsumed under the no-harm principle. If our only obligation is not to harm others or at most to prevent harm, the only form of parentalism worth considering is protective. It should be noted that even with this restriction, the range of values to be taken into consideration in contemplating a parentalistic action is vast. As James Childress remarks, the concept of harm is as broad as that of interests. Harm may be done to health, property, liberty, reputation, domestic relationships, and many, many other goods.[13]

There is no reason to deny that beneficent actions can be parentalistic. Once again, the broader conception is preferable to the narrower one. Certainly the parental analogy supports the former. As Geoffrey Scarre notes in criticizing Francis Schrag, "Normally adults do a great deal for children in the way of providing them with food, shelter and protection, in the absence of which services the survival and happiness chances of children, especially of the younger ones, would be seriously diminished; yet this aspect of adult-child relations is not mentioned in [Schrag's] model."[14] The point is obvious, but it needs to be made in face of the effort of many authors to circumscribe the kinds of parentalism that must be taken into consideration in a theory.

There is a more direct reason for acknowledging beneficent parentalism. An agent who cares for a subject must often weigh protection of her from some harm against the provision of some positive good for her. Then the choice is between modes of parentalism. Whether to act either way and hence parentalistically at all is a second one. It is no argument against this conception to point out the difficulty of weighing goods against harms for another. In pursuing our own welfare, we often decide whether the good we may achieve will outweigh the harm we may suffer. We are forced to do this in prudential calculations, and there is no reason to prohibit it in moral calculations of the welfare of others. On this point, Dan Brock's comment on exceptions to prohibitions of parentalism typically allowed by rights theorists are relevant. Such theorists claim that parentalistic interferences are permissible only when the subject threatens to harm herself due to some encumbrance or incompetence which prevents her from acting autonomously. Brock observes:

> The prevention of harm is the motivation of the moral-rights theorist allowing any paternalistic interference at all with persons acting as they wish. . . . Why, at the level of basic moral principles, should only the avoidance of major downside risks and harms limit possession and exercise of moral rights? Persons undertake activities in the first place in order to obtain the benefits the activities promise, and not merely to avoid the potential danger they carry. They seek to promote their good quite as much by obtaining such benefits as by avoiding such harms, and the former is equally relevant to their capacity or competence to promote their good effectively in an activity. They may fail to promote their good as much by failing to secure the benefits they seek as by failing to avoid harm.[15]

Like Brock, I see no reason why intervening in a person's life to prevent her from failing to gain an important good is any less justified than intervening to prevent her from harming herself.

Parentalistic Measures

P's intention to benefit *S* is a necessary but not sufficient condition for her action to be parentalistic. Parentalistic actions are restricted to measures relevant to the subject's condition of subordination and need. The parentalist must be solicitous for the subject's welfare under the impression that she has the power to promote it in ways he cannot accomplish for himself.

The one form of intervention covered by all discussions and the only one that many authors have in mind is coercion. However, actions on or for unconscious or unknowing subjects may also encroach on their autonomy. In acting for a subject without his consent and doing for him what he might have done for himself, the parentalist must weigh the value of his autonomy against the values to be achieved by sacrificing it in all of these forms of intervention.

Moreover, the three—coercing, doing to, and doing for—are often alternatives among which the parentalist must choose in pursuing the subject's welfare. She must weigh them in the same balance. At first glance it might seem that coercion is always the most undesirable option, but this is not the case. It at least requires the subject to be aware of the threats leveled against him, whereas doing to and doing for him may involve deceiving him or keeping him in ignorance. Such measures are offensive for different reasons than coercion and in some instances more offensive since coercion gives the subject the opportunity to resist while deception or ignorance denies it.

The offensiveness of alternative available means must be weighed not only against each other but against not acting at all. If the available means are all too offensive, it is better not to act. It is appropriate, then, to consider all the alternative means under the same heading, parentalism, and treat the choice among them as a decision of how to be parentalistic in contrast to the choice to eschew all of them as a decision not to be parentalistic at all. Moreover, parents typically blend coercing, doing to, and doing for in their care of children, so the parental analogy suggests that they be considered as alternative means to the same end and belonging to the same category of action defined by the intention behind them. For these reasons, I take a view of parentalism that comprehends a wide range of measures as possible means.

Coercion may be characterized informally as the issuance of a threat to induce the subject to perform an action to which he would not otherwise be inclined. In some instances, a threat compels an action much like physical force: approaching a person in a menacing way may induce him to step out of the way of traffic or put down a poisoned cup as effectively as pushing him from the street or knocking the cup from his hand. In some instances a threat may restrain the person from acting much as a physical impediment: it may prevent a pedestrian from walking onto an unsafe bridge as effectively as handcuffing him to a light post. The violence done the recipient's freedom of action by threats thus can be similar to that done by physical compulsion and restraint. Moreover, both kinds of measures vary in degree and hence justifiability is a function of the strength of the subject's desires which they frustrate, the severity of the measures, and the magnitude of the goods and harms produced.

Compelling and restraining, whether by threats or physical force, differ in significant ways and involve different kinds of drawbacks. As Beauchamp remarks in reference to new methods of biobehavioral control, "the distinction between actively requiring a person to do x and passively not allowing a person to do x is worthy of notice. . . . Such passive coercion is likely to be the most subtle, least noticed, and most widely prevalent form of paternalism."[16] The fact that the parentalism of an act escapes notice and hence critical examination is a mark against it. Just as a parent should make clear to the child to the extent the latter is capable of understanding why she is caring for it in the way she is, so the parentalist owes her subject an explanation of her actions and the opportunity to review and assess what is being done to or for him. When circumstances make this impossible, it is a reason for desisting from the action.

There are ways of controlling a person's decisions besides the issuance of overt threats. Some have come into particular prominence in modern times, such as physically by drugs, electric shock, and surgery and psychologically by hypnotism, brainwashing, and indoctrination. Technology constantly expands the power to control, and it is important to be on the lookout for new techniques as well as traditional ones. These may not fall under the strict definition of coercion, but their effect can be similar. Beauchamp is suggesting that they be subsumed under an expanded category of coercion when he refers to them as "coercively controlling human mentation."[17]

Coercion forces a person to act against his will. Parentalistic coercion forces him to act for what appears to the coercer to be his own good. A number of moral philosophers write as though this destroys the subject's autonomy. However, when coerced to choose between unpalatable alternatives, a person still is choosing, acting, and exercising autonomy in some form and measure. He is passive when the parentalist acts on or for him, not against his will, but independent of it. The subject may not consent because he is ignorant of what is being done, or his consent may be fabricated by deception and so not represent an effective volition. Thus coercion is a subset of a wider category of actions that affect a subject independent of his informed consent.

To determine what counts as parentalism in its various forms, we must consider what constitutes consent. For a person to consent to an action, it is necessary for him to be aware that the agent proposes to perform it, he must know what it entails, and he must make feelings about it known to the agent. The weakest form of consent is acquiescence. In stronger forms, the subject actively wills that the agent perform the action. Parentalism is action taken independent of whether consent in any form is present. It is obvious that nonresistance to or toleration of the action and even active solicitation of and gratitude for it do not make it nonparentalistic. As a number of authors point out, actions for which consent has been "manufactured" may be parentalistic. The consent of a hypnotized subject clearly does not negate the parentalistic dimension of the suggestion that he perform a self-beneficial act, nor does what a person agrees to in a drugged or drunken stupor. If the subject is insane, exceedingly dimwitted, or drastically uninformed, he may be incapable of consenting in the sense necessary to make an action on his behalf nonparentalistic.

As we multiply the types of manufactured consent, it becomes problematic exactly what kind of consent does take away the parentalistic character of an intervention. How competent and knowledgeable must a person be before her consent is free and informed? What methods must the agent use in obtaining consent? Moreover, I have defined parentalism as action independent of the subject's consent, not as action without his consent. He may offer perfectly free, informed, and rational consent and the parentalist not take it into consideration in deciding to act. Exactly in what way, then, must the agent take the consent into consideration before deciding to act for an act to be parentalistic? These are questions we must take up again when we consider the justification of parentalism.

The assumption that coercion and consent are diametrically opposed is simplistic. Consider the similarities between coercion and the use of positive inducements to persuade a person to act in a way that another thinks best for him but to which he is not initially inclined. In coercing a person, the other adds penalties to the consequences of alternative courses of action to dissuade her from them and induce him to follow the course which she deems best. To coax him to follow that course, she adds rewards to that alternative. In both cases, she affects his autonomy by altering the choices he faces. In both cases, she leaves him with alternatives and hence a sphere of autonomy.

Few authors have thought it necessary to evaluate the parentalistic use of rewards to attract a person to do things for his own good. Since their concern has been to judge morally questionable cases, they have assumed that rewards can be ignored. Rewards enrich the recipient's life while penalties add to its burdens. Intervention by reward may seem unobjectionable and not worthy of attention. However, the primary objection to parentalism is that it infringes on the subject's autonomy, and both penalties and rewards alter the conditions of choice and both leave a choice. They are thus on a par in respect to autonomy. If coercion can be parentalistic, so can inducement by rewards. Thus B.F. Skinner's ideal society in *Walden Two*, which relies entirely on positive reinforcement, is archetypically parentalistic. Would those who run such a society respect the autonomy of its members any more than those who run coercive societies? Or, better put, do those who run coercive societies take the autonomy of its members any less into account than those who run a Skinnerian society? The preferability of the Skinnerian system lies in the pleasing nature of the arrangements by which the members of society are controlled, not in any greater concern for the "freedom and dignity" traditionally associated with autonomy.

In support of assigning a role to rewards under the concept of parentalism, we should reflect that parents use rewards as well as punishments to control their children, and good parents use rewards more than punishments. The parental analogy here again speaks for a broad conception. Moreover, similar criteria are relevant to evaluating positive and negative control. Both must be judged in terms of the intrinsic qualities of the actions required of the parentalist and the actions induced or inhibited in the subject and the external consequences of the actions for the subject's welfare.

Like rewards, rational persuasion is ignored as a tool for parentalism. If a person convinces another by sound reasons that her actions are in his interest and induces him to cooperate with them, then they would seem to be paradigmatically nonparentalistic. But perhaps the assumption behind the neglect of rational persuasion is the same here as with rewards: it seems that rational persuasion hardly needs justification. Thus, while Mill vehemently condemns compulsion of individuals for their own good, he not only permits but urges us to remonstrate, reason with, and entreat them to avoid harm, and he does not think that such efforts collide with his principle of liberty. More problematic is Mill's denial that it is coercive to point out to a person that his behavior will incur disapproval or ostracism as long as the speaker does not issue the threat to deter the behavior. The parental analogy shows that this proposition is questionable. Approval and disapproval are powerful tools in the hands of parents. The mere possibility of ostracism or denial of affection may be overwhelming to the child. Confronting it with the possibility can be coercive, whatever the intention of the parents. The same is true in many parentalistic relationships. The subject is in a position of subordination and dependency. Hope for care may bind him to the parentalist. Her mere announcement that he will incur disapproval if he does not change his ways or accept help may intimidate him as effectively as a threat. Even if the parentalist only calls attention to the fact that others will disapprove, this focuses the pressure of public expectations on him and constrains him. In such a situation the parentalist cannot evade a measure of responsibility for the way the subject reacts. She has no justification for calling his attention to the consequences of his actions if she does not intend to alter those actions. In general, it is hard to imagine cases in which it is legitimate for persons to make their disfavor known or mention the disfavor of third parties when they do not intend to alter the choices confronting the person.

Rational persuasion in this instance consists in pointing out to a person the consequences of his action that one knows he will not welcome in order to dissuade him from the act. Hence, the measures approved by Mill—remonstrating, exhorting, and reasoning with people to dissuade them from self-harmful courses—can be parentalistic, and his principle of liberty, which encourages the use of such measures in preference to coercion, allows more parentalism than appears on the surface.

The most important reason not to deny rational persuasion as a parentalistic measure emerges when we examine an assumption behind a remark of Dworkin in which he explains why he excludes from consideration

> measures such as "truth in advertising" acts and Pure Food and Drug legislation . . . are often attacked as paternalistic but . . . should not be considered so. In these cases all that is provided—it is true by the use of compulsion—is information which it is presumed that rational persons are interested in having in order to make wise decisions. There is no interference in the liberty of the consumer unless one wants to stretch a point beyond good sense.[18]

The assumption here is that there is no interference in the liberty of consumers when they would welcome the action if they are rational. Now, it is a tautology that completely rational persons welcome rational arguments. Actual persons frequently do not welcome ones that dissuade them from a course on which they have set their mind. They resist attempts to show them what is in their best interest. The caring person may have to intrude on their thoughts, and they may resent the intrusion as an invasion of privacy or encroachment on their autonomy: "Why are you telling me that?" "It's for your own good." "Who are you to tell me what to do?" "I'm just trying to get you to think for yourself." "Mind your own business!" However reasonable the advice, the advice-giver is altering the other's choice-situation by forcing him to face facts. She pushes a new responsibility upon him, that of making an informed choice, when he may prefer to avoid it.

We should remind ourselves that persuasion, like rewards, is a basic tool in the parents' kit. It is their duty to counsel and instruct their children, as well as to tell them what to do and discipline them. Children are sometimes as resistant to guidance as to commands. Parents are expected to take the child in hand and say,

"You *will* hold still. You *will* listen to what I have to say." They may also have to wheedle and bribe prudent behavior from their children until, at last, the children are amenable to rational persuasion and perhaps even seek advice about what they should do.

Analogous treatment of adults—rewards, remonstrances, unwelcome argumentation—is sometimes justified and sometimes not. Depending on the circumstances, it can be proper to induce an adult to take care of his own interests by offering him unusual rewards or pressing unwanted advice upon him rather than letting him flounder in his poor judgment, just as it can be proper or improper to hector him into prudence by nonrational measures such as threats or emotional appeals.

To conclude the discussion of ends and means of parentalism, parents both coerce their children for their positive welfare ("You *must* go to school today") and promote that welfare noncoercively ("Honey, if you brush your teeth, we'll increase your allowance"; "Let's start setting aside money for Baby Jane's college education") and likewise they protect them from harm by both sorts of measures ("You will stay out of the street or you will get no supper tonight"; "Honey, if you don't brush your teeth, you'll get cavities"; "We should enroll Jimmy in Our Lady of Perpetual Vigilance to get him out of the drug scene at P.S. 13"). So also people who care for others parentalistically may either promote goods for them or protect them from harm and may use either coercion or noncoercive measures.

A broad conception of parentalism brings into relief the relevance of the full range of goods and harms and possible measures to the decisions of the full range of possible agents toward possible subjects. To bring all of these considerations into an effective encounter with one another in the prospective parentalist's mind, it is necessary to cast wide the net of a comprehensive definition.

Under my conception, parentalism is defined by its aim. An action is parentalistic if and only if the agent believes it will benefit the subject and performs it for this purpose, independently of his wishes. The aim is made central to the definition because it determines the appropriateness of the measures the parentalist chooses and the success of her effort. Where actions have mixed motives and complex effects, it is important to distinguish the parentalistic aim and identify the measures and consequences due to this dimension of the action.

The parentalistic aim may be to provide a positive good or prevent a harm. The values involved may be physical, material, psychological, social, moral, or any other sort, though in formulating principles simple enough to be practicable and general enough to apply to all subjects, it is necessary to concentrate on primary or basic goods and evils shared by most people. In doing this, we should remain alert to the possibility that the particular subject of parentalism may have an idiosyncratic schedule of values in which goods basic for others have a lower place for her.

All of the goods and harms of the subject which may enter the aim of the parentalistic agent and all of those entailed in the measures which she contemplates must be considered in evaluating her decision. Values of the most diverse character must be weighed against one another. For example, the parentalist may have to decide whether the subject's moral development warrants infliction of corporal punishment, confinement, or a monetary penalty. She may have to decide whether respect for autonomy warrants forbearance from interference in the subject's participation in a dangerous sport to protect him from a serious injury or humiliating defeat. If she decides to intervene, she may have to weigh the evils of coercing against those of deceiving or acting behind the subject's back in choosing means.

The parentalist can act as a private individual by virtue of a chance relation to the subject or by virtue of an official or semi-official position in a group. In the latter case, we say that the group is acting parentalistically. Parentalistic groups range all of the way from families, cliques, and friends, through formal organizations and institutions, to the state or its ruling element.

The parentalist, whether acting as an individual or for a group, must be a person to have aims and perform acts in the strict sense. In addition, the parentalist must occupy a position that affords the power to intervene in the recipient's life and generates a concern for his welfare. There is no need for her to assume any kind of superiority. Similarly, the recipient can be any individual or group as long as he is subordinate to the parentalist and seems to need help.

A parentalist may coerce the subject to do or refrain from doing something, she may act on his person or possessions, or she may act in his place. She may act on him directly or indirectly through laws, rules, institutions, practices, control of physical conditions, or anything else that affects him. The action may affect him alone or also third parties, aiming at some good or harm for them or merely affecting them in such a way as to promote his welfare.

Parentalism as conceived here thus covers a wide range of caring acts. The responsibilities of solicitude are subtle and complex in view of the diversity of values that must be taken into consideration and the immense range of measures available to pursue them. Guidance based on humanity's long centuries of experiments in care is needed by the individual enmeshed in a web of commitments, loyalties, and obligations to himself, particular others, and human beings as such.

6

The Evaluation of Parentalism

On the inductive model suggested in Chapter 2, the ability to account for firm and widely shared intuitions is an important test for moral principles. A principle should explain why actions in core cases are right or wrong, decide hard cases, and explain why the hard cases are hard. Thus Dan Brock claims that his consequentialist principle of parentalism meets all of these conditions: it captures the core intuition behind the question, "When my conduct harms no one else, and I bear its full consequences, why is it anyone's business but my own, and what gives anyone else a right to interfere?" It settles hard cases—for example, the propriety of deterring persons from smoking cigarettes or entering an unwise marriage; and it makes clear why informed observers disagree on the cases.[1]

However, the dialectic of parentalism is more complex than the model suggests. It is spiral rather than linear. Principles cannot simply be induced from an inventory of intuitions. We must oscillate between harmonizing our principles with intuitions and restocking our intuitions in the course of putting principles in action. The process should move us toward (to use John Rawls's phrase)[2] a reflective equilibrium between principles modified to conform to our responses to concrete cases and responses refocused by carefully thought-out principles.

Critical intuitions about any sphere of action such as parentalism should be informed by general conceptions derived from intuitions in other spheres. The inductive base for norms for a particular category of actions is enlarged by bringing the norms into accord with the basic principles of a coherent ethical theory and the norms which they entail for other categories of action with their own bodies of intuitive data. Guidelines for a specific category are to be validated, we may say, by looking down at cases, up to principles, and across to guidelines for other departments of life. Moral norms in this respect resemble the more sophisticated scientific hypotheses, which are compatible not only with specific data but also with accepted basic theories and are formulated with an eye to their unification with laws of other sciences.

Consequentialism Salted with Deontology

Before I propose a principle and strategy for evaluating parentalism, I will explain the general ethical theory which shapes my own thinking. Theoretical positions in the literature on parentalism fall, though not neatly, into the standard categories of deontological and consequentialist. Deontologists condemn parentalism on the basis of the right to autonomy in self-affecting matters. Extreme deontologists categorically prohibit parentalism as a violation of a putative absolute right to autonomy. Consequentialists condemn most parentalistic acts as failing to benefit the subject in the way the parentalist intends, but they reject absolute prohibitions. They sanction exceptions to antiparentalist rules because parentalism may provide benefits such as life, health, and moral development which outweigh their diminution of goods such as autonomy and pride of self.

Consequentialists tend to define parentalism more broadly than deontologists since they see that similar consequences must be weighed against each other in problematic cases as in cases on which most people agree. The broad definition brings more hard cases under the same principles as core cases, thereby bringing the reasons that decide core cases to bear on the hard cases. More narrow definitions tend to restrict core cases to obviously wrong ones and hence bias decisions about hard cases toward condemnation. In contrast, the broad definition leads us toward a somewhat greater tolerance of parentalism.

It would be misleading to suggest that there is a sharp distinction between deontological and consequentialist prohibitions of parentalism. Only in extreme forms do the two approaches diverge widely. Reasonable deontologists recognize a number of considerations that overrule the right to autonomy and permit parentalism. Reasonable consequentialists recognize the harmfulness of a wide range of parentalistic acts and propose stiff rules against them. Thus the most sophisticated theories, those best adjusted to critical intuitions, fall between the extremes, and the judgments they sanction overlap extensively. The consequentialist position advanced here falls in this middle zone.

The position is predicated on the premise that caring is essential to a truly human existence, even though people differ in the way they care and what they care about. This entails that a generic feature of objective goods is that they are related to people's cares. Goods are features or products of caring activities or of things that enable the agent to carry out his cares effectively. What else should concern the caregiver but the impact of her efforts on the objective well-being of those for whom she cares, that is, their consequences?

An adequate consequentialist position must incorporate insights from deontological theories since these have been particularly sensitive to the harms done by parentalism. For one thing, such a position considers not only whether an action, practice, or rule promises to maximize the means to happiness for those who are affected, but whether it will result in a fair distribution of these means. That is, it takes into account justice as well as other ingredients of welfare. It considers just distribution one of the principal values to be maximized.

There is often a tension between justice and other values. Richard Arneson notes that classical utilitarianism is distribution-insensitive. It enjoins us to maximize welfare but disregards how the components of welfare are distributed, thus sanctioning unjust treatment of some individuals to enhance the welfare of others. Arneson calls for a distribution-sensitive alternative with "rules of trade-off between the norms of 'Maximize welfare!' and 'See to it that welfare is equally distributed.' "[3] Among the possible rules he mentions, I like Paul Weirich's[4] because it is informed by the ideal of a caring society in which the good things of life are not only maximized through the cooperative efforts of all, but distributed in a fair manner to all and a fair contribution is exacted from each.

In the consequentialist position here, happiness is conceived in Aristotelian terms as a life of activity that brings satisfactions to the agent because it engages his human faculties. It does not identify happiness with pleasure or satisfaction per se but takes these only as (fallible) indices of the possession of objective goods. This allows us to acknowledge that the consequences of a good life include the intrinsic satisfaction of being a principled person and performing actions that are burdensome and painful. Since autonomy is a basic condition for these activities, the autonomy of both the parentalist and the recipients of care must be weighed in evaluating parentalistic acts.

One critical difference between deontology and (liberalized) consequentialism is that the deontologist tries to determine the moral status of actions solely by their intrinsic characteristics apart from their external consequences—for instance, whether they conform to a formal principle or have a right motive or spring from a noble character or obey an authoritative command. The consequentialist acknowledges that actions with deontological characteristics are among those with important intrinsic value, but maintains that the value has to be weighed in the same scales with the instrumental value of the act to determine whether on balance it should be performed. Important values will be lost if either intrinsic or instrumental values are considered without the other.

The satisfaction we receive from making choices is a function of our basic nature as centers of consciousness and points of origin for changes in the world. At the same time, caring requires us to interact with others, and we achieve our highest satisfactions by participating in caring relationships. The satisfaction of acting autonomously thus reflects our existence as both independent beings separate from one another and interdependent beings whose welfare depends on one another.

The Principle

Let me now turn to the task of formulating a principle for the evaluation of parentalism within the consequentialist framework predicated on the centrality of care. Like the definition of parentalism in Chapter 5, the principle is simple in form but broad in scope. It applies a modified principle of utility to acts whose primary intention is to help others independent of their consent.

Principle of Parentalism (PP): *Persons are justified in acting parentalistically if and only if they believe that the expected value of the action for the recipient is greater than any alternative and they have reason to trust their own judgment despite the opposition of anyone, including the recipient.*

PP refers to two sets of variables: (a) objective, the values that may result from the act and the probability that they will result, and (b) reflexive, the grounds the agent has for trusting her judgment in face of contrary judgments. In parentalism the objective focus is on values of the recipient rather than the agent or third parties, since it is his autonomy that is encroached upon, but the latter must be considered in real situations. This qualification calls for its own qualification to do justice to supererogatory acts. It is sometimes praiseworthy to sacrifice one's own interests for the sake of others. Acts of sacrifice have intrinsic value for the agent and instrumental value for others. Either of these may be important enough to counterbalance what otherwise would be a greater loss (to the self-sacrificial agent) than gain (to the beneficiary).

Some corollaries of PP merit emphasis in view of the intrinsic value of autonomy and generic features of the situations in which one person is called on to help another. I will state the corollaries briefly and discuss them at length.

- *Corollary I*: A person contemplating intervention in another's life should seek consent, if possible.
- *Corollary II*: When a subject's disabilities or encumbrances justify intervention, the intervention should extend only to the affected areas.
- *Corollary III*: The parentalist should hold the encroachment on the subject's autonomy to a minimum even at a sacrifice of some of the benefits she is attempting to provide.
- *Corollary IV*: If possible, the parentalist should act to enhance the subject's future autonomy, terminating the parentalistic relationship as soon as the subject is capable of self-care.
- *Corollary V*: The parentalist should take into consideration the effect of the act on her own habits and the practices of others.
- *Corollary VI*: The parentalist should remain open to help from others when it is needed.

Corollary I calls attention to the distance between interventions to which the subject rationally consents and coercion. It reminds us that actions are evaluated according to their means as well as their ends. To anticipate the later discussion, consenting is a significant exercise of autonomy, though less important than the activities that may be denied the subject by an intervention. Respect for the subject's autonomy dictates that the intervener seek consent. It is possible to justify acting when she fails to get it, but acting without consent is harder to justify than acting with it. The attempt to secure consent is an attempt to make the act nonparentalistic. It is dictated by the prima facie objection to parentalism as an infringement on the subject's autonomy.

Corollary II is based on the premise that only reasonable and informed acts of consent have very much intrinsic value for the subject. It is proper for the intervener to engage in action that lacks the subject's rational and informed consent — by disregarding his wishes, manufacturing his consent, or acting in the face of his objections — only if it is not possible to obtain such consent and the good to be achieved is important enough to proceed without it. The parentalist must remember that there are particular evils attendant to all of the alternatives to rational consent. Coercion does violence to autonomy, is painful to the subject, and leaves him resentful. Deception is required to manufacture consent and may arouse resentment. If it is necessary to keep the subject in the dark about what one is doing, the parentalist should remember that ignorance is an evil.

In respect to Corollaries II and III, when a subject's incompetencies do warrant parentalistic care, the parentalist should control only those parts of the subject's life in which he is incompetent. She must not use the subject's incompetencies and encumbrances as an excuse to encroach on other areas, and she should attempt to restore his competency.

Corollary IV spells out the importance of autonomy. It is an important value, and the parentalist's attempt to maximize the subject's well-being should include reasonable efforts not only *not* to encroach on it in the present but to enhance it in the future.

In respect to Corollary V, a parentalistic "practice" is a set of actions prominent members of which are parentalistic and which are performed as part of a recognized social role. It is important to distinguish practices from individual acts because, while comprising predominately parentalistic actions, they typically include pseudoparentalistic actions in which the agent attempts to benefit herself. She may get away with it precisely because most people who engage in the practice are genuinely parentalistic. Thus a practice must be evaluated differently (in this case, as less justified) than the actions that typify it. The ease with which parentalism becomes a cover for exploitation is a reason to discourage parentalistic practices. The precedent that an action provides must be taken into account in evaluating it.

In respect to Corollary VI, the parentalist's aim should be to foster relationships of mutual care and interdependence. She should not always be the giver and never the taker. One-way relations reduce others to dependence and expose them to domination. Moreover, the moral agent needs to view her actions from the standpoint of others, especially the recipient, and only by receiving care can she know what she is doing when she gives it. Hence, she should cultivate her own openness to help and encourage the caring impulses of others and maintain mutuality in her relationships.

Judging the Good of Another

We turn next to considerations that must be taken into account in applying PP to cases. The principle and its corollaries are intended for people who actively care for others and struggle to determine whether parentalistic means are appropriate—that is, for reflective persons who are trying to be fit members of a caring society. This includes both agents who take care of others directly and bystanders (ethicists, legislators, moral leaders, advisers, and so on) who assess the efforts of primary agents to determine which should be encouraged and which discouraged.

First note that PP is a guideline rather than a rule. It is formulated in terms of variables whose values must be assessed by the agent in the particular context in which she is acting. It instructs her in what she should take into account; it does not provide categorical rules or mathematical formulas to follow algorithmicly. This feature of PP does not preclude the institution of strict rules for specific contexts, such as medical practice or public education, where the value of coordinating the efforts of people in standardized relationships is great; it does leave the individual responsibility to decide whether to support such rules, whether to participate in such relationships, and whether to live up to their expectations.

In pure parentalism, where the values of the parentalist and third parties are not significantly affected, the objective welfare of the recipient of the action is the sole concern. To rate consequences in terms of the recipient's objective welfare, the agent must compare the expected value of the parentalistic action with the expected values of its alternatives. (Expected value as the sum of the products of the goods which the action may produce times the probabilities that it will produce them, less the sum of the products of the harms it may produce and the probabilities that it will produce them.) In impure parentalism, which comprises most cases in real life, the intrinsic value of the action for the agent, together with that of any actions that may be inhibited or elicited from the recipient, must be fed into the calculus. So also must be the goods and harms for the agent and the recipient produced as extrinsic consequences of these actions. So must goods and harms for bystanders. In the more complex cases, the agent must make comparative estimates not only of the effects on different people but also of the value of disparate effects, including the good of such different things as autonomy, health, and affection. The second objective variable is the probability of each outcome for each possible action, when some are immediate and obvious and others remote and problematic.

Among the reflexive variables the agent must consider is the strength of her evidence that each of these diverse primary estimates is correct compared to the evidence available to those who oppose the action. Another variable may be the soundness of the arguments by which she reaches her conclusion—for example, that she should take parentalistic action—compared to those of anyone who opposes it.

I am couching my explanation of PP in quantitative terms, which can be represented by abstract models of rational decision theory. However, the contingencies described in such models are seldom realized in real life. Rankings of the expected values of alternatives in concrete situations can only be crude and qualitative. Not all arbitrary elements can be eliminated from decisions. The agent is obliged to estimate the parameters without being able to analyze them in detail, to measure them by any standard unit, or to sum them by a formula. All that can be asked of conscientious agents, therefore, is that they investigate the most important factors of a situation, think through the issues, bring critical intuitions to bear in the light of considered principles, and draw inferences as logically as possible within the limits allowed by the urgency of the action. This procedure itself is appropriate only when there is time for reflection and significant benefits are promised from an analysis of the situation. In most routine decisions, as well as in emergencies, the agent must fall back on habits and unanalyzed "experience."

These crude guidelines will disappoint anyone who expects a mechanical decision procedure from consequentialism. However, the indeterminacies in the calculus are no greater than those in approaches that require the agent to balance rights, duties, rules, intentions, or qualities of character against one another. Consequentialism at least tells us what objective factors to look for in the concrete case.

By its very nature, a parentalistic action flies in the face of some of the recipient's wishes. What weight should the prospective parentalist give to them? In discussing this issue, most authors distinguish between wants or inclinations and stable and considered desires. The recipient's momentary want may be a response to immediate stimuli which reflects limited understanding of the situation and allows strong emotions to generate fallacious inferences. Considered desires, formed at times of reflection and tested by experience, may bring more of the person's understanding to bear and be more likely to be directed toward his true goods. Yet even his considered desires are not perfect indices of goods since no one has absolutely comprehensive understanding or is immune to mistakes in reasoning. To promote a person's true welfare, therefore, it may be necessary to overrule most well thought-out aims, even his entire life plan.

The prospective parentalist is faced with a fundamental procedural decision. Should she try to satisfy the subject's wants of the moment, his considered desires, or his objective welfare? PP requires the last. It is the caregiver's obligation to provide for the care receiver's objective good, his true welfare, as best she can whatever his desires. It is hard to see how anything else could be argued.

However, this is not the final word. The most accessible evidence about what is good for a person is his expressed desires. The most reliable evidence is his settled desires, since in reflective moments he is more likely than any outsider to know what is best for himself. Hence, the parentalist must take the subject's wants as evidence of what is good for him and his considered desires as better evidence than his wants. On the other hand, the parentalist sometimes has reason to dismiss even the subject's considered desires as misleading. The subject may display such lack of understanding or defective reasoning that they should be positively discounted. Or the prospective parentalist may simply have no firm evidence about the subject's desires. Then her knowledge of human nature may take priority over the subject's desires in her estimate of his welfare. She knows, for example, that by virtue of being a human being the person needs life and health, though he acts as if these do not concern him. She has good reason to deter him from endangering himself in a reckless escapade. At the same time, the rational parentalist knows that objective goods as well as desires vary from person to person. She knows something of the ways people differ. She takes into account available evidence of the individual's idiosyncracies in respect to what is good for him. Perhaps in this case excitement is truly worth the risk of life.

To make clear where the discussion is going, let me discuss the evaluation of the subject's autonomy. The position of the present work, which is defended at length later, is that autonomy has great value for most human beings most of the time, but not absolute value. It is sometimes right to encroach on a person's autonomy for his own good in face of his desire to be left alone, and it is also sometimes right to force autonomy on him in face of his desire to escape responsibility. Some people value autonomy highly, and others apparently could not care less. The prospective parentalist must look beyond the desires of the subject to determine how valuable his autonomy really is.

One basis for the parentalist's judgment in the particular case is the general importance of autonomy for human beings. A second is such evidence as she has of the satisfactions which the particular exercise of autonomy which she is about to curtail offers the subject. These satisfactions must be weighed against the other goods which he would fail to obtain by exercising autonomy if, for example, he lacks the ability to achieve his goals or if the goals he pursues are not really good for him.

At the same time, the parentalist should realize that her knowledge about the subject is limited and her judgment is fallible. Hence, she should be cautious about relying on her own ideas of what is good for the subject when they conflict with his considered desires. Consider the example of moral parentalism. A parent, confidant, teacher, or legislator undertakes to inculcate moral virtues in a recalcitrant child, friend, pupil, or citizen, for the person's own welfare. Suppose there is ample justification for doing so. PP dictates that such measures be limited to the area of the person's deficiencies (Corollary II) and include provisions for the elimination of his need for the measures by helping him overcome the deficiencies (Corollary III). It is essential to realize that the person, though not yet (highly) autonomous, has forms and degrees of autonomy that can be nourished and enlarged. Moral instruction therefore should be administered in such a manner as to allow the recipient to exercise autonomy in his ongoing life as much as possible as a way of developing it for its responsible exercise in the future. This might justify, for example, a dialectical "values clarification" approach to moral instruction in the schools in preference to a dogmatic program of indoctrination. The temptation is to indoctrinate mores for sex and drugs when parents, teachers, and the public become alarmed, to inculcate the habit of "Just say No" rather than trusting the ability of young people to make informed judgments. Unfortunately, this does not prepare them to deal with other problems in life or even to resist the tempter who says "Why not? It's fun."

The parentalist must keep in mind that the boundary between autonomy and subautonomy is arbitrary; it is not a natural and unbridgeable chasm. People achieve full autonomy in incremental steps. They should not be permanently barred from crossing the boundary by disabling forms of parentalism, but neither should they be catapulted over it before they are ready. Almost everyone can be led on a safe route of gradually expanding responsibilities. When one helps them do this, there is little danger they will crash to their doom, nor is there is any reason to hold them back from the brink of autonomy in fear that they will.

Other Strategies

One moral of the present reflections is that a self-critical person is alert to the kinds of bias to which she is prone. The parentalist can be seduced, for example, by the self-congratulatory feeling that she is a good gal who knows best. The feeling can swamp empathy for the chagrin of the recipient at needing help or having his own judgment ignored. Such a parentalist can be blinded to the world in which the recipient lives and become incapable of judging what is truly best for him. Then her very solicitude may rob him of his proper cares and humanity. The complacency of parentalism can be countered by taking to heart Sissela Bok's advice offered in reference lying. Bok observes that people prone to deception chronically shut out the perspective of the deceived. To maintain our moral balance, she says:

> We need to learn to shift back and forth between the two perspectives, and even to focus on both at once, as in straining to see both aspects of an optical illusion. In ethics, such a double focus leads to applying the Golden Rule: to strain to experience one's acts not only as subject and agent but as recipient, sometimes victim. . . . We all know what it is to lie, to be told lies, to be correctly or falsely suspected of having lied. In principle, we can all readily share both perspectives. What is important is to make that effort as we consider the lies we would like to be able to tell.[5]

Likewise, when tempted to parentalism, we should recall what it is like to be subject to it.

The negative side of objectivity is to reflect on our biases and seek to counteract them. The positive side is to look as hard as we can at the relevant features of the external world. These have to do with true interests of person we are trying to help and the causal connections among events relevant to the attempt. The wishes of the subject and his competencies weigh against parentalistic intervention and usually provide a prima facie objection to it. What objective factors are sufficient to overcome this objection?

The burden of proof that there are such factors rests on the parentalist despite or even because of the purity of her motives, and it is a heavy burden. The magnitude of the prospective benefit necessary to justify encroachments on autonomy is difficult to specify. Some authors consider the threat of irremediable harm or irretrievable loss of opportunity to be either necessary or sufficient. They oppose most forms of intervention, but concede that one ought, for example, to use force to prevent a person from committing suicide due to clinical depression or pressure him to take advantage of his last opportunity to escape the morass of poverty due to lack of education. My intuitions about such examples are not strong enough to persuade me that irremediability of a harm or irretrievability of an opportunity are either sufficient or necessary to justify parentalism: *They are not always sufficient*. A harm which a person inflicts on himself, such as tattooing "Mother Love" on his forearm, may be irremediable but not important enough to compensate for the indignity of being prevented from tending to his own business. *They are not always necessary*. It may be right to prevent a person from harming himself even though the harm might be remedied later if it is serious enough and the encroachment on his autonomy would be minor—for instance, forcing a friend to listen to information about someone he trusts to deter him from investing in a poor venture even though he could make up the loss later.

What then is the relevance of irremediability and irretrievability? In a sense, all harms and all lost opportunities are beyond remedy. The past is unalterable. What is done is done and cannot be undone, and what has been left undone is not done and can never be done. There is no way to make a harm not to have happened or a missed opportunity to have been taken. It is proper, nonetheless, to say that some harms are "remedied" and that some opportunities "come again." Something damaged can be restored to its former state; today's evil can be balanced by tomorrow's good; a deferred satisfaction can be enjoyed at a later time; an opportunity of a similar kind can come again. The original harm is still a harm, but it is balanced by a later good. This is not the case with harms that are "irremediable" in the ordinary sense. For one reason or another, they cannot be matched by later goods. When we see that a person about whom we care is making a mistake, we must weigh the harm he will bring on himself against any goods his action may achieve and which we will sacrifice by interfering, including the opportunity to learn from a mistake. We have less justification in intervening to prevent a self-harmful act if the harm will be matched by compensating goods without our intervention. But if the harm is truly irremediable, there are no future goods to consider, and this certainly counts in favor of intervening. The point is the magnitude of the harm, not the mere fact of irremediability.

The aim of what I call the institution of morality in Chapter 3 is to promote objectively good actions. Its guidelines affect behavior insofar as the agent is aware of the factors to which they refer. Hence, institutions with moral functions should maximize the probability that agents will see situations in the correct light. They should motivate them to be observant and reflective and teach them how.

PP requires the prospective parentalist to examine her judgments to assure herself that her beliefs, intentions, and reasons are as sound as possible and that she has better reasons to rely on her judgment than on that of anyone who opposes her action, including the recipient's. The parentalist must ask herself, What evidence do I have that the action will have the consequences I intend? that their probabilities are what they seem? that the consequences will really benefit the other? that what I take to be his interests are his true ones? that he has not (or has) consented to my intervention? that he was not (or was) rational in refusing to consent (or consenting)? that I am sincere in my desire to help him? that I have thought through all that the action and its practicable alternatives involve? that I have fully considered their effects on other persons?

PP thus demands not only objective judgments about actions and their consequences but also reflexive judgments about the objective judgments. Moreover, it demands that the objective judgments be well grounded. To overcome the prima facie objection to parentalism, the apparent consequences of the action must be sufficient to outweigh the apparent harm of curtailing the recipient's autonomy and the agent must have good reasons for believing that these will be the real consequences. These are demanding requirements and further justify our practice of treating parentalism as prima facie objectionable.

Reflexive judgments evaluate objective judgments by logical standards of evidence and inference. The obligation to follow these standards falls under the ethic of belief or more broadly what I will call the *epistemic ethic*. It is a tautology that we act according to our beliefs, since action by definition is the behavioral expression of intentions, and intentions are shaped by beliefs. It is a contingent matter whether our beliefs are sound. Our moral obligation is to make them as sound as possible. To put it another way, while we can only act according to the way things seem to us, we should strain every mental muscle to make them seem the way they really are. Moreover, we should exercise special caution when we make judgments about complex and problematic situations where there are prima facie reasons not to act on impulse, which often motivates parentalism.

An Illustration

Let us bring these considerations down to earth with a concrete example. One of the most wrenching decisions imaginable is to intervene to prevent the suicide of an apparently rational friend. Suppose that Elizabeth has a colleague of many years standing, Harry, who has lost close members of his family and recently his wife. He suffers chronic ill health and no longer finds satisfaction in his work. He is depressed and has every reason to be. He confides to Elizabeth that he may end it all. Elizabeth sympathizes, tries to cheer him up, and pleads with him not to think of such a thing, but to no effect. He remains gloomy and withdrawn. In the ensuing days she keeps an eye on him. He goes about his affairs and gives no evidence of emotional disturbance. He speaks matter-of-factly about the justification of suicide. Absolute respect for Harry's autonomy would dictate that Elizabeth limit her efforts to rational dissuasion. She might, for example, enlist Harry's relatives to urge him to consult a psychiatrist. Suppose, however, that he does, and the psychiatrist judges him to be mentally competent and discounts his talk of self-destruction. The absolutist does not interfere with the choices of a competent person: he would advise Elizabeth to step aside.

In contrast, PP sanctions more active and persistent intervention. It justifies the intuition that Elizabeth should use all of the emotional rhetoric and psychological pressure at her disposal to prevent Harry's suicide. His life is too precious to others and potentially to himself to stop short. She should urge him to defer a decision. She should help him see that he has much to live for and try to give him more. She could attempt to persuade him to change his basic values, for example, to convert him to her own optimistic philosophy or hopeful religion. If she can convince those with the legal authority to have him committed for counseling and medication, perhaps she should do so. Yet eventually she would have to step aside. She is not Harry's wife or child or parent; she cannot assume responsibility for his life. But until she reaches the limit, she should not stand passively by and let him destroy himself.

As a variation of the case, suppose that Harry agrees to receive therapy from psychiatrist Karl Miller, whose therapeutic ideology causes him to take seriously attempts, threats, and even hints of suicide. He interprets these as "cries for help," which express a desire to going on living even when the patient believes that he wants to end it all. Miller might be justified in utilizing what he has learned about Harry's values and innermost thoughts to appeal to his religious or moral scruples against self-destruction even though he, Miller, does not have the scruples himself. This would be a form of deception, but it seems legitimate.

Under the concept of the cry for help, it seems permissible for Miller to take the initiative in persuading Harry's family to have him committed to a mental health facility and plied with antidepressant drugs.

Miller's efforts might be justified, yet eventually Harry would have to be released and allowed to follow his own light even to self-destruction. Harry's friends and psychiatrist must see that it is not in his interest to be incarcerated against his will and follow a regimen managed by others.

With plausible variations in the circumstances, we can imagine that a friend or counselor could discover that Harry has good objective grounds for wanting to die and allow him to do as he would. Numerous cases of rational suicide have been reported in the public media in the last few years:

- Henry P. Van Dusen, former president of Union Theological Seminary, suffered a disabling stroke at the age of 72. His wife, Elizabeth, developed severe arthritis. They took their lives together when he was 77 and she 80, explaining in a letter, "We still feel this is the best way and the right way to go."
- Wallace Proctor was a 75-year-old dermatologist with Parkinson's disease. Before committing suicide, he visited the office of the district attorney to eliminate any suspicion of foul play.
- Artist Jo Roman made known her views on the desirability of suicide in the face of terminal illness some 15 years before she developed breast cancer. When she did develop it, she wrote a book and made a videotape, subsequently shown on the Public Broadcasting System, justifying the act. Then she killed herself.[6]

Assuming that the facts are what they seem, it would surely have been an offense against the individuals' autonomy and quite problematic in respect to their other objective interests for anyone to have forcibly prevented them from carrying out their acts of self-destruction.

The amount of intervention to prevent suicide sanctioned by any principle is a matter of judgment. We cannot draw a line at a definite point where someone committed to PP would push ahead and one committed to an alternative principle would desist, or the second point where the adherent to PP would also desist. All that can be said is that PP encourages more active and extensive intervention in the lives of those in desperate need than most of the alternatives on the market.

III

AUTONOMY

7

The Anatomy of Intervention

Any reasonable ban on parentalism based on respect for autonomy must be replete with exceptions because the forms of autonomy vary in degree and importance and some deserve much more respect than others. We will next examine the nature of autonomy, its value, the points at which it can be affected by intervention of others, and how all of this relates to justification of parentalism.

The Absolutist Dilemma

Those who would categorically ban parentalism on the basis of the right to autonomy face a dilemma. Autonomy in its maximal form entails complete rationality, self-control, knowledge of relevant facts, and other demanding conditions internal to the agent, as well as freedom and resources to act. Maximal autonomy might vie for the title of the highest good, but unfortunately it is a prerogative of God. If autonomy is conceived in maximalist terms, few if any human actions will be autonomous and they are not the ones that need protection. The principle that it is wrong to curtail the liberty of autonomous agents is rendered morally otiose.

The second horn of the absolutist dilemma is to define autonomy so weakly as to cover the bare process of opting. But then autonomy no longer deserves respect per se. Wild and stupid behavior merits disgust, apprehension, and pity, not admiration. Its intrinsic value for the agent is insignificant compared to the harms he may inflict on others and himself. Moreover, absolutists acknowledge that a person's autonomy must be limited to protect the autonomy of others. There is something odd in the view that it is permissible to interfere with actions in order to protect third persons but not to interfere with similar actions to protect the agent himself. If prevention of harm justifies restrictions of autonomy in one case, why not in the other? For these reasons, a categorical ban on intervention on all autonomous behavior carries no moral authority.

The absolutist's dilemma is that if one defines autonomy so that it always deserves respect, no one is autonomous; and if one defines it so that everyone is autonomous, it does not always deserve respect. However, an intermediate concept of autonomy involving a threshold concept of competence is popular in the literature and used to justify a strong ban on parentalism. We must explore it to clarify what the right to autonomy entails and what kind of ban on parentalism it warrants.

The first thing to observe is that autonomy is variable along several dimensions: it involves resources, opportunities to act, and the cost of each act, along with rationality in the form of an ordered set of preferences, sound beliefs, logical powers of inference, and self-control. Each of these may be present in any number of quantitites or degrees. Each varies not only from person to person but in a given person at different times. Autonomy, then, is a matter of type and degree, not something that some individuals possess and others lack in toto. Deficits in particular elements can be balanced by exceptional amounts of other elements. What must be respected is the person's aggregate autonomy realized throughout her lifetime. What must be considered about a parentalistic intervention is its effect, as far as this can be anticipated, on her future stream of autonomous actions and satisfying experiences.

No one would be so foolish as to claim that quanta of autonomy can be measured and aggregates summed, but gross differences can be discriminated. This person has more resources on one occasion than on another; she is more in control of herself, has sounder information, or faces lighter penalties for doing what she wants. Such intuitive comparisons cannot rank degrees of autonomy in linear order: Is a person more autonomous when she has many resources, or when she has fewer but is in control of herself? when she has her values straight, or when she is confused but knows more about the contingencies? One can only estimate. Despite these limitations, one who intervenes in the life of another can often judge well enough whether his action will enhance her autonomy in a significant way by providing her more resources, reinforcing her self-control, helping her sort out her values, providing her information, etc. Similarly, he can see ways in which an action will detract from her autonomy. The important thing is to take all dimensions of her autonomy into consideration. Interventions are often condemned for reducing some while overlooking the way the act enhances others.

Those in search of strict rules forbidding parentalism for entire categories of people while permitting it for others are uncomfortable with such complexities. They want to discuss autonomy in dichotomous terms, to be able to classify people as autonomous or not; if autonomous, as competent or not; and if competent, as encumbered or not. This approach puts phenomena into neat bins for analysis, but distorts them and confounds our intuitions. More important, assigning people to precisely delimited and homogeneous categories rather than taking account of the subtle differences among them is harmful in practice.

I will distinguish two conceptual approaches to autonomy and competence which affect attitudes toward parentalism. I will call one *relativistic* and the other *threshold conceptions*.[1] According to relativistic conceptions, mental capacities vary continuously among people. The most we can say about an individual is that he is relatively autonomous or competent. Daniel Wikler notes that standard competence measures such as IQ tests take the relativistic conception for granted. Only because the labels are controlled by people with average capacities valued in a given society do people of lower capacities come to be categorized as "impaired" or "retarded" and treated in special ways. Average people would be treated the same way if the gifted were to assign the labels. The dividing line between overall "competence" and "incompetence" is drawn arbitrarily for ideological purposes.

According to threshold conceptions, the distinction between competent and incompetent is based on a natural, if broad or vague, division. The difference between the people on two sides of the boundary are much more important than differences among those on each side. All of those above the threshold of competence are equipped to meet the challenges of the world and are classified as normal. Those below are unable to meet them: if incompetence is due to injury or congenital defects, they are classified as incapacitated, handicapped, or retarded; if it is due to youth or temporary impairment, they are classified as immature or ill. All "incompetents" require extensive care by normals.

Dan Brock labels the threshold and relativistic conceptions of competence as "competence$_t$," and "competence$_r$." Under the concept of competence$_t$ it makes sense to institute distinct rigid policies respecting parentalism for three categories of human beings: normal adults, the impaired, and children. Brock observes that the trichotomy is utilized to establish strict schedules of rights:

> It is true that most of the usual rights to liberty(ies), autonomy, or self-determination are commonly not extended to young children, the retarded, and mentally ill persons, yet are fully extended to all normal adults, however much they differ in intelligence. This alone strongly suggests that it is competence$_t$ that is assumed by the rights theorist to be necessary for a person to possess rights. Competence$_t$ seems generally understood as a minimal requirement, and as implying capability for a minimally satisfactory performance.[2]

Most moralists realize, however, that competence$_t$ should not seal a person off entirely from parentalistic care. Competent persons often act contrary to their own interests under the encumbrance of ignorance or an eruption of emotion. This ought to lead those who espouse the concept of competence$_t$ to competence$_r$, but it only causes them to treat encumbrance as a threshold property. They enlarge their categories to four: competent-unencumbered adults, competent-encumbered adults, impaired adults, and children. The goal remains to formulate a simple set of rules by treating each category as homogeneous.

Benn's Threshold Concept

To explain why I utilize relativistic concepts, I will examine an analysis of parentalism which opts for threshold ones. S.I. Benn distinguishes three levels of self-rule: "subautarchy," "autarchy," and "autonomy proper." He prescinds from the variations in human powers within each level and from the way that each shades into the next so as to treat them as discrete homogeneous wholes. This allows him to formulate different rules of intervention for the different levels. If a person is above the subautarchy-autarchy threshold, one is fully autarchic wherever one falls in that level; and if one is above the autarchy-autonomy threshold, one is fully autonomous however little one is beyond it.

Subautarchics include neurotic and psychotic persons, who are "inner-impelled," and hetarchic persons, who have been subjected to conditioning approximating brainwashing. Benn maintains that subautarchics do not make choices in a strict sense and hence there is no difficulty in justifying parentalism toward them.[3] At the other extreme, there is little temptation to justify parentalistic interference with fully autonomous persons: we cannot imagine how outsiders could direct their affairs better than they do themselves. The critical category, therefore, is the great middle group, the autarchics. These may be called "natural persons" since there are few subautarchics and full autonomy is a personality ideal which even fewer people realize. Autarchy is normal in both the statistical sense of the most frequent condition and the normative sense of a nondefective one.

Benn's Principle of Respect for Autarchy governs interactions between natural persons. It says: "manipulating a person's actions by means that short-circuit his decision-making capacity does him wrong, unless overriding justification can be found."[4] This acknowledges that there are overriding justifications, but Benn does not assert that these may pertain to the subject's good, so it is not clear that he rejects a categorical ban on parentalism. His remarks on the value of autarchy to the individual suggests that he favors one.

What is most interesting in Benn's paper is his argument for his principle.[5] He describes its structure in this way: "I shall argue that for someone who has a normal conception of himself as a natural person in a world of natural persons, the conceptual sacrifice to which he would be committed by denying the principle of non-interference would be extremely punishing." The argument runs: (a) We natural persons so value our autarchy that we base our claim to moral agency on it. "Seeing ourselves as natural persons, or makers of projects, in a world with other persons, we have developed a conception of ourselves as moral persons too, entitled to a degree of forbearance from any other natural person conceptually capable of grasping our self-perception." (b) Consistency requires us to respect the personhood of others. "Claiming respect—moral personality—on the grounds of natural personality, we are then committed to extending it to anyone else satisfying the same conditions." (c) To claim moral status for ourselves without acknowledging it for others would be to deny that others are persons and "the cost would be enormous. There would be so much of human behaviour to explain away: and such a strategy would, in any case, be rather like the paranoid, forcing the subject back into a private world."

Central to Benn's argument is the assumption that autarchy is a basic interest of human beings, that it is a fundamental element in their welfare whether they recognize it or not, and hence anyone concerned with their welfare should respect it. But wherein lies its value? Benn locates it in the consciousness of being the initiator of events and therefore a person. "A man's consciousness of himself as author is essential to his conception of himself as a person."[6] To be conscious of being an author of events in this sense one must apprehend situations in the light of preferences, which presupposes a preference set. Having a preference is the initial moment of autarchic acts, regardless of whether the preference and the further moments of the act are informed by facts or reasoning—that is, what distinguishes autonomous acts. The autarchic person may receive his preferences from others, while truly autonomous persons are authors of their own preferences, but both autarchic and autonomous persons participate in their own development since they actualize potentialities by initiating changes in external things. Hence, autarchic and autonomous acts are valuable both intrinsically for the satisfaction of performing them and instrumentally for what they contribute to self-realization.

What are we to make of the principles of justification precipitated by these dichotomous concepts? Benn traces the value of both autarchy and autonomy to our ontological status in the world. So far, so good. But he implausibly assigns an absolute value to autarchy:

> To take seriously one's conception of oneself as a chooser is to assign a kind of higher-level importance to being the kind of agent capable of arranging his conduct according to the importance he attaches to various states of affairs. To find that his choices were manipulated would amount to finding he did not choose at all. Thereafter nothing could count for him as important at the lower level; he would be left with a conception of himself as a set of dispositions to behave, but to none of them could he sensibly attach importance. But the higher-level importance of being a chooser would not be similarly dissolved. It would manifest itself in a sense of lost identity, of having been deprived of that element in one's self-perception that had given its particular kind of coherence to all the rest.[7]

I construe this to be the strong claim that autarchy has priority over all other values except autonomy since a person would find nothing of value without autarchy. If this is the claim, it ignores important passive values. A person who discovered that he had been raised to be a puppet might cease to evaluate his actions according to a preference set that had been implanted in him, but this need not make him indifferent to what happened next. He might care whether he was scheduled to suffer excruciating pain or exquisite pleasure, whether his robot existence was contributing beauty and insight or ugliness and confusion to the world, whether fellow robots were programmed to be affectionate or hostile, whether he had been designed to be immortal or wear out in time.

But let us assume for argument that autarchy is the supreme value. An absolute ban on parentalism is still not dictated. To deprive a person of autarchy, a parentalist would have to robotomize him. Nothing short of brainwashing or lobotomy would do. Ordinary parentalism does not traffic in such measures and hence is not a threat to autarchy. Interventions affect only a fraction of the subject's stream of life. Normally they affect only some aspects of her action of the moment. Thus they do not deny her minimal autonomy (drive her below the threshold of autarchy). The most violent form of intervention, coercion, consists in altering the costs of her options but even it leaves her options. Moreover, minimally autarchic persons such as children, retardates, asylum inmates, and prisoners make choices and initiate actions. What is distressing is not that they never use their faculties, but that they are unable to use them to pursue important values without excessive costs. Their choices are limited to lesser evils and minor goods. In short, respect for autarchy does not dictate condemnation of parentalistic acts en masse. There are no grounds to imagine that every intervention robs the person of the sense of being an initiator of events or the dignity of being a person.

Let us return to Benn's universalization argument to locate the point at which his Principle of Autarchy fails. Recall that it is a premise of the argument that we claim to be entitled to noninterference by other people on the basis of our consciousness of ourselves as natural persons. This premise does not prove what Benn wants. The fact that autarchy is valuable does not entail that we are entitled to it; entitlement implies a moral obligation on the part of others, not just a strong desire or demand on the part of the title holder. A framework of moral rules is necessary to show that we ought to be provided what we want. The proper framework, according to my light, must be founded on relations of mutual caring that are realized in the good society, that are demanded of us in building a good society, that are our principal consolation in the kind of society that we have, and that are a fundamental source of satisfaction and necessary condition for happiness whatever our society. If we accept that the function of morality is to provide conditions under which people can live authentically and authenticity requires people to care for and be cared for by one another, then what is important for each is a concern for every other. Each is entitled to care which includes but is not confined to respect for his autonomy.

It is a peculiarity of autonomy that one usually helps another to enjoy it by forbearing from intervention in his life. But Benn's overevaluation of low-grade autonomy obscures the additional truths that in some circumstances one can further higher levels of autonomy by intervention and in other circumstances there are values at stake that warrant the sacrifice of low-grade autonomy.

A Relativistic Concept

The difficulties in Benn's analysis spring from his threshold concepts. They mandate relativistic concepts according to which competence and encumbrance are matters of degree. Relativistic concepts still allow us to draw lines to single out less competent persons in special contexts, but they deter us from imagining that the lines are natural or absolute. Nothing is more designed to strangle discriminating care in its cradle than categorical labeling of persons as *either* entirely competent and unencumbered and hence needing no care at all *or* completely incompetent or irrational and hence needing total care.

In defending relativistic conceptions, I will reconstruct the progression from the lower and more heteronomous levels of volition to the highest and most autonomous. The distinctions I will make are conceptual and normative. It is a task for the developmental psychologist to determine their actual sequence in the growth of the individual. There is no suggestion here of a chronological sequence, nor do I try to show how instances of processes at one level affect instances at another.

At the lowest level, humans merely respond differentially to external and somatic stimuli. Their acts fall below the margin of autonomy. *Opting* is the most rudimentary form of deciding, in the sense of cutting off all but one alternative in such a way as to release the organic urge to action. It involves apprehension of at least one possibility in a situation, followed by an intention to realize it. It is a matter of convenience whether one calls the action that ensues "voluntary" or not. In higher forms of action, *decision* is the terminal moment in the apprehension of multiple alternatives and the initial point of behavior on one of them. Every decision is made in situ. Objectively, a situation involves things perceived in terms of their possibilities; subjectively, it involves the perspective that determines which things and possibilities are singled out to become factors in the subject's action. Significant forms of autonomy begin to occur when the possibilities that spring up are shaped by one's beliefs and goals. These transform facts into opportunities and threats, resources and obstacles—that is, into conditions for possible actions. Bare choice, then, involves discrimination of facts, negation of them to apprehend possibilities, valuation of facts and possibilities, and finally decision, which cuts all possibilities but one so that the urge to act is channeled in its direction.

At this primitive level, the distinctive patterns of care emerge. Decisions are governed by the concerns of the individual: what one cares about and how he strives to take care of it.

At this low level, choice is scarcely distinguishable from automatic response to a stimuli. It can hardly be called voluntary. A single possibility enters the agent's awareness and he pursues it. His preferences may be unstable—he may prefer X to Y one moment and Y to X the next. His beliefs may fluctuate—he may see A as a means to X one moment and as an obstacle at the next. Nevertheless, he chooses because he has the power to perform alternative acts and preferences shape his intentions in a way that an unordered set of nebulous feelings or an anomic state would not.

Self-control involves more than an instantaneous apprehending-opting that eventuates in action. It involves a stable set of preferences and beliefs that empower the agent to sustain intentions through a sequence of steps. The more extensive the action—the greater the number of its steps—the more stability is required in the self. Moreover, self-controlled actions require a degree of stability in the environment. Actions initiate processes to accomplish intended ends. Conditions must remain constant through the phases of the action to sustain these processes to successful conclusion. The agent must be able to count on this to perform a complex series of steps leading to a remote end.

The dynamic character of the human condition precludes absolute permanence in the self or stability in the environment. The agent moves from situation to situation, and situations evolve. The truly autonomous self is not static, but flexible enough to adjust to shifting circumstances. Moreover, self-control requires more than a dynamic equilibrium between enduring but adaptable preferences and beliefs and relatively stable conditions in the evolving environment. To stay on the course despite obstacles and distractions, the agent must have his affective reactions in hand to focus his conative drives on the course of action which his cognitive faculties endorse. Self-control, then, means control by one part of the person (the rational) over the rest (emotional and volitional).

Self-control is not a gift of nature; it is won through commitment to action, trial and error, and habituation. To attain the higher levels of autonomy, a person must acquire good habits, considered tastes, enduring commitments and loyalties, determinate ideals, and effective models—the whole apparatus of the moral life. But even when these capabilities and possessions are secure, most choices remain unreflective. The circumstances of the action, along with the agent's preferences and beliefs and intentions sustained for the duration of a project, may be kept *in* mind without being kept *before* the mind. Consciousness may be focused on the situation, the goal, or the action rather than on the process of choosing and the considerations in terms of which the agent chooses. The agent chooses *for* reasons, rather than attending *to* them. Deliberation brings reasons to the foreground of attention. It measures goals and means, opportunities and threats, and resources and obstacles against norms in the form of rules, ideals, objectives, and paradigms.

The agent may also reflect on his norms in order to improve his judgments. We can now speak of evaluation and truly voluntary action in addition to valuation and decision. Moreover, reflective norms enable the agent to actively seek out relevant factors of a situation rather than reacting to ones that accidentally or routinely affect him. He can search for side effects of alternative actions and remote consequences of possible goals. He then becomes aware of the costs of acting different ways. He discovers that actions have consequences besides the specific goods at which he aims, so that to choose the goods means to accept the other consequences. He learns that to perform any action, he must forego certain other actions with their costs and benefits. Thus he moves in the direction of awareness of all of the alternatives for action and all of their costs and benefits in a given situation in the total matrix of causes and effects in which it is located.

Reflection introduces the note of truth and knowledge. Full autonomy entails not only initiation of an action, but carrying it through to completion. Actions can be initiated by a false apprehension of the situation or false beliefs about causal connections in it. Successful actions depend on accurate perceptions and true beliefs. To be autonomous in any sense worthy of the name, an agent must have some knowledge of the external world. Single autonomous actions require knowledge of particular situations. The succession of actions that constitutes the autonomous life requires knowledge about the whole spectrum of life situations.

As demanding as all of this is, it still does not ensure the highest level of autonomy. An agent's goals may prove to be unsatisfying when achieved, and this inhibits his tendency to act the same way the next time around. His preferences shift. By virtue of this process, an ongoing pattern of successful actions requires a continuing readjustment of preferences to see that they are directed to things that truly satisfy the agent. The agent becomes aware of the distinction between objective and apparent goods.

Most of life is conducted on the basis of beliefs that are partially uninformed or misinformed and preferences that are partially indeterminate or misdirected. The individual receives most of his beliefs and preferences from other people, so they are not neatly tailored to his individual makeup. Reflection offers a route to transcend second-hand mental equipment and routines. It enables the individual to learn from his own experience, modify his beliefs, and revise his preferences to fit his individual makeup. It allows him to develop a plan of life that will maximize success in concrete situations and lead to lasting satisfactions. It raises the prospect of that total condition, so difficult to define and elusive to attain, yet so central to life, that we call happiness. It challenges the reflective individual to its intelligent lifelong pursuit.

Good plans do not guarantee successful outcomes. Fortune may subvert the best conceived programs, and weakness of will prevents individuals from following them consistently. Autonomy in the fullest sense, the self-governance of an entire life in accordance with a rational plan, requires not only the cooperation of the environment but a developed and integrated personality. It requires a stable character in which intellectual and moral virtues are firmly fixed. Self-control thus presupposes the development of strength and constancy in the ego and domination of the psyche by its natural ruler. Highly autonomous persons have the mental faculties that enable them to review and evaluate alternatives and the self-control to stick to a course in the face of difficulties through changing circumstances.

Faculties and self-control, however, are only potencies or powers. Autonomy is actualized when freely chosen actions are carried out, and this requires favorable external conditions. It does little good to run over alternatives if they are few and all bad. It does no good at all to strive resolutely for goals that are doomed to failure. Autonomy is thus a function not only of the agent's subjective powers but also of his external resources. To exercise autonomy he must find or create an environment with resources to overcome the obstacles that cannot be eliminated.

The ability of the parentalist to affect the autonomy of his subject is a function of his control over the two sorts of factors, internal and external. Since there are many elements in each sort, intervention can take many forms. The parentalist can influence the subject's preferences and beliefs, help her reasoning or disrupt it, foster her self-control or incite her to go out of control; and he can change the costs of the subject's options or alter the options themselves by providing or removing resources or erecting or razing barriers.

Conditions of autonomy can be divided into categories on the basis of the analysis proposed above. I will refer to external factors as *facilities*. They include (1) resources, (2) the costs of alternatives, and (3) the condition of the agent's body. Internal factors or *faculties* include (4) experience, (5) rationality, (6) knowledge, and (7) self-control.

Facilities

Resources

External resources include wealth, the accessibility of facilities and equipment, social status, influence, friends, and allies—everything that empowers a person to carry out her wishes. The liberty of action of impoverished, imprisoned, friendless, politically impotent, and socially despised people is limited. Smug antiparentalistic refusal by the privileged to help such people on the pretense that they must learn to stand on their own feet rings hollow. In other cases privileged parentalists forget how precious the little autonomy left to the deprived may be as they fulfil some more obvious need for them.

One can affect another's autonomy by controlling resources. Thus one may avoid feeding a friend's drug habit by reneging on a debt, refuse to return a handgun to a suicidal neighbor, or forego an opportunity to use political influence to obtain a position for a relative to protect her from getting in over her head or being corrupted. The notion of resources is broad. Parentalists and pseudoparentalists deny people social opportunities to which they have a formal right in the name of preventing them from engaging in self-harmful activities. For example, a temperance mob wrecks a saloon to protect working men from demon rum; bigots blackball Jews from their club to protect them from discomfort. In connection with this point, we may observe that the contextualist notion of legal rights provides a utilitarian ground for Mill's opposition to enforcement of contracts in which a person sells himself into bondage:[8] society thereby discourages such contracts and denies the subject the opportunity to enter a self-harmful relationship, although contracts are enforced for a wide range of other relations.

Costs

Autonomy is conditioned by the cost of options. The causal nexus of a situation determines the effort an agent must expend to reach a particular goal, the other goals that must be sacrificed, and the harm that will ensue if the action fails. A subject does not choose between actions *simpliciter*, but between actions with their probable consequences. The term *costs*, while standard, is too negative. As we noted in connection with the measures available to the parentalist, benefits must also be considered in understanding how the subject's actions can be influenced by others. One can intervene by adding not only to the harms resulting from acts one wants to deter, but to the benefits resulting from the act one wants to encourage. Control consists in inducing someone to do what he otherwise would not do, either by penalizing the alternatives or rewarding the action. The extreme forms of control are coercion, which makes the cost of an unwanted action prohibitive by severe penalties, and seduction, which makes a wanted action irresistible by extraordinary rewards.

Both negative and positive weighting leave the subject's power of decision intact and the same options available. But this needs qualification. Extreme weightings can so damage the subject's powers that his autonomy itself is diminished. Suppose that S must choose between X and Y. X is abhorrent to him. C, who wants to deter him from Y, adds cruel penalties to it, confronting him with an impossible choice. He is thrown into panic or despair and is no longer able to think rationally.

The impact of extreme coercion on autonomy and the harm inflicted by any form explains why antiparentalists have centered their opposition on coercive parentalism. Reward intervention is preferable where it can achieve the same result. If P adds rewards to X, she will present S with two savory alternatives. S is already attracted to Y, and P has made X attractive. S will receive positive goods whichever he chooses, and his emotions are less likely to get in the way of a rational choice between them. In that case, the question of justification of P's action is not likely to arise. Yet rewards do affect S's choices. Is his choice of X any more free if he is motivated by an extraneous reward than if he is dissuaded from Y by an extraneous penalty? Alternatively, is he any less free in avoiding Y than in choosing X?

Both coercion and rewards, though external, affect conduct by altering the subject's internal condition. S.I. Benn notes that both are functions of the subject's values, so what constitutes duress (and seduction) is a function of his preferences. Jeffrie Murphy likewise notes that coercion is effective only if the subject desires what is threatened; he retains autonomy under coercion though the options under his schedule of preferences are curtailed.[9]

The Subject's Body

Little has been said about the state of the subject's body in discussions of parentalism, though a few authors mention incarceration and bodily injury as reductions of resources. Two who cite direct assaults on a subject's body are Beauchamp, who refers to psychosurgical passification of violent individuals as an alternative to imprisonment, and Gert and Culver, who imagine a mother mutilating her son to prevent him from enlisting in the Marines.[10]

The point is that the condition of a subject's body—health, strength, speed, agility, perceptual acuity, grace, beauty, and so on—and its physical circumstances, such as being at the right place at the right time or being an object of admiration, provide resources for action in the world. The parentalist can enhance the subject's autonomy by adding to these resources and diminish them to achieve other goods for her. Existing deficiencies, impairments, or restraints reduce the value of the subject's residual autonomy, making it easier to justify parentalistic intervention.

Faculties

The internal conditions of autonomy—experience, rationality, knowledge, and self-control—can be cross-divided into psychic capabilities and states. To act autonomously, one must first be endowed with capabilities and then have them brought into a state of readiness. An extended process of development is required to become fully autonomous, which is why it is easier to justify parentalistic care of children than of adults.

In this connection, we should keep in mind a basic point made by Benn: personhood is the foundation of autonomy. To be a person and carry out long-term activities, one must preserve his identity through time. This is quite a long time in the implementation of a plan of life. Faculties such as memory and imagination are necessary to devise a course of action, anticipate its consequences, and keep them in view while the necessary steps are executed. One also needs reason and judgment to form the beliefs and values that provide content for plans. The richer the subjective life of the agent, therefore, the greater is his potential autonomy.

The integrated complex of psychic abilities and possessions which is the necessary instrument for action make up the "self." The stability of this self through time constitutes personal identity. Autonomy is a sequence of actions that express the perduring self, the self with a stable personal identity, by utilizing its enduring abilities and possessions. Thus, Feinberg, hearkening back to Aristotle, observes that autonomous actions "not only have their origin 'in the agent,' they also represent him faithfully in some important way: they express his settled values and preferences. In the fullest sense, therefore, they are actions for which he can take responsibility."[11] The more settled the agent's character and the more enduring and integrated his self, the wider the range of actions open to him. The weaker his character and less integrated his personality, the less autonomous he is, however favorable the external conditions.

Experience

Subjective possessions may be sorted into groups in relation to analytic phases of fully rational decision. The first possession is breadth of experience. A person's ability to receive and retain perceptual material and understand that of others provide data on which he can form beliefs and values. His autonomy, therefore, can be restricted by limits on his experience due to impairments such as blindness and learning disabilities and to lack of opportunity, for education or travel, for example.

Thus Mill admits an important exception to the proposition on which he insists, that individuals are the best judges of their own interests: "The presumption in favor of individual judgment is only legitimate, where the judgment is grounded on actual, and especially on present, personal experience; not where it is formed antecedently to experience, and not suffered to be reversed even after experience has condemned it."[12] This remark should be taken in conjunction with Mill's explanation that he does not intend for the principle of liberty to apply to children, backward societies, or "any state of things anterior to the time when mankind has become capable of being improved by free and equal discussion." A person severely limited in experience or education is in a comparable condition in regard to many matters important for his welfare.

Rationality

One basis for the higher forms of autonomy which has received extensive attention is rationality. For example, among Benn's conditions for autarchy is the ability to recognize canons of evidence and inferences warranting changes in beliefs. The treatment of normal adults as equal members of the moral community presupposes some concept of competence in which rationality plays a part. Individuals may be deficient in rationality in a variety of ways. Daniel Wikler in discussing retardates and Francis Schrag in discussing children make clear how hard it is to determine the ways in which groups are deficient in justifying parentalistic attitudes toward them.[13] The problem is complicated by the differ- ence between natural deficiencies and episodic interruptions such as emotional disturbance and neurosis.

The flaws in preferences may be due to lack of knowledge or lack of rationality to use knowledge. Michael McDonald distinguishes between ratio- nality of means and rationality of ends and two correlative forms of "self- regarding failures"—not getting what one wants and seeking the wrong things. The first produces frustration; the second, dissatisfaction. A subject's dissatisfac- tion due to faulty preferences warrants intervention as much as frustration due to faulty causal beliefs.[14]

Knowledge

The autonomous agent acts on the belief that actions will produce various consequences with particular degrees of probability. She utilizes beliefs about the causal efficacy of factors in the context, such as how things will go if she initiates a chain of causation in the world or if she lets things slide. She utilizes notions about the goods and evils intrinsic to particular actions, their conse- quences, and other factors in the situation. A fully autonomous agent is one who knows the objective importance of different values in particular situations and who shapes her preferences accordingly.

Even persons of limited competence may have goals determined by an ordered preference set in the light of which they make choices. The fully autonomous person in addition subjects his values and causal beliefs to critical reflection:

> The autonomous man is, in Rousseau's phrase, "obedient to a law that he prescribes to himself." His life has a consistency that derives from a coherent set of beliefs, values, and principles which govern his actions. These are not supplied ready-made like those of the heteronomous man; they are his because of a still-continuing process of criticism and evaluation.[15]

Knowledge of self as well as the world is essential to autonomy in its higher forms. Rationality is valuable to a person because it makes it more probable that she will acquire knowledge, and knowledge enhances her chance of choosing actions that will succeed in their purpose. Ignorance and false beliefs compro- mise the autonomy of even the most rational person and make it easier to justify parentalistic intervention. However, the intervention is easier to justify still if it takes the form of enlightening the beneficiary about facts or values so that she will voluntarily avoid the harmful act in the future—in other words, if the parentalistic act ultimately enhances her autonomy.

Self-Control

The endowments just described do not guarantee that an agent will act suc- cessfully. She needs the strengths and capabilities that are lumped together as "self-control." Imagine a contemplative rational being who lacks the capability of acting because she cannot come to any decision on the possibilities opened by her knowledge or sustain intentions through the period required to carry out decisions. A person is deficient in autonomy if some internal compulsion, inhibition, or disability prevents her from carrying out her intentions. She is likewise deficient if she reacts impulsively to immediate stimuli without surveying possibilities. Act she must and reason she may, but her actions are not geared to her reasoning because they do not express her enduring self.

Fragmentation of the personality and lack of self-control are often described as division of the self against itself. The person is pictured as acting contrary to the beliefs and preferences of her "true" self. The person may herself use the gambit to avoid responsibility ("I was not myself," "It was not the real me"). But after all, what is the self but that which acts? On the other hand, without a notion of internal division, what does it mean to talk of self-control and weakness of will? It posits a self that is quiescent before forces of the moment that confront it as alien powers. The true self is the part of the person that *should* rule the whole. Since reason is the complex of powers which can discover what is best for the total person, the true self is the part which exercises and obeys reason. If this element is too weak to commit the whole person to action, the person is deficient in autonomy and is a candidate for parentalistic care.

8

The Value of Autonomy

Nothing rings out more clearly in the literature on parentalism than praise of autonomy. Many philosophers take it to be the distinctive trait of persons, the source of human dignity, and a basic human right. They claim that it deserves respect, and they sharply distinguish respect from affection or esteem, which may be due animals and things.

The more eloquent the rhetoric and the more it resonates with our feelings about ourselves and other humans, the more assiduous should we be in tracking down what it entails. We should not let the fact that autonomy is extremely valuable in many of its forms and respects entice us into assuming that it is supremely valuable in every form and respect.

Mill on Human Dignity

There is no better place to begin the discussion than Mill's remarks since it is largely he who first defined the issues of parentalism. Since 'autonomy' is not his term, we must look at his treatment of related matters. This includes what he has to say about the ability to act according to norms, which distinguishes our species; the process of choosing and pursuing what we desire, which provides us the fundamental experience of being human; and the rationality and morality of some of our choices and success in carrying out rationally chosen actions, which bring us higher forms of pleasure and culminate in happiness.

Mill discusses not only the instrumental value of these aspects of autonomy—they are essential to securing other ingredients of happiness for the agent and those for whom he cares—but also their intrinsic value. In his familiar distinction between qualities of pleasure, he maintains that the better ones involve the higher or distinctively human faculties such as reason, imagination, and volition. These are precisely the faculties that are operative in autonomous acts. Generally speaking, the more we use the higher faculties, the more autonomous our acts; and the more autonomous our acts, the more satisfying they are.

In *Utilitarianism* Mill asks why a being of higher faculties accepts frustration and discontentment rather than allowing himself to sink back to a lower grade of existence. While it may be attributed to pride or love of liberty, power or excitement, "its most appropriate appellation is a sense of dignity, which all human beings possess in one form or other, and in some, though by no means in exact, proportion to their higher faculties, and which is so essential a part of the happiness of those in whom it is strong, that nothing which conflicts with it could be otherwise than momentarily, an object of desire to them."[1] Note that dignity is a variable. Those who exercise the higher faculties have greater dignity, and enjoy greater happiness, than those who settle for a lower mode of existence. This is one reason Mill puts such stress on education: it inculcates the abilities and virtues that are the key to dignity along with useful knowledge.

While higher faculties are possessed in some measure by all normal humans, their specific form, degree, and combination differ, and each individual utilizes them in a unique way. Mill prizes individuality very highly and defends its value at length in chapters 3–5 of *On Liberty*. Arneson points out that Mill praises at least three distinct things: the uniqueness of each person, making for diversity in the human species; the development of human traits, accentuating diversity and allowing each person to enjoy what he is most suited for; and self-cultivation of traits, which enhances dignity.[2]

Respect for individuality requires sensitivity to individual differences and bars uniformity of treatment. Mill says:

> It is not by wearing down into uniformity all that is individual in themselves, but by cultivating it and calling it forth, within the limits imposed by the rights and interests of others, that human beings become a noble and beautiful object of contemplation; and as the works partake the character of those who do them, by the same process human life also becomes rich, diversified, and animating, furnishing more abundant aliment to high thoughts and elevated feelings, and strengthening the tie which binds every individual to the race, by making the race infinitely better worth belonging to.[3]

Note several things that Mill says in this pregnant passage. First, fine acts and qualities have intrinsic value not only for the agent, but for others as noble or beautiful objects for contemplation. This is Mill's way of explaining the respect that is due to persons and moral agents. This aesthetic concept (respect as a feeling aroused by a beautiful object) is not Kant's magisterial one (a feeling toward something which exercises power over the will), but in it Mill like Kant recognizes respect as a basic moral phenomenon. Individuality has aesthetic value in regard both to the sheer variety of the human beings which it produces and the particular specimens of excellence which emerge among them. Those who cultivate uniqueness and excellence whether in themselves or others are artists. "Among the works of man, which human life is rightly employed in perfecting and beautifying, the first in importance is surely man himself." We would not exchange humans for automatons even if they could get our "houses built, corn grown, battles fought, causes tried, and even churches erected and prayers said."[4]

Second, despite Mill's appreciation of the intrinsic value of individuality, he directs attention mainly to its external benefits. Individual differences lead to experiments in living, new ideas for the common stock of knowledge, innovations in custom, and so on. This argument is enmeshed in his defense of freedom of thought and speech. He discusses at length the instrumental value of the talent, heroism, outstanding deeds, and exceptional personalities that are multiplied under conditions of liberty. Nevertheless, he clearly finds a great deal of intrinsic value in both liberty and individuality.

Third, the statement does not prohibit parentalism, and elsewhere Mill notes that compulsion is sometimes necessary for the individual's own good. It is obviously needed to ensure the development of children. He thinks that less coercion of adults is needed because it is more effective to educate them to deal with the problems of life. Thus he protests against the view that society has "no means of bringing its weaker members up to its ordinary standard of rational conduct, except waiting till they do something irrational, and then punishing them, legally or morally, for it. Society has had absolute power over them during all the early portion or their existence: it has had the whole period of childhood and nonage in which to try whether it could make them capable of rational conduct of life."[5] Nevertheless, he concedes that society fails to educate its members perfectly and people do act irrationally. They obviously have to be coerced and forcibly restrained to keep them from injuring one another. Mill does not say whether the cost of letting them injure themselves is always warranted by the gain in their liberty and autonomy by refraining from coercing and restraining them. It is clear that he thinks it very often is, but we do not find him issuing a categorical prohibition of parentalism and the way he puts his principles leaves the door open.

In a society more complex than Mill's, even an ideal system of education might not be able to equip its members with the knowledge necessary to tend to their own welfare in many areas of their lives. Clearly, actual educational systems fall far short of doing this. As a result, Mill's restrictions on parentalism for his society might not work as well for ours and even less for more complex ones of the future. I do not shrink from this conclusion. The more complex a society and the more numerous the skills needed to deal with its complexities, the more areas of one's life have to be taken under the care of institutions which he does not directly control if space is to be made for the relationships of mutual caring on which authentic human existence and community depend. But, correspondingly, more safeguards will also be needed to maximize the freedom of individuals to choose how to relate to the institutions, on the one hand, and to keep the parentalism of the institutions in bounds and see that their powers are not used for exploitive purposes, on the other hand.

Moreover, as the complexity of life and society grows, it becomes ever more important to cultivate mutual care. It is important that those who care for others are cared for in their turn and are conscious of that care so that hierarchies of dependency do not evolve. Dependency is a mark of failure or deficiency in human relations; interdependency is a mark of success and fulfillment.

Whether or not Mill would accept particular kinds of institutionalized care found in contemporary society, with their parentalistic dimensions and often weak safeguards, is problematic. He expresses his opposition to comparable arrangements of his own time. For example, he protests against the treatment of "the laboring classes" as children to protect them against alcohol by measures such as prohibition. He opposes the requirement of a prescription by a physician to obtain "poisons" (presumably he means dangerous medicinal drugs), which makes them expensive and difficult to obtain. He believes that "it would be giving too dangerous a power to governments, were they allowed to exclude anyone from professions . . . for alleged deficiency of qualifications." He thinks that "degrees, or other public certificates of scientific or professional acquirements . . . should confer no advantage over competitors, other than the weight which may be attached to their testimony by public opinion."[6]

All of these practices are widely accepted today. If Mill were alive, he might still condemn them, but it is possible that he would judge them desirable in the new context. The proliferation of technical expertise and artificial substances makes it ever more difficult to equip people to take care of their health and well-being or even know to whom to go for help. Some parentalistic protections of the consumer seem justified. We cannot know what Mill's views on particular measures would be, but we can be confident that he would not be dogmatic. He would try to determine empirically what practices are most beneficial in the concrete setting.

The reader should understand that I am not claiming Mill's authority for my own judgments about these measures. Mill was impressed with the difficulty of cultivating individuality in a complex society where it is both hard for individuals to acquire the wide range of expertise necessary to express their individual natures effectively and the institutions of society have the power to cultivate and enforce uniformity. If he would concede a parentalistic role to institutions at all — as I suspect he would, but cannot prove — he would put greater emphasis on safeguards for the autonomy and individuality of those benefited by them. While agreeing with me that specific measures need to be rethought as empirical conditions change, he might very well disagree strongly with my judgments about those measures.

This leads to my fourth observation about the quotation from Mill. It maintains that diversity and genius flourish in an atmosphere of freedom. Liberty ought to be assured in a broader range of activities than his society allowed and than does ours. With this I agree. However, I wish to point out that parentalistic guidance sometimes works better than hands-off toleration to produce diversity and certainly to develop genius. The protection of autonomy in most areas of life does not preclude parentalistic intervention in a few to bring out the unique talents of the individual.

Fifth, I would want to tell Mill that diversity is not an unmixed blessing. Many forms of human personality and action are ugly, offensive, and harmful. A greater number of ugly personalities may emerge in an individualistic society than in a conformist one. Mill maintains that freedom is worth the price in his society, but he does not claim that it is worth it in all societies. He suggests that societies surrounded by enemies and primitive societies incapable of self-rule need benevolent despots. Regardless of whether we agree about these cases, we should admit that a directive government might be needed in a society in which complexity became so great that the harms of certain freedoms outweighed their benefits. A call for more freedom was in order in Mill's time and it is in order in our own, but there is no reason to absolutize the concept. Mill does not claim, or need to claim, that exactly the same practices respecting toleration and liberty are appropriate for societies significantly different from his. We miss his point if we uncritically apply his recommendations to conditions he did not anticipate. Rather, we should follow his example and weigh the consequences of particular measures *in context* to determine which forms of parentalism are legitimate and which illegitimate under actual conditions. Once again, however, we should not assume, and I do not claim, that Mill would agree with our judgment on particulars, nor is there any reason to appeal to Mill's authority in judging the particulars.

Self-Development and Success

Humanity and human powers are only valuable for, revealed through, and developed by their use. Mill recognizes that humans must act humanly to fulfill their humanity and take satisfaction in it. In often quoted passages, he says, "it is the privilege and proper condition of a human being, arrived at the maturity of his faculties, to use and interpret experience in his own way" and "if a person possesses any tolerable amount of common sense and experience, his own mode of laying out his existence is the best, not because it is the best in itself, but because it is his own mode."[7] There is room for misunderstanding here. Mill praises the act of choosing—he recognizes the intrinsic satisfaction of being the initiator of events—but he bestows greater praise on choosing wisely. His reader must take care not to transfer his higher praise to choice as such. Moreover, while Mill defends practices that allow people to choose badly and harm themselves, he does not say that the good of making a choice always outweighs the evil of choosing badly. Rather, the self-inflicted suffering of some is a price that must be paid for practices that allow other people to work out their destinies successfully. This is not to say that the individuals who suffer in the process are better off for having suffered.

I have asserted that the value of choosing prescinded from the wisdom which informs some choices is not sufficient to merit respect. Mill appears to recognize this. He wants a wide scope for the exercise of autonomy not because he attaches supreme value to bare choosing, but because he recognizes that protections for choice at all levels are necessary to ensure the opportunity for choice at high levels. Moreover, he argues that learning by mistakes is necessary for personal development in two important ways.

First, only by choosing do people develop their rational faculties and master the art of choosing wisely. They cannot learn all they need to know from the successes and failures of others; they need to learn from their own. Since society is forced to limit their choices to protect other people from their mistakes, it should restrict it as little as possible in self-affecting matters.

Second, persons, despite their ignorance and venality, are more likely to make good choices for themselves than anyone else will:

> [The individual] is the person most interested in his own well-being: the interest which any other person, except in cases of strong personal attachment, can have in it, is trifling, compared with that which he himself has [and] with respect to

his own feelings and circumstances, the most ordinary man or woman has means of knowledge immeasurably surpassing those that can be possessed by any one else. . . . [T]he strongest of all arguments against the interference of the public with purely personal conduct is that when it does interfere, the odds are that it interferes wrongly, and in the wrong place.[8]

Here Mill advances several empirical generalizations. They admit numerous exceptions, as he implies in his references to "strong personal attachment" and "the odds." In rare cases others are more concerned about the individual's welfare than he is and know better than he what needs to be done for it. One can oppose parentalism in most cases without opposing it in all cases. If individuals are afforded freedom to make their own choices in most self-affecting matters, especially where they are equipped and motivated to act more wisely than anyone who might act for them, they will develop their rational faculties, respect themselves, and acquire the wherewithal to be happy as far as fortune permits. Restrictions on their choice in a few severely self-harmful actions will not prevent self-development or self-respect.

To tie down the point, let me refer to McDonald's criticism of Benn for failing to recognize that it is choosing rationally and acting successfully that contribute to self-respect. Chronic frustration (missing a chosen target, failing to get what one wants) and dissatisfaction (choosing the wrong target to aim at, failing to be gratified by what one does get) destroy it. The first kind of failure reveals limitations of intellect or will, for which one cannot respect oneself. The second affects the person's self-image: "with dissatisfaction the defect may run so deep that it affects, in a way that frustration doesn't, one's sense of identity. So that in the more extreme cases, one may well wish that one were a different sort of person."[9]

One last point: Many of the satisfactions that attend the pursuit of one's own welfare also attend the pursuit of the welfare of others. One can gain self-respect by successfully helping others. Using one's reason in both sorts of choices develops one's faculties. Consequently, in a society of interdependence and mutual caring, all may enjoy self-respect if all have the opportunity to act as intelligent parentalists though they are also recipients of parentalism.

Respect for Persons

Our analysis of the value of autonomy has been conducted in terms of its consequences in the broad sense of both the intrinsic value and external effects of actions that utilize human faculties at different levels. These reflections have led to the position that parentalistic encroachments are usually but not always unjustified. To determine which is the case in concrete circumstances requires difficult assessments, and many philosophers seek a basis in a right to autonomy in self-affecting matters founded on the respect due persons as autonomous beings. The difficulty they encounter in cashing in the notion of respect to determine the scope of rights may be due to inclarities in their concepts of autonomy and respect. Is it actual or potential autonomy that deserves respect? If potential, is it the degree of potentiality found in the particular individual or in the species which he represents? If actual, is it his exercise of it at any level or only the higher ones? If only at higher levels, what encroachments on lower levels are legitimate to enable the subject to realize her potentiality for the higher levels or to achieve other goods?

There is similar obscurity in what is meant by "respect." Important variations are evident from dictionary definitions, which suggest three clusters of meaning: to respect is (a) to esteem or prize a being because of some quality deserving of honor; (b) to manifest such esteem publicly; or (c) to treat the being in an appropriate way. Proper treatment includes refraining from interfering with expressions of the quality by the being and honoring the demands that go with its expression.

Autonomy in its higher forms deserves respect in these senses. It is a quality which is a basis for our esteem for persons. We should express our esteem publicly since this helps them develop and exercise the quality. And we should treat beings endowed with the quality a special way. It is not clear that we should respect autonomy in its lower forms the same way. The concept of respect is too nebulous to decide the dividing line. We should value autonomy and value it more in its higher forms, but we must appeal to other principles to determine what forms of conduct honor it properly.

To see this better, let us look at an attempt to base antiparentalism on respect for autonomy. VanDeVeer[10] asserts that when the parentalist overrules the judgment of his recipient about what is best for her, he "imposes" his concept of values on her. He treats her

> as a "good receptacle" or "utility location," but persons are not just that. They are arbiters of their own well-being, and not merely sentient, computing, devices to be kept in good repair. They both assess their competing lower order, self-regarding desires, determining which is most urgent, and form moral preferences as to the extent to which their own interests or urgent self-regarding desires should be promoted, cultivated, repressed, or thwarted in cases of conflict with self-regarding desires and interests of others.

When we impose our values on others, we treat them as different sorts of beings than ourselves and not persons.

> [T]o treat them *as if* they lack what we have and expect to pursue, namely a conception of the good, is to deny them a certain *moral equality*. For if, as paternalistically inclined agents we invasively interfere with nonconsenting competent persons when they wrong no others, we act on our own conception of the good while subverting the efforts of others to act in like manner. . . . [It] is to act as if others are clay to be sculpted and not, as we regard ourselves, active sculptors of unique lives.

Respect for a person requires us to defer to his desires when it comes to promoting his welfare.

In criticism of this position, I will first note the ambiguity of the phrase "to impose one's values." The parentalist perforce consults his own standards of good and evil in deciding to act contrary to the subject's desires, and his conception of good or his judgment about specific measures under a common conception may differ from hers. Equally, he must follow his own standards in deciding to act as she desires or not to act contrary to her desires. In neither case does he need to require her to adopt his values, except in rare instances where he must alter her values to carry out his action. Even then it is difficult if not impossible for him to "impose" his values in the invidious sense posited by VanDeVeer. Ordinary acts of parentalism only alter limited portions of the subject's life by diverting her from particular goals or activities; they do not change her values wholesale. The agent has no opportunity or wish to subvert her plan of life, much less undermine her power to choose. It is perfectly possible for him to retain respect for her autonomy as it relates to most other circumstances.

The vagueness of the notion of respect is due to the failure of its sponsors to give attention to the variations in different forms of autonomy. The prospective parentalist should certainly respect the subject's autonomy if "to respect" means to give due weight to the value of particular concrete exercises of it in the context of appreciation of other goods. But little about behavior can be deduced from respect in the abstract. Does respect dictate that a person's wishes of the moment be honored or sacrificed to her hypothetical more competent ones? that she be allowed to pursue paths doomed to frustration and loss of self-respect or self-confidence rather than be diverted to more promising ones? that her present autonomy be curtailed to enhance her future autonomy? that her consent waives her right to autonomy or transfers some of her basic responsibilities to the parentalist?

Respect and the Right to Autonomy

Let us now consider whether the appeal to rights on the basis of respect for persons clarifies matters. One of the questions at issue is whether there are any absolute human rights in Feinberg's sense of "generically moral rights of a fundamentally important kind held equally by all human beings, unconditionally and unalterably."[11] Specifically, is there an absolute human right to autonomy in self-affecting matters, an unconditional negative right to forbearance from intervention by all members of the community? Whatever the assumptions behind the claim for such a right, it speaks to the widely shared intuition that respect for persons prohibits parentalism.

Feinberg's list of kinds of treatment incompatible with dignity suggests that dignity is the foundation of the right to autonomy, but also suggests that it does not prohibit all restrictions on autonomy. Dignity bars actions that reduce a person to the level of an animal. Persons have the negative right not to be brainwashed, made into passive instruments for the purposes of others, or transformed into domesticated animals. Feinberg observes that these are probably the only rights that are human rights in the strongest sense—that is, unalterable, absolute (exceptionless and nonconflictive), and universally and peculiarly human. Note that the practical implications even here are not completely negative. The right not to be brainwashed might justify intervention to prevent a person from submitting to it, for example, rescuing him from a religious cult and "deprogramming" him. If so, absolute respect for human dignity justifies parentalistic actions. More generally, when we ask whether various forms of parentalism infringe on rights, we must consider the possibility that some are actually required by them, whether they be rights to autonomy or welfare. If, for example, people have a positive right to a certain level of well-being, other people—those assigned by virtue of a social role such as legislator, custodian, guardian or physician, or those who chance to encounter them in times of need—have the duty to provide certain benefits even without the right-holder's consent. Rights have to be balanced against one another in deciding when to respect a person's autonomy in the sense of refraining from encroaching upon particular forms.

Very difficult calculations are required if one is to decide about parentalistic actions in terms of consequences. For example, the considerations that justify parentalism to prevent harm (preventive or negative parentalism) are relevant to justifying that to provide benefits (promotive or positive parentalism), and frequently the choice has to be made between preventing a harm and providing a benefit. Such choices are difficult and in some cases indeterminate, but they have to be made. The point is that they are not obviated by framing them in terms of rights: one must decide whether the negative right to noninterference in the name of autonomy takes priority over the positive right to other elements of welfare.

I have recommended that the notion of rights be utilized in evaluating parentalism but in a contingent and contextual way. Feinberg provides the fragment of a thesis that helps articulate what rights are basic for humans, including the right to some degree of autonomy. He is discussing political rights that are to be respected by public officials:

> The most vital interests in a personal system of interests are those I choose to call "welfare interests" in the indispensable means to one's ulterior goals whatever the latter may be, or later come to be. In this category are the interests in one's own physical health and vigor, the integrity and normal functioning of one's body, the absence of distracting pain and suffering or grotesque disfigurement, minimal intellectual acuity, emotional stability, the absence of groundless anxieties and resentments, the capacity to engage normally in social intercourse, at least minimal wealth, income, and financial security, a tolerable social and physical environment, and a certain amount of freedom from interference and coercion.[12]

Observe that "a certain amount" of freedom is a welfare interest. Welfare interests share "the common character of bare minimality." In this form they are "indispensable means to one's ulterior goals whatever they may be." One needs health, for example, to pursue other things. Welfare interests are thus valuable not only in themselves but as conditions for autonomy.

It is easy to think of situations in which a rational person might sacrifice some portion of welfare above the minimum to enhance some form of autonomy. She might risk her health for excitement in a sport or success in work. She might give her life to serve a noble cause. What I would like to insist is that the same is true of autonomy. A person might reasonably accept limitations on her autonomy for an ulterior good as long as the restrictions did not drive her below a minimal level—for instance, she might choose to become a nun or serve in the armed forces with the discipline required. Likewise, the parentalist is morally permitted and sometimes obligated to curtail the autonomy of a subject to promote other goods, but likewise he should never drive it below the minimum necessary for a human form of existence.

It is in the definitions of minimum autonomy rights that threshold concepts seem appropriate. However, if rights are conventional and contextual, it is not necessary to declare everyone above a threshold of general ability "competent" and defer to their autonomy wherever they exercise it. Rather, the point is that no one should be driven below the threshold or be allowed to sink below it if others can prevent it.

The conception of minimum welfare rights can be articulated in terms of an ideal system of rules. The system would stipulate minimum welfare interests—such as a certain level of health and possessions—as positive rights and allow them on some occasions to defeat negative rights of exemption from interference. The evaluation of parentalism thus must take into account that there are rights to receive care that compete with rights of freedom from intervention. We cannot simply assume that if there is a right to autonomy, it is never to be violated for the sake of other values.

However, minimal autonomy is not the only form at issue. The higher forms are important for the well-being of people, not only those who value them but those too obtuse to do so. The antiparentalist who thrusts autonomy upon those who shun it is a parentalist in deed. Respect for autonomy demands that we *not* keep hands off people who flee their own autonomy, as well as not off those who do not respect the autonomy of others. It is the drift of our analysis that while respect for autonomy dictates a right of the individual to be generally free of parentalistic intrusions, it also requires intervention on some occasions to see that she does not abandon her cares or her responsibility for herself and others.

The critical pragmatic question is whether insistence on the limited right to autonomy nurtures the right kind of solicitude by helping discriminate between legitimate and illegitimate occasions for parentalism. A system of properly conceived and effectively guaranteed rights, that is, one empirically adjusted to the context in which a particular group of people are interacting with one another, can contribute to an infrastructure that will restrain selfish persons from abusing one another or taking advantage of caring persons. Such an infrastructure will provide security in which mutual solicitude can wax strong. It will also provide individuals something to fall back on to fend off improper forms of solicitude.

To exercise full autonomy, a person's entire life stream of actions would have to express maximum power and rationality. She would have to enjoy all of the conditions for autonomy at a high level: resources, opportunities to act, bodily integrity, breadth of experience, logical habits of thought, and self-control. To enjoy total welfare a person would need sound health, substantial material possessions, and supportive human relationships throughout life. Clearly, full autonomy and total welfare are unattainable. They are approximated only by a privileged few. It is beyond the power of society to guarantee them for everyone, and it would be unfair for it to allow the few to approximate them at the expense of the remainder. But it is both practicable and proper to guarantee a decent degree of both autonomy and welfare for everyone and maintain restrictions to prevent anyone to achieve more than this minimum by driving others below it.

It is customary to refer to the practicable levels of autonomy and welfare as "autonomy" and "welfare" *simpliciter*. If the ultimate moral aim of individual action is to maximize happiness and distribute it fairly among all of humanity, its fundamental proximate aim is to promote the practicable level of autonomy and welfare for those whose lives one directly influences. This can be viewed in a rough way as respecting their rights, including both their negative right to autonomy and their positive right to welfare.

I have not formulated my guidelines in terms of rights, but my position accommodates a conditional and contextualist concept. Autonomy is an important interest for human beings. Its exercise brings irreplaceable satisfactions, and it serves the individual in pursuit of other goods. Rights to specific forms of autonomy feasible within the given physical and social context are central to any system of rights. But autonomy is a complex and variable phenomenon. Only some forms or conditions can be guaranteed. Among the first autonomy rights that come to mind in relation to parentalism in our complex, technical, mass, and impersonal society are the right of the individual to learn about everything of importance to her life; the right to choose a rewarding occupation that utilizes her talents from the range of socially useful ones; the right to adopt a sexual orientation suited to her needs and to establish a family or not; the right to raise children according to her lights as long as she respects their basic rights; the right to participate in the political process of her community; the right to seek a satisfactory relationship with the ground of her being, God or whatever she conceives it to be; the right to leisure and choice of leisure activities; and the right to die when and how she chooses. Most of these rights would be important in any imaginable society. What is contingent and contextual is the way in which the opportunity of the individual to exercise them must be balanced against restrictions and obligations imposed to protect or promote the well being of the other members of society.

There is no stronger or widely shared moral intuition than that of the importance of autonomy for human beings. Most people hold their own autonomy dear, and we must suspect that the few who do not do not know what is good for them or have somehow been defeated by life. Hence, there is a prima facie objection to any interference with a person's autonomy. While everyone realizes that interferences to protect third parties is necessary, interference in matters that affect the person herself is harder to justify. Solicitude for a person tempts us to intervene when she threatens to harm herself or some harm impends which she is unwilling or unable to forestall. We are also tempted to intervene when she is on the verge of missing an opportunity for an important benefit. Our first impulse is to rush to her aid. On reflection, that very solicitude tells us that we may harm her more by intervening than by standing back. Her autonomy is too important for us to encroach upon it cavalierly.

Caring people thus need guidelines to judge when and when not to intervene. Some philosophers attempt to derive rules from respect, the attitude they think is proper toward persons and their autonomy. They maintain that autonomy deserves treatment not accorded by society for other goods because it is what makes the biological human a person and a moral agent. However, declarations of respect are too encompassing and vague to mandate particular practices. When the anatomy of autonomy is examined, it proves to be a complex phenomenon with many dimensions and many degrees in each dimension, and its value varies with its forms and degrees.

Following Mill, we have identified two major values of autonomy for the agent—intrinsic and instrumental. The exercise of autonomy is intrinsically satisfying. Making decisions and carrying them out are essential to being human. A completely heteronomous life, if it were possible, would be subhuman. Instrumentally, autonomy is the best guarantee that the individual will secure what is best for himself in most contexts since it is he who knows and is most concerned to get what is good for him as a unique individual. Moreover, some of the satisfaction brought by autonomous activities is due precisely to the fact that they work. They bring the agent to a destination she has set for herself.

However, not all ends are objectively good. The agent may only too often pursue false goals. It may be possible to provide some objective goods for her, and they may be worth providing even at the cost of denying her the satisfaction of pursuing them or alternative goods for herself. Moreover, her ineffectual pursuit of some goods with the attendant experience of failure may negate the intrinsic satisfaction of being able to pursue them autonomously.

In both actions which are performed for their own sake and those which are performed to achieve ulterior goals, satisfaction is the result of competence, a function of the rationality and self-control of the agent and the intellectual and physical resources available to her. The internal conditions of competence engage the higher or distinctively human faculties, which are also the faculties that make autonomy possible. Roughly speaking, the more competent the agent, the more autonomous. From this it follows that the higher the level of autonomy at which an agent operates, the more rewarding its exercise, both in terms of internal satisfaction and external achievements. This, of course, is not universally true; misfortune can frustrate the most rational endeavors and good fortune can bring success to the most foolish. But the equation still holds: the more one's higher faculties are engaged, the more satisfying are likely to be one's life activities and the greater their chance of obtaining other goods.

9

The Role of Consent

The consent of persons affected by an action is an important consideration in justifying it. According to the guidelines in Chapter 6, the prospective parentalist should make a reasonable effort to get her subject to agree to her efforts to help him. However, his consent is neither necessary nor sufficient to justify intervention. It can be right to help him without his consent or in face of his opposition, and it can be wrong to help him even though he badly wants it.

To defend this position it is necessary to address the following questions: What are the major forms of consent? How does each bear on whether an action is parentalistic? What is the value or function of each? How does this bear on the justification of intervention?

Current Consent

There are significant differences between yielding to, concurring in, and cooperating with another's actions, and there are further differences between merely consenting to and prompting, enticing, urging, inciting, or commanding actions. However, the effect of these variations on the justification of intervention is a matter of degree, and in most cases it is obvious how they should be handled under the principles that pertain to full-blown consent. I will therefore concentrate on the latter.

As we have noted, the extreme position makes autonomy in self-affecting matters absolute. Since absolutists concede that many interventions are justified, they must specify conditions under which the right to autonomy is inoperative or abrogated. A favored condition is the subject's consent at the time of the intervention, or what I will call *current consent*. The rights theorist thinks that this either waives the right to autonomy or converts the intervener into the subject's agent and her actions into exercises of his autonomy. Thus VanDeVeer asserts, "If there is a presumption that individuals have a right not to be coercively interfered with, then, foregoing utilitarian type appeals, it would seem that the only way to justify coercive interference of a paternalistic sort would be to show that under certain conditions the presumption fails."[1] VanDeVeer thinks that consent is such a condition. Gerald Dworkin and Rosemary Carter maintain that it is the only condition.[2]

In assessing these claims there is a conceptual problem at the outset. If parentalism is coercive by nature, consent would seem to make an action nonparentalistic. This disposes of justification by definition: only consent can justify intervenion; if a person consents to it, it is not parentalistic; hence, no parentalistic act is justified. So much for parentalism!

However, according to the broad conception of parentalism, an action is parentalistic when the agent performs it independent of whether or not he consents. While we are prone to think of cases in which she acts in the face of his objections or coerces him, there are others in which she acts on or for him without his knowledge or is determined to proceed regardless of what he wants. Moreover, the subject may consent only in a qualified way. A number of variations have been discussed in the literature, including consent a significant time prior to the intervention; approval of it after it has occurred; authorization of a range of actions that include the intervention without the subject's awareness that it is included; consent that he would have given under contrary-to-fact conditions, such as if he had been better informed or more rational or a different sort of person; proxy consent by someone else; and consent which a rational and informed person would have given. While the subject's explicit current consent taken into account by the intervener makes the intervention nonparentalistic, other forms of consent do not, and they bear in a number of ways on the justification of intervention. The careless notion that consent in any form waives the right to autonomy and justifies all interventions and the correlative notion that they are justified only when the subject has waived his right dissolve under analysis.

Consent in the strongest sense is given to an action with full knowledge of what it entails and explicitly expressed in unequivocal terms at the time. Near equivalents include consent a brief period before the act; current consent that is implicit but obvious, such as from the subject's demeanor; and consent to the main elements of the action without detailed knowledge of its particulars. Whether or not these forms technically make an act of intervention nonparentalistic, all absolve the agent from the charge of coercion, deception, or taking advantage of an unwitting subject.

It may seem unproblematic that an action for a person's welfare to which he currently consents is justified. The agent acts for the subject and extends his ability to achieve his goals much like a surge of power, a new resource, or a good tool. These empowerments are morally neutral, so why are not the agent's efforts? Consent does not necessarily justify even nonparentalistic acts. Setting aside cases in which the agent helps the subject harm others, she may become a party to his self-inflicted harm. Failing to prevent harm to one for whom one cares (for example, standing by as a friend drinks excessively or endangers his health by a crash diet) is bad enough; collaborating with his activity or providing him the means to carry it out (providing the alcohol or diet) is worse.

Moreover, current consent does not eliminate every element of encroachment on the person's autonomy. The agent is autonomous; she cannot become a *mere* instrument of his will. She must exercise discretion, apply her knowledge, consult her own values, draw conclusions, and perform actions her own way.

Though he agrees to her action, it is *her* action, not *his* and it replaces acts which he might have performed. Though his consent is an exercise of his autonomy, it is not the one which the act of the agent replaces. In consenting, the subject thus forgoes some autonomy. How is this choice to be evaluated? It is essential to one's consciousness of being a person to make a difference in the world by entertaining goals, forming projects, and engaging in enterprises. In doing so, the person experiences success and failure. When he consents to let another act for him, he may get satisfaction from her success as "his" physician, guardian, leader, or advocate. These satisfactions, however, can hardly bring the sense of achievement and personhood that comes from being the prime initiator of major life-affecting actions and important changes in the world.

This is not to say that consenting is unimportant in other ways. It may produce major benefits. It plays a central role in the conventions pertaining to rights since it is declared to be a primary way of abrogating them and absolving an intervener of the duty of noninterference when other values are at stake. Moreover, it is an important lubricant for reciprocal caring relationships. Our efforts to help one another go much more smoothly when there is consent. The point, however, is that the consenting does not negate the reduction of autonomy produced by the action taken on the consenter's behalf. Naturally, the reduction is less when he consents than when he does not, but there is a reduction nonetheless.

Actions in the face of the subject's dissent not only reduce his autonomy, they arouse his frustration and resentment. They may make him feel inferior or worthless. They erode the ties of care. Solicitude thrives only when it is met with some measure of gratitude and reciprocity. If all that a helping person ever meets is resistance and resentment, her urge to care will wane. Moreover, positive concern for the other's autonomy nurtures caring relationships. Those whom we help are made appreciative of our care, or more tolerant if they consider it misdirected. We are moved to learn more about their lives and deepen our relationship with them. We become better able to judge what is truly good for them and more effective in promoting their welfare by securing their collaboration.

When people consent to the good offices of others, those who care and help can operate in an atmosphere of approval and cooperation. It is important in the caring society that help be freely accepted as well as given. Mutual care, reciprocity, and voluntary cooperation are necessary to sustain a matrix of relationships in which exceptional acts of one-way care can do their work without evolving into psychological despotism on the one side or dependency or blind rebellion on the other.

Actual Rational Consent

Restraints may be justified on people who are running extreme risks or deliberately harming themselves. The initial reason is to determine their true wishes and obtain their consent for efforts to protect them. Almost everyone would agree that it is permissible to restrain them until it can be determined whether they are rational, can regain competence or shed an encumbrance, or at least review their course calmly. In this vein, Feinberg endorses a weak legal parentalism to the effect that

> the state has the right to prevent self-regarding harmful conduct only when it is substantially involuntary or when temporary intervention is necessary to establish whether it is voluntary or not. When there is a strong presumption that no normal person would voluntarily choose or consent to the kind of conduct in question, that should be a proper ground for detaining the person until the voluntary character of his choice can be established.[3]

Beauchamp endorses the wider principle that "a person ignorant of a potential danger which might befall him could justifiably be restrained, so long as the coercion is temporary and only for the purpose of rendering the person informed, in which case he would be free to choose whatever course he wished."[4] This enables Beauchamp to condemn all interferences with knowingly dangerous acts. He argues that a subject ignorant of a danger is not actually choosing the dangerous act, so restraint is not interference with *it*. I believe this idea misses its mark. For example, while Mill's pedestrian is not choosing to fall into the river, he is trying to cross the river and he is stepping onto the unsafe bridge as a start. The police officer who restrains him keeps him from trying to do what he wants (to step on the bridge) even though he does not know the consequences of what he wants (the collapse of the bridge). If parentalism were restricted to interference with acts where the subject knows all the consequences, there would be no parentalism since there are no such acts.

The valid point about restraint follows from the obligation to seek consent. Respect for the person's autonomy requires an intervener to seek his approval before acting. She is sometimes justified in restraining him to do so. Once she determines that he does not wish her to act or that it is impractical to ascertain whether he does, she must consider whether there is sufficient reason to act without his consent. Likewise if she restrains him until she determines that he knows the danger in what he is trying to do, she must decide whether to let him run the risk knowingly.

While consent in all of its forms brings benefits, those of some forms are not unalloyed. The subject may be led to consent by misinformation or ignorance or wishful or fearful thinking and these are generally harmful. This point stirs up a nest of new problems. What forms of "manufactured" consent are possible and how are they distinguished from rational consent?

Manufacturing consent involves deception and hence it is a positive evil. It not only contributes nothing to the justification of the act under consideration, it detracts from it. However, the parentalist may find it necessary to manufacture consent to carry out an act which is strongly justified by other considerations. Fewer odious measures are required when the person can be persuaded by his own view of the facts or impelled by his feelings. Such consent, however, may still be uninformed or irrational, and the agent may know that it is. It may be as objectionable for her to play on the subject's ignorance or irrationality as it is to manufacture his consent.

We sense intuitively that it is the agent's responsibility to explain to the subject what she is trying to do, even when this may transform his unthinking consent to a wise measure into dissent and opposition to it. For example, a patient who puts himself in his physician's hands may be repelled or frightened by details of proposed therapy, and this may tempt the physician to keep these details to herself. She may ask herself, what is the value of rational and informed consent when it frustrates the larger scheme to promote the person's welfare? In response we may point out that rational and informed consent is more valuable in every respect than irrational and manufactured forms.

In the first place, it is more satisfying as an act of autonomy. It proceeds from knowledge rather than ignorance or error. The consenter has a richer sense of the context and the actions affecting him. He has more reliable assurance of the intervener's good will. He has a firmer sense of her agency as an extension of his own power to control his life and world. He has a better reason for congratulating himself on his choice of agent. He sees more clearly the concordance of what she is doing for him with his own aims and values. The satisfaction he takes in her efforts is likely to grow as time passes, whereas ill-informed or manufactured consent will turn into regret and resentment.

In the second place, a person is likely to be the best judge of what is objectively good for himself. His wishes and preferences, therefore, are usually the best evidence which the intervener has of the goods which she should promote. His consents and dissents are indices of his preferences. But wishes and preferences are reliable indices of objective values to the degree that they are informed and rational. Therefore, a person is obligated to inform the beneficiary of her efforts and appeal to his rational faculties to persuade him to accept them as much as circumstances allow, though as with other forms of consent this obligation can be overruled by the obligation to help.

Prior Consent and Subsequent Approval

Current consent in any but its fullest form does not prevent an intervention from being parentalistic, and it is neither necessary nor sufficient to justify the intervention, though its presence counts in favor of intervention and its absence must be countered by strong reasons before intervention is justified. The role of a number of other kinds of consent and acquiescence have been discussed in the literature. To keep chronological relations straight in this discussion, I will designate the time at which an action is performed as t_2, any earlier time at which the recipient consents to it or the agent does something to prepare him to accept it as t_1, and any time after the act at which anything else happens relevant to its justification as t_3.

When the recipient explicitly consents at t_1 and the agent has no reason to think that he has changed his mind by t_2, it is reasonable for her to consider the consent to be in effect. Such prior consent is on a par with current consent. It has some intrinsic value as an exercise of autonomy. It has some evidential value in determining what is good for the recipient and ways to promote it. The practice of seeking consent in either form (current if practicable, prior if not) prompts subjects to reflect on their interests, which in turn develops their faculties and makes parentalistic help less necessary in the future. It also forces the would-be parentalist to reflect on her own intentions to see whether they are sincere. There are thus many reasons to seek the subject's consent prior to acting for him, though like current consent prior consent is neither necessary nor sufficient to justify an action.

Difficult questions arise when a person consents to an action, but changes his mind or events occur that would have changed his mind had he been able to take them into account. Hidden conditions of autonomy play a role here. Persons with a stable personality are more capable of entering into agreements and binding themselves over longer stretches of time and greater changes in circumstances than are unformed and malleable persons. The institution of morality assigns stable persons greater responsibility, trusts them with greater autonomy, and shields them more from parentalistic meddling. Conversely, greater parentalism is warranted toward unstable persons. When such a person changes his mind about whether to allow another to protect him from self-harmful impulses, the prospective parentalist is forced to decide what his "true" wishes are, what the "real" person wants, as more reliable clues to what is truly good for him than his transient desires.

At t_1 the person welcomes an action in his behalf and at t_2 he objects to it. Which attitude expresses his real values? Not necessarily the later one. His wishes at different times express different elements of his nature, and his later wishes do not always reflect the better ones. The agent who respects his autonomy will give priority to his highest, albeit intermittently exercised, powers of decision and action even if this requires her to disregard some of his wishes. She will give priority to those wishes that reflect his basic character and settled aims whether it is they which induce him to consent to A at t_1 or to resist it at t_2. This judgment flies in the face of the intuition that current consent and dissent are more important than prior. The basis of the intuition seems to be that the person's later attitude is more likely to be better informed about the proposed action. If this is not the case, his prior attitude should be honored over his current one.

A caveat is in order in view of a "statute of limitations" for responsibility for one's choices in any rational system of morality. Suppose at a cool moment a person consents to a future action in his behalf. When the time comes for the act, he objects to it. If the interval is great, he may have changed radically and his objection at t_2 may be as rational and informed as his consent at t_1 but simply made on different values. Then he should be treated as if he were a different person, and the action should be considered against his will. If the action is justified despite this, it is because it promises sufficient benefits for the "new person" to outweigh the violation of his autonomy, not because the "old person" consented to it.

Should a person's approval of an action after it has been performed be counted in evaluating it? The term *consent* is not appropriate since endorsement after the fact bears little resemblance to consent proper, so I will refer to this as *subsequent approval*. VanDeVeer observes that while it does not waive the right to autonomy, it has other functions: "It may declare to the world that the one treated paternalistically forgives the committer of the prior right-violation. It may waive a right to complaint or compensation for the earlier "injury." None of this requires that there was no rights violation at an earlier time."[5] Subsequent approval helps relieve the person's frustration at having been prevented from performing actions and his resentment at having been subjected to actions against his will. It helps reconcile him with the parentalist after the rupture which the latter's actions has caused. It helps fortify the caring relationship between them. While it is better to avoid the subject's frustration and resentment by securing his consent prior to interventions, it is desirable to ease them afterward by securing his approval.

These are consequentialist considerations. To perform an act and seek a reconciliation with the recipient has better results than to perform the act and ignore reconciliation. To perform an act that eventually wins the recipient's approval has better results than to perform another which achieves the same end but never wins his approval. The agent is more justified in performing an act if she has grounds for anticipating that she will be able to secure the recipient's approval than if this is not probable.

The recipient's approval of the action at t_3 has a certain epistemological value for the agent. It confirms that the parentalistic act was indeed beneficial for the recipient. This does not add to the justification of the action, for the agent had to decide to perform it on the evidence available at the time she acted, not on the basis of the evidence provided by the recipient's post facto approval. But it is relevant to her justification for performing actions at future times. ("In the past he has come to realize that I was right. I know that he will this time as soon he gets over his anger.")

Dispositional Consent

All forms of consent discussed thus far involve actual acts. They are exercises of autonomy which have some value to the one who performs them and materially facilitate the efforts of the one who is trying to help him by providing clues to his true welfare and assuaging his resentment. These benefits should figure into the calculations of the parentalist.

Now, it is intuitively evident that some interventions are justified in the absence of actual consent. Our guidelines, combined with a recognition that benefits for the subject can be more important than a limited diminution of his autonomy, rationalize these intuitions. However, this consequentialist rationale is denied those who maintain the absolute value of and inviolable right to autonomy. To accommodate intuitive cases, they are driven to seek some form of consent other than actual by which the subject waives his right. Kinds of nonactual consent considered in the literature are the disposition to consent on the part of the subject (dispositional consent), consent which he would have given under conditions that did not obtain (hypothetical consent), and consent which a perfectly rational person would have given (rational consent).

Carter maintains that the subject's disposition to consent to an intervention waives his right to autonomy even if he never expresses it. She includes the disposition to consent upon receipt of relevant information ("He would approve if he only knew a little more about what I am doing"). Contrary to Carter's intention, this sanctions almost any intervention by the enthusiastic parentalist ("I could get his approval if I could just talk to him for a while" where "a while" is an hour, day, year, or lifetime). Moreover, even where minor information would win consent, the value of the unexercised disposition is unclear. How can it compensate for the negative consequences of the actual dissent of the subject?[6]

Carter thinks that dispositions which waive the right to autonomy can develop after the interventions they justify. The subject's approval at time t_3 retroactively alienates his right to autonomy at the time of the intervention, t_2, a notion I have rejected. This and the notion of waiver by disposition imply that a subsequent unactivated disposition to approve alienates the right — for example, if the subject dies without receiving the information which would have caused him to approve.

John Hodson advances a dispositional theory that does not involve retroactive waiving. He asserts that the only thing relevant to the justification of intervention is evidence that the subject would have consented had his will not been encumbered:

> Paternalistic interventions are justified if and only if (i) there is good evidence that the decisions with respect to which the person is to be coerced are encumbered, and (ii) there is good evidence that this person's decisions would be supportive of the paternalistic intervention if they were not encumbered. . . . A person's decisions are encumbered whenever those decisions are made in circumstances which are known to affect decision-making in such a way that the person making the decisions sometimes comes to believe that the decisions were mistaken or unfortunate.[7]

Encumbrances include ignorance, emotional stress, duress, mental illness, and impaired consciousness. Evidence for what the subject would have supported if he had been unencumbered is empirical, but not direct. His consent can only be inferred from what he has done in the past, his values, and the nature of his encumbrances. Conclusions can only be hypothetical, so Hodson refers to the inferred disposition as "hypothetical unencumbered consent."

This modification does not resolve the problem we found in post facto consent and disposition to consent. The possible cannot cancel the actual. Hypothetical consent cannot waive the subject's actual right to autonomy. What then does a disposition to consent under the contrary-to-fact condition that the subject has all of the relevant information (Carter) or is unencumbered (Hodson) add to the justification of a parentalistic act? It does not have the intrinsic value of actual consenting, nor does it prepare the subject for acting autonomously in the future. Moreover, neither dispositional nor hypothetical consent before, at the time of, or after the intervention will ease the subject's resentment or reinforce the caring relation between him and his benefactor. Finally, no imaginary consent has evidential value as a clue to the subject's true good since it requires the same evidence to determine the subject's dispositions to consent as what he wants and with both further evidence is required to determine what is objectively good for him.

Ideal Rational Consent

Actual consent, then, is what counts. A person who would intervene in another's life should put greater weight on his rational and informed consent than other forms. Such consent, however, must be sharply distinguished from the consent a hypothetical rational being would give if he were in the person's shoes, as discussed by Dworkin. Dworkin begins with the premise that abridgments of a person's autonomy can be justified only by consent. This turns out to be the consent a rational subject would have given rather than that which the actual subject has given. Consider Dworkin's "agreement schema" that he develops in connection with "social insurance policies":

> [S]ince we are all aware of our irrational propensities, deficiencies in cognitive and emotional capacities, and avoidable and unavoidable ignorance it is rational and prudent for us to in effect take out "social insurance policies." We may argue for and against proposed paternalistic measures in terms of what fully rational individuals would accept as forms of protection. Now clearly, since the initial agreement is not about specific measures, we are dealing with a more-or-less blank check and therefore there have to be carefully defined limits. What I am looking for are certain kinds of conditions which make it plausible to suppose that rational men could reach agreement to limit their liberty even when other men's interests are not affected.

The "we" who take out social insurance policies are the prospective recipients of parentalism. Dworkin also specifies principles which prospective parentalists ought to follow. To do so he sketches

> types of situations in which it seems plausible to suppose that fully rational individuals would agree to having paternalistic restrictions imposed upon them. It is reasonable to suppose that there are "goods" such as health which any person would want to have in order to pursue his own good—no matter how that good is conceived. . . . [O]ne could agree that the attainment of such goods should be promoted even when not recognized to be such, at the moment, by the individuals concerned.[8]

It is the consent of a hypothetical rational subject which justifies a parentalistic act in the face of dissent by the actual subject rather than the latter's prior, subsequent or dispositional consent.

As we have seen, the value of actual consenting is proportional to its rationality. However, the consent of the imaginary rational person has nothing to do with the actual subject. It certainly cannot alienate his right to autonomy. Nor does this imaginary act of consenting have any value for him. It is his actual rationality that adds to the quality of his life and his actually irrationality that detracts from it. The consent of a hypothetical rational subject, therefore, adds nothing to the justification of an intervention in the actual person's life, and appealing to it may even be a bad thing if it makes the infringement on his autonomy seem less than it is.

We must wonder what these authors are groping for in their appeals to dispositional and hypothetical consent and the imaginary consent of a perfectly rational subject. I can only guess the following. While the "consents" add nothing to values achieved by a parentalistic action nor magically waive the right to autonomy, reconstructing what they would be may help the parentalist assess the values that *are* affected by his action. The parentalist needs to identify the true interests of the subject whom he wants to help. These are the very interests that the subject would want furthered if he were perfectly rational. It may be helpful for the parentalist, therefore, to think in terms of why a rational subject would consent to her act as well as directly about the values which the act promises to achieve for the real subject. It may also be useful heuristically to think about what the actual subject would consent to if he were better informed or unencumbered.

Consider the situation. A completely rational judge of what is best for a person would be equipped with his history, body, and circumstances. He would be fully informed about the person's needs and be able to transcend his biases to determine how to promote his true interests. This is precisely the perspective which the parentalist seeks in trying to transcend her own biases. There may be heuristic value in imagining herself first as the person sans his encumbrances and then that person become completely rational.

A crucial point, however, is that the rational judge is not an independent oracle who can tell the parentalist things she does not already know. As a creature of her imagination, his perspective is no better than that which she actually achieves in trying to understand the person she wants to help. The rational judge is simply the parentalist trying to be rational. What she thinks the rational judge would decide is precisely what she thinks is rational by her own standards. The rational judge carries the authority of her own reason, no more and no less.

Can the Right to Autonomy Be Waived?

I have surmised that it is an uncritical evaluation of autonomy that has led moralists to postulate an absolute human right to autonomy in self-affecting matters. They believe that infringements on autonomy cannot be justified by other benefits for the right-holder. To accommodate cases in which intervention is intuitively justified, they look for an autonomous act of consent that waives or alienates the portion of the subject's autonomy which is diminished by the intervention. Since actual consent is not found in all of the intuitive cases, they are driven to the incoherent notion that some imaginary or hypothetical form can waive the right to autonomy. Our guidelines for parentalism justify the intuitive cases without resort to this notion. They also point to the values found in actual consent and why those who want to help others should try to obtain it while forging ahead in some cases when it is not forthcoming.

While consent counts in favor of intervention and dissent counts against it, neither is decisive. The authors we have examined consider consent to be decisive not only negatively (they think it wrong to intervene without consent) but positively (they think it permissible to intervene with the subject's consent). Since rights are claims sanctioned by valid rules, the issue is whether there is a rule in rational morality that allows people to waive their claim to noninterference in self-affecting matters. Under such a rule there would be no reason to regret the intervention's diminution of S's autonomy. But if, on the contrary, diminution is always a cause for regret, automatic alienation of the right to autonomy by consent should not be accepted as a rule of morality.

What reason might be given for such a rule? Philosophers countenancing self-alienation of rights may have in mind an analogy between having autonomy and owning property. Under customary rules people are permitted to give away their possessions and the recipients are permitted to treat the objects as their own. Also, it is considered praiseworthy for the recipient to use the gift to benefit the donor. Similarly, people can authorize others to act for them and, under the analogy to property, this is conceived as ceding autonomy and as conveying the right to act to the other. The other is permitted to use it as she chooses, and it is praiseworthy for her to use it to benefit the donor.

The analogy, however, is not as tight as the argument requires. A possession remains the same object when title is transferred, but an agent's action is not numerically the same as that which is relinquished by the one who authorizes her to act for him. Moreover, the two actions are quite different in character. When an agent acts in another's place, her action shares only goal (his welfare) and a few external features (managing his affairs, forestalling some danger, and so on) with his. The actions differ in intention: he would have acted to achieve something for himself, the agent acts to achieve the good of another–the one action is self-interested, the other is selfless. Moreover, the circumstances of the actions and the way they are carried out are bound to differ substantially, and what the agent ends up doing is likely to be quite different from what the person would have done for himself. Ceding autonomy thus is quite unlike transferring property, and one should not expect the moral rules that govern the one to be the same as those that govern the other.

The traditional rights of property that form the basis for this analogy are not unexceptionable. We can imagine a society in which property would be entrusted to persons precisely on the condition that they *not* give it away, but use it constructively. It might be confiscated if its owner tried to unload it on others. To the extent that there is an analogy between autonomy and property, it would be immoral for persons to relinquish autonomy, for instance, by voluntarily entering servitude or burdening others with the responsibility for caring for them. It would also be immoral for others to collude with such persons in their dereliction.

The analogy between autonomy and property thus does not support rules allowing self-alienation of autonomy. The very value of autonomy condemns the use of autonomy to escape itself. Under the importunings of the parentalist, a person may consent to a severe curtailment of his autonomy for some benefit such as security, piety, peace of mind, or moral purity. But autonomy is a responsibility that no one should shirk except in extremis. That it is a right does not mean that it is not also a duty or that persons are permitted to eschew it at will. Hence, others should often refuse to accept it from the person.

In sum, to the extent autonomy is important to its possessor, there are reasons to reject the concept of self-alienation. Autonomy is a burden that one ought to carry unless extremely strong needs force him to abandon it. Correlatively, strong reasons are required to warrant another person to encroach upon it, and his consent is not sufficient to do so. When abandonment or encroachment are warranted, the fact is a reason for profound regret.

Still, there are reasons to allow people to forego autonomy in some circumstances. Let us relate the discussion to the consequentialist conception of rights developed earlier. Rights are claims warranted by valid rules. Moral rights are claims warranted by the rules of rational morality. Such rules are not the same for all societies, but are relative to the concrete circumstances of particular ones. They are the rules that would maximize goods and ensure that they are distributed fairly in those circumstances. Rules—and therefore rights defined by those rules formulated in terms of rights—are thus contextual.

Moreover, the ultimate aim of morality (maximum goods fairly distributed) is not always best promoted by strict rules. A fortiori this is true of the rules required to assign rights and correlative duties. In some spheres of life, behavior is better shaped by the other instrumentalities available to morality, including ideals, character, loyalties, and affections. Hence, the scope of rules and rights itself must be delimited for the circumstances of each society.

Rules are ineffectual unless they are articulated, proclaimed, and widely accepted in a community. The formulation of moral rules in terms of rights can help to make them effective by giving the members of society leverage to demand what is due them, though it can also be counterproductive in encouraging adversarial relationships and militating against caring ones. Hence, the invocation of rights must be assigned its proper sphere rather than being made the centerpiece of moral life. The institution of rights is often useful in impersonal relations between people where ties of mutual solicitude and care are weak. It is often damaging when those ties are intimate and strong. In cases where the definition of rights and assignment of specific behavior to specific individuals are especially important, rules should be enacted as laws and the apparatus of the state mobilized to apply them to cases. Here legal rights occupy center stage. Analogously, it is expedient for institutions and organizations that depend on routinized behavior of their participants to adopt formal rules of procedure and codes of conduct. Specific quasi-legal role-specific rights can have an important place in organizational life.

Laws and codified rules must be formally adopted, authoritatively promulgated, and effectively administered. They tend to be precise and detailed and produce experts to whom the individual can appeal to determine what they require in concrete cases. For good reasons, societies also employ informal moral standards to control conduct. Some take the form of rules that assign rights as well as responsibilities, but moral rights are generally quite different in character from legal rights. They are less well defined. There are differences among the community as to exactly what they are and require. Interpretation and adjudication are loose, informal, and negotiated by those who are in the process of honoring them.

The looseness of customary autonomy rights opens the door to a wide range of parentalistic interventions. Given the offensiveness of much parentalism, the question naturally arises, should not the mores be made more strict and codified to make them more like positive laws? Would a truly rational morality not be composed of detailed rules, universally accepted and authoritatively adjudicated, which assigned precise rights and duties to each and every member of society? My answer has been negative. The use of the legal model for all interrelationships in life would be disastrous. Laws, rules, and rights are indispensable for particular purposes, but they are fatal to others. The looseness of moral rights prevents them from smothering solicitude among the members of society.

We have suggested the place for stricter rules. Where those who intervene in the lives of others are likely to have limited knowledge of those whose welfare they affect, rules are needed, and they will often require consent to sanction intervention. Elsewhere consent should be taken as a factor in the assessment of goods and harms, but neither as a necessary or sufficient condition to negate the consenter's right to autonomy or to justify the interventionist act.

In opposition to the single-minded valuation of autonomy over other goods, elevation of actual consent to the status of necessary or sufficient condition for justification and otiose appeal to dispositions, to the hypothetical unencumbered will, or to the consent of the perfectly rational subject, I propose the following.

In evaluating an intervention in a person's life, gains and losses in actual autonomy are what count. These include his exercise of autonomy if he consents, his loss of the autonomy which would have been exercised in the acts supplanted by the intervention, and the effect of the intervention on his future autonomy. The subject's prior consent, generic or specific, and subsequent approval enter into the equation only if they are actually given. His disposition to consent, what he would have consented to if his will had not been encumbered, and what a perfectly rational person would have consented to do not enter the cost and benefit equation.

A person contemplating an act on behalf of another has the obligation to attempt to persuade him rationally—that is, to secure his rational and informed consent. If he consents and the intervener has good reasons to think that the act will benefit him, it is hard to see how the act could be wrong. Nevertheless, the intervener does take away some of his autonomy. The parentalist may not be able to secure the subject's consent. The latter may be absent, unconscious, or impervious to persuasion. If his needs are great and the parentalist has made a good faith effort to secure his rational consent, failure to do so is not an absolute barrier to action. The parentalist may even be justified in manufacturing his consent by misinforming him or playing on his ignorance, emotions, or prejudices to forestall his active opposition or resentment. If so, she should keep in mind that manufactured consent is worthless as an exercise of autonomy and may vitiate the subject's powers of rational choice for the future.

IV

ANTIPARENTALISM

10

Varieties of Antiparentalism

This whole discussion is animated by the vision of a caring society whose members are bound together by voluntary ties of mutual solicitude rather than the provisions of a contract or the categorical commands of an authoritative master. In the ideal caring society, people help one another because they want to, not because they are obliged to.

In the actual world, however, unfortunately people do not care enough for one another to enable society to rely on solicitude as the sole basis for communal life. It is forced to lay down rules that define rights and duties, and it must impose sanctions to see that the rules are obeyed. It is driven to develop institutions which indoctrinate new generations in their duties and coerce recalcitrants to respect the rights of others.

The purpose of rules for rights and duties is to protect caring relationships from laceration by people whose emotions or intellects are too stunted to participate voluntarily. Paradoxically, rules, rights, and duties are also needed because some care all too well, but unwisely. Their solicitude overflows its proper banks, and they harm those whom they would help. Solicitude must be disciplined for the very reason that arouses it, to take care of those with whom the parentalist's life is intertwined.

Restraints on parentalism are necessary because recipients of care are autonomous agents, not dumb animals or complex machines. They have cares of their own. They need the strength to discharge them and the opportunity to take satisfaction in them. That is, they need to attain and retain a significant measure of autonomy, and they must not be robbed of autonomy in the name of their well-being. Authentic concern takes the autonomy of the other into consideration along with further elements of his welfare. Hence, the urge to parentalism, while well-meaning, must always be viewed with suspicion. A mild degree of generalized antiparentalism is demanded precisely in order to fine tune the caring society.

Antiparentalism in the Liberal Tradition

The general posture of antiparentalism seems to have originated in the political arena. As we have noted, the term *paternalism* is pejorative in ordinary usage. I now wish to point out that the term is popular among liberal thinkers of a democratic bent and not among those with more elitist philosophies. This perhaps is explained by Kleinig's historical thesis that the concept dates back to the replacement of the patriarchal society of the Middle Ages by liberal social forms. The ideology of feudalism pictured the sovereign as a patriarch of a family; his paternalism was so taken for granted that it was not even named, much less subject to critical scrutiny. Paternalism became a focus of debate only when the liberal ideology was developed to justify the overturn of feudalism. The new ideology replaced the father-child model of the sovereign with the model of an agent assigned limited authority by a contract with equals. The notion of paternalism was devised as a bête noire to combat the remnants of the patriarchal attitudes.[1]

The thesis that the notion of paternalism originated as a weapon to combat monarchy is questionable, since the term came into currency only in the twentieth century. There is no question that self-avowed liberals now use the concept with special vigor to argue for limitations of the power of the state, but the notion of a liberal tradition is nebulous. The term covers philosophies all the way from an idolatry of liberty which leads to absolute antiparentalism (what I will label "libertarianism") to sensible forms of "hard" antiparentalism prominent in the literature, to my softer antiparentalism. I will now turn to the range of possibilities in order to place my own stance.

The possible attitudes toward parentalism are four. In defining them, I take my departure from Dworkin, who distinguishes two of the attitudes in a way that has become standard. He says, "By soft paternalism, I mean the view that (1) paternalism is sometimes justified, and (2) it is a necessary condition for such justification that the person for whom we are acting paternalistically is in some way not competent. . . . By hard paternalism, I mean the view that paternalism is sometimes justified even if the action is fully voluntary."[2] The two brands of limited parentalism (paternalism) are also brands of limited antiparentalism since both condemn most forms of parentalism. That is, soft parentalism is hard antiparentalism: it opposes parentalism toward everyone except seriously incompetent persons. Hard parentalism is soft antiparentalism: it sanctions some parentalism toward competent persons, though condemning most. In both cases, the label "parentalism" is a misnomer because the emphasis is on opposition to the practice. Hence, I will refer to the positions as *hard and soft antiparentalism*.

Two extreme positions may be added to the moderate ones: *absolute parentalism*, which sanctions intervention in the lives of others for their own good whenever the parentalist has the urge, and *absolute antiparentalism*, which condemns intervention no matter what. There is no support for absolute parentalism, and I will ignore it and deal only with absolute, hard, and soft antiparentalism. My own position falls into the category of soft antiparentalism, but when it comes to cases, I do not see much difference between it and more popular hard antiparentalisms. My position is that parentalism is prima facie suspect, and I condemn most of the cases which the hard antiparentalist condemns. Hence, I question whether the distinction between hard and soft is as important as the literature suggests. I will treat it here merely as a platform to launch a discussion of the issues.

The absolute position may be reduced to the following essentials. Rational morality sanctions the claim of each person to be allowed to act or refrain from acting as he chooses in pursuit of his basic interests—that is, morality bestows universal rights. Rights take priority over other interests (utilities) of both the right-holder and others. No combination of utilities can outweigh a right. Rights are ordered lexically (A, B, C, . . .) so that prior rights in the series must always be satisfied before posterior ones. Autonomy is the supreme interest for everyone: it is the highest order intrinsic value and a condition for all other values. The right to autonomy in self-affecting matters, therefore, occupies first place in the order of rights. Therefore, it is always and categorically wrong to abridge autonomy. Therefore, parentalism is always wrong.

A few authors speak wistfully of absolute antiparentalism because it simplifies the moral universe by promising a way to make decisions without messy utilitarian calculations. Two authors who succumb to the temptation to adopt it are Pollock, who explicitly assumes an extreme position on the right to autonomy and categorically condemns parentalism, and Arneson, who does so obliquely by criticizing the strong antiparentalisms of Dworkin and Feinberg and maintaining (implausibly) that Mill espouses absolutism. I have dealt with Arneson's argument elsewhere. It will be instructive to see where Pollock's argument goes on the rocks, though it is hardly worth attention on its own grounds.

According to Pollock, moral principles are provisions of a contract among self-interested agents which regulate exchange of services. The basic provision is the freedom principle, according to which "each person ought to grant to other persons an equal right to be free. . . . Thus, interactions between myself and others should be based on mutual consent."[3] This means that morality is essentially negative: it tells us only not to infringe on the freedom of another except to prevent him from infringing on the equal freedom of still others. Pollock denies that we have moral obligations to help others except when we have promised to do so or have incurred the obligation by bringing children into the world. Compassion and generosity are not moral motivations but sports of nature. They even disrupt morality when they lead the compassionate person to neglect his own interests.

Pollock thinks of freedom in the negative and external sense of the absence of interference in the individual's life by force, threat, and deception. These all induce him to pursue what he does not (otherwise) value or most values. Pollock concedes that the reduction of autonomy of people torn by emotion or impaired by drugs or ignorance may justify interference if the purpose is to cause them to behave in accordance with their own values. However, he vacillates about what this means. At different points he implies that "their own values" means what is objectively good for them, what they desire in reflective and informed periods, and what they happen to want at the moment. This vacillation allows him to condemn measures that he apparently wants to condemn on ideological grounds, such as the social security program, occupational licensure, and regulation of drugs, as typical of what he calls "big brother" (and nonlibertarian thinkers call "the supportive state"). At the same time, it allows him to avoid the counterintuitive condemnation of egregiously heartless strictures on social and personal assistance for those in need. That is, he is able to reconcile a dogmatic absolute antiparentalism with widely shared moral intuitions by fudging basic concepts.

To generalize from Pollock's example, absolute antiparentalism is untenable because it values a single good—autonomy—above all others. No single feature of human existence merits such adulation. Values come in clusters, and no single value outweighs all combinations of others.

Mill's Antiparentalism

Kleinig notes that many philosophers in the liberal tradition have drawn back from extreme antiparentalism because of their recognition of human interconnectedness and the inadequacy of the social atomism of the libertarian position. They have realized that absolute opposition to parentalism is "a doctrinaire and uncompassionate overreaction, contrary to our humanitarian impulses and good sense."[4] This realization, however, is not incompatible with the recognition that there are grounds to oppose parentalism in most instances and hence to establish restraints on it. I will now turn from easy criticism of the extreme view to the more difficult constructive task of delimiting an antiparentalism upon which reasonable deontologists and consequentialists might agree.

My approach is consequentialist, but it is a form of consequentialism that recognizes the intrinsic as well as instrumental value of autonomous actions. In this I agree with Mill and will again use him to introduce my view. In *On Liberty* Mill is not primarily interested in the isolated actions of individuals. He wishes to promote practices that have high utility, and he employs all the rhetoric at his command to gain currency for these. Focus on practices leads him to be concerned about the precedents set by particular actions and the generalizations that people draw from them. Many of his reservations about parentalism stem from this. Thus he warns that even legitimate acts of care feed the offensive inclination of people to insist that others live just as they. He argues that it is better to lose the benefits of intervention if examples of restraint help deter "intrusively pious members of society" and "every government and every public, who have the pretension that no person shall enjoy any pleasure which they think wrong." He remarks, "The disposition of mankind, whether as rulers or as fellow-citizens, to impose their own opinions and inclinations as a rule of conduct on others, is so energetically supported by some of the best and by some of the worst feelings incident to human nature, that it is hardly ever kept under restraint by anything but want of power" and hence it is necessary to "raise a strong barrier of conviction . . . against the mischief."[5]

Mill is particularly disturbed by the growth of state power and its coalescence with public opinion. Concentration of state power bureaucratizes and homogenizes social processes and soaks up talent that would otherwise flourish in private pursuits. The processes legitimize the tyranny of public opinion and render individuals more and more incapable of thinking for themselves. This is Mill's final warning in *On Liberty*.

Mill's focus on practices and state actions limits what he has to say about interactions between individuals who enjoy caring relationships with one another. His principles have to be adapted, and I believe softened, as we move from the impersonal and generalized relations with which he dealt to the more personal and individuated relations that are our principal concern in this volume. The following are what I take to be his considered views that are pertinent to parentalism in all of its forms and which I incorporate in my own position. Once again I should warn the reader that Mill might well object to the way I use his ideas, and in no way am I claiming his authority for their validity.

Choosing and acting are necessary for self-respect, but not sufficient to obtain it. Choosing rationally and acting successfully are essential. It is they which provide the higher pleasures and contribute to real happiness. The faculties that make rational action possible are developed by use. Individuals should be afforded a wide space for acting according to their own lights though they make many mistakes. Since liberty in the area of other-affecting actions must be restricted to protect society, it should be maximized in the area of self-affecting actions. Society should err on the side of granting too much liberty rather than too little, to combat the ever-present temptation to moralistic intrusion.

However, guarantees of liberty are not enough. To promote general happiness, institutions are needed that motivate the individual to contribute to others and teach him effective ways of doing so. He should be taught to use rational persuasion where possible, but that compulsion is sometimes necessary. Whichever he uses, persuasion or compulsion, he must keep in mind that the primary objective is to help the recipient of his attentions to exercise freedom in a rational manner. Interference with her liberty in self-affecting matters should be a measure of last resort when education and persuasion have failed. Some parentalism is necessary, but the need must be strong and obvious and its boundaries clearly delimited. Just when it is necessary and what its limits in the concrete situation should be must be determined empirically.

Mill's specific proposals for his society are relevant for us to the degree that our society resembles his; his principles themselves warrant different practices to the extent that our society differs from his. Those principles warrant further differences for societies that differ even more. As conditions change, more parentalism may be needed than in his day—or conceivably less. Mill is no less vigorous an antiparentalist because he recognizes exceptions to rules against parentalism and the relativity of the rules to concrete conditions. The fact that parentalism is legitimate on a few occasions does not make it less harmful on the many occasions on which it is not.

Despite the qualifications that Mill not only allows but spells out, his stand against parentalism is ardent. He marshals decisive reasons for the sober conclusion, "Mankind are the greater gainers by suffering each other to live as seems good to themselves, than by compelling each to live as seems good to the rest."[6] This advice should be kept in mind as we cautiously endorse particular sorts of intervention. Our stance should remain generally antiparentalistic.

A Compendium of Arguments

It is very important to realize that the antiparentalist of any stripe is in the same
boat as the parentalist in dealing with the values of others. He judges that one of
their interests (in his case, their autonomy) is so important to their well-being
that others of their interests must be sacrificed to it. This is parallel to the
judgment of the parentalist that others of their interests are sufficiently important
for them to sacrifice their autonomy.

Many people not only unwittingly misuse their autonomy to pursue false
goods but also sometimes flee autonomy and its cares. Hence, solicitude rules out
any blanket acquiescence to their preferences, and respect for autonomy demands that others *not* keep their hands entirely off their lives. The absolute
antiparentalist would thrust autonomy on people regardless of the cost to them.
The reasonable antiparentalist would thrust autonomy on them only to the extent
that promises to be essential to their happiness, and he is ready to curtail their
autonomy if other important values are at stake for them.

This all means that reasonable antiparentalists are also reasonable parentalists. They are concerned with people's total welfare and weigh their autonomy
against other values. This dictates a mild antiparentalism in that it counsels a
prima facie suspicion of every parentalistic proposal, since parentalism by
definition abridges autonomy; at the same time, it sanctions a mild parentalism in
countenancing parentalistic acts under special circumstances.

Much of the literature is devoted to debates about exceptions to rules against
parentalism. Kleinig provides a useful survey of the major arguments. Some if
valid would condemn parentalism wholesale. Others are counterarguments that
sanction particular forms of parentalism and therefore require qualifications of
antiparentalism.[7] A review of the dialectic between the two batteries of arguments will help me explain the implications of my position and assess its cogency.

The antiparentalist arguments in Kleinig's review identify autonomous activity with individualism and hence parallel Mill's defense of individualism in *On
Liberty*. They indict parentalism as the mortal enemy of autonomy and hence of
individualism and declare that no compromise with it can be tolerated in a
libertarian society.

What follows is a simplified summary of Kleinig's formulations. After each
argument I will explain how I come to terms with the issues that it raises.

The Argument from Oppression of Individuality

All persons who have reached the age of discretion possess the capacity for
rational choice. Rational choice entails self-evaluation and self-determination.
By using these powers, the person can be improved by rational persuasion until
she becomes the source of reasons for her own actions and an end valuable in
herself. In contrast, parentalism transforms her life-pattern into a construction of
another. It therefore violates the demands of individuality and subverts the
subject's standing as a chooser.

Kleinig observes that this argument is "within walking distance of Kant" and ties the argument to a Kantian version, the Argument from Disrespect for Persons. This seems reason enough to him to reject the argument, but he does not make clear why. He does point out that persons neglect and abuse their capacity for rational choice, so the disposition to choose rationally is an ideal to be pursued rather than a natural endowment. In criticism of the absolutist position, I have argued that it is a mistake to transfer the profound respect due ideally rational choice to the imperfect choices of actual people. The latter deserve a much more qualified respect. I have also pointed out that limited restrictions on choice do not destroy autonomy or prevent its exercise in the greater part of life. The status of a person as an autonomous moral agent depends on the aggregation of her choices, particularly the more rational ones, over the course of a lifetime. Curtailments on occasion do not necessarily entail a lack of (the appropriate degree of) respect for overall autononomy or autonomy per se. The recipient's future autonomy itself justifies some restrictions on her present autonomy, and other components of her welfare justifies many more.

The Argument from Paternalistic Distance

Conditions for self-development vary among people. The individual has a greater interest in her own development and better knowledge of its conditions and constituents than anyone else. Hence, she is the individual who is best equipped to provide what she needs for himself. Parentalistic efforts are bound to benefit her less than she can benefit herself. Hence, we should avoid them in her own interest.

Kleinig points out that there are many exceptions to the above generalization. I have argued that parentalism is justified under some of the exceptions, but at the same time have taken account of the fact that the generalization is true for the most part by incorporating an epistemic clause in guidelines for parentalism. The parentalist must have evidence that he knows more or is more concerned about what is objectively good for the subject than the subject herself before he is justified in intervening in her life. In lieu of such evidence, the presumption is that the subject knows best. While this does not erect an absolute barrier to parentalism, it establishes a prima facie objection to it.

The Argument from the Developmental Value of Choice

Rational choice is an art which people must master. They learn by doing. So to master the art of choice, they must be allowed to make choices and succeed or fail. Parentalism prevents them from learning by trial and error.

We have taken note of the obvious, that most interventions while denying the individual some choices leave her innumerable opportunities to make others. Under normal circumstances, she acquires a great deal of practice in choosing. Parentalistic care must be carried to an extreme, it must reach some critical mass that is quite large, before it stunts development. At the same time, a person with no parentalistic protection may make mistakes that deny her vital goods, destroy her self-confidence, and interfere with her development. Intervention to prevent the more egregious mistakes may contribute to development rather than militate against it. So discrete intervention limiting her present autonomy may be necessary to prepare her for greater autonomy in later life.

Consent-Based Arguments

Kleinig reviews five arguments for making consent either necessary or sufficient for justifying intervention. Taken together they would make it both necessary and sufficient and hence would condemn all parentalism since any interventions to which the subject consents are not parentalistic.

The Argument from Prior Consent

If a person in recognition of her own weakness asks another to restrain her or submit her to corrective treatment when she is tempted to self-harmful behavior, the agent is authorized to do so.

Prior consent is equivalent to concurrent consent if the person agrees in advance to precisely the agent's action and experiences no change of values in the interval. But then the action is not parentalistic and not to be evaluated as such. On the other hand, a person may consent in advance only to the general type of treatment, in which case the act is parentalistic and the consent has less substantive value and evidential weight in justifying it than concurrent consent. Moreover, the degree to which consent, whether prior or concurrent, generic or specific, is rational and informed affects its significance in both respects, substantive and evidentiary. Thus, prior generic consent which expresses the settled values of a rational and informed subject can count more than her current dissent to the intervener's specific action if the dissent is impulsive and ill-considered. In sum, prior consent contributes to the justification of an action but does not suffice to justify it by itself.

The Real Will Argument

A person's actual volitions ("real will") may differ from her manifest wants ("empirical will"). Though she consciously wants A, which is harmful to her, she really values B, which will help fulfill her true nature as a rational being. Society should give priority to B, so the parentalist is not wrong in interfering with A.

We have observed that the claims in this argument can be taken two ways, both of which are objectionable. Kleinig emphasizes the idealist interpretation, which is too problematic to use in practical life and which, as Kleinig charges, encourages totalitarianism by reducing the individual to a replaceable organ of society. The second interpretation does not employ the metaphysical concept of a superpersonal real will, but is misleading in its own way. The person's settled values should be afforded more consideration than her transient preferences and indeed may be treated as what the real person wants. Actions to promote her settled values are more likely to bring her genuine satisfaction, and her settled values are better indications of what is truly good for her than actions to provide her what she momentarily prefers. In the end, however, it is her true good that the parentalist should promote in the face even of her settled values.

The Arguments from Subsequent and Anticipated Consent

The approval a person gives after someone has acted for or upon her either makes the act nonparentalistic or waives the person's right to autonomy and makes the imposition not an intrusion on autonomy. To the extent that the agent can anticipate the subject's approval, he is justified in imposing his services.

Approval after the fact is not consent, and it cannot retroactively rescind an earlier violation of the right to autonomy. Moreover, whether or not the approval is forthcoming depends on factors beside the will of the person. External accidents cannot determine whether an action is right or wrong. The notion of subsequent consent is so unstable that its advocates shift attention from it to the person's disposition to consent. The cogency of the two arguments turns on the significance of consent which the subject would have given under possible circumstances whether or not she actually gives it. It may be helpful heuristically for the parentalist to reflect on the subject's dispositions in trying to assess her values, but dispositions have no substantive value or independent evidential weight. Actual subsequent approval has some value in easing the subject's resentment. If the agent can anticipate that it will be forthcoming, it is one of the consequences he should consider in calculating the expected value of the action.

The Argument from Hypothetical Rational Consent

Impositions are justified which fully rational individuals would accept.

The hypothetical acceptance of a person's action by rational persons does not diminish the infringement on the actual subject's autonomy. What the "rational person" or the subject if she were fully rational and her choices unencumbered would will has none of the value of her actual volitions (preferences, decisions) as exercises of autonomy and evidence of her true welfare.

Stratagems to Accommodate Intuitions

Most philosophers concede that the foregoing arguments fail to make a case for absolute antiparentalism. In particular, they recognize that intervention is justified when the subject's capacity for rational choice is so defective that it is not worth exercising or will not be significantly affected by the intervention or will be subsequently enhanced by it. However, these concessions are not sufficient to support strong parentalism. They still permit strong antiparentalism.

To see whether there are reasons for intervening in peoples lives when they are not seriously defective, Kleinig turns to counterarguments in defense of various forms of intervention. The first set of counterarguments, while they take a toll on the arguments of extreme antiparentalism, technically do not justify parentalism since they are designed to show that certain intuitively justified interventions are not really parentalistic.

The Argument from the Self as Other

We become and act as individuals only when embedded in a matrix of social relationships. Kleinig formulates the argument proceding from this fact:

> Thus our good is not to be adjudged by reference to some individual nature of our own, but rather by reference to some generic nature whose individual characteristics are determined by their location within the ongoing demands of the community. On this view, self-destructive behavior that is not sanctioned by the transcendent purposes of the community does not constitute an act of merely self-regarding significance, but is first and foremost a violation of the community's prior claims. Our lives, therefore, are not our own to dispose of as we see fit, but differentiations from and subordinate to the community in which we live, move, and have our being.[8]

What are condemned as parentalistic impositions are actually attempts to protect the social organism from the wanton self-destructiveness of its parts.

I have quoted Kleinig's summary because the argument is murky, and I am not able to clarify it. It presupposes an idealistic conception of society, without which it reduces to the genetic fallacy. It is true that persons are what society makes of them—that is, their talents and values develop through interaction with other people, and this is shaped by social institutions. It is true that their primary scene of action in life is social: they act in a network of relationships with individuals and groups, their primary choices bear on interactions with them, and these interactions are channelled by the institutions of society. But nevertheless it is the individual subject who acts. Social influences on her behavior work through her. The locus of decision is in her. Actions issue from her decisions as she expresses herself in the world. The satisfactions brought by her actions occur in her and in other individuals. Thus, without individuals there would be no actions and no values. The group does not act; the individual does. There is no general welfare other than the aggregate well-being of individuals. It is mystification to speak of the whole acting on the individual or the good of the whole transcending the goods of individuals. When "society" must be protected from the individual, it is to prevent him from harming other individuals. When it is right to intervene parentalistically to protect him, it is to prevent him from harming himself as an individual, not as a part of society.

The Arguments of the Other as Necessary for Survival and for Flourishing

These arguments take account of the interconnectedness of people without converting them into mere organs of society. Since a person's survival and well being ("flourishing") depends on others, he has a stake in their existence and development. This gives him a reason to interfere when they threaten to harm themselves or fail to develop as they ought.

The two arguments give reasons for interfering in the lives of others in ways that do benefit them, but the interference is not parentalistic; its motive is self-interest. Hence, the argument does not deal with the cases of concern to us. Moreover, it is odd to think that interventions in the lives of others for their benefit are less justified than interventions motivated by self-interest. The argument also fails on its own terms. Only in rare circumstances does the well-being of one person depend so directly and importantly on the development of another that it would pay him to interfere to ensure her development (the rare example might be parent who nurtures his daughter solely so that she will care for him in his old age). In most instances, her development will benefit herself or third parties without particularly benefiting the person caring for her.

The Argument for Protection of the Future Self

Persons change over time, so the person who runs risks at a given time is different from the person who is harmed by the risk taker's mistakes. Under the harm principle, we have an obligation to prevent persons from injuring other persons. Hence, we are obligated to prevent persons from taking risks for their future selves.

Again, the actions covered by the argument would not be parentalistic and so it does not contribute to the justification of parentalism. However, the concept of self in this argument makes shambles of the notions of personal identity and responsibility in the context of practical action. If A_1 and A_2 (individual A at t_1 and t_2) are different persons, why should A_2 be held accountable for anything A_1 does? Why should she benefit from what A_1 does? Why should one keep his promises to A_1 when he deals with A_2? Indeed "he" is no longer the one who made the promises any more than "she" is the person to whom they were made. These implications reduce the premises of the argument to absurdity.

The Arguments from the Instrumentality of and Enhancement of Freedom

Freedom is a necessary condition for people to obtain benefits for themselves. Moreover, free activity is satisfying. But the value of freedom in both respects is proportionate to the extent that the subject is rational, informed, and self-controlled. Hence, when subjects are deficient along these dimensions and their deficiencies endanger important values, intervention is legitimate. They are not benefiting from their freedom in the area of intervention anyway, and it may protect or enhance it in that area or other areas for the future.

Kleinig is doubtful that this argument defeats the antiparentalistic Argument from Oppression of Individuality. I have argued that the latter relies on a notion of respect that is too vague for cogency. More important, parentalistic measures clearly can enhance the subjects's subsequent autonomy and may be dictated by respect as properly conceived.

The Argument from Personal Integrity

It is supremely important to each individual to develop her unique capacities, form a plan of life, and live by it in her own way. Benevolent interference is necessary in her early years when she has not yet formed a life-plan or adopted settled objectives. From time to time in later life intervention is necessary when "self-regarding vices" (carelessness, impulsiveness, etc.) jeopardize her stable projects. Intervention, however, should be a strategy of last resort after education and persuasion have failed.

Kleinig characterizes this argument as "valid, but not necessarily sufficient" to justify strong parentalism and hence sufficient to demote antiparentalism from hard to soft because it sanctions only relatively minor impositions. However, there are occasions where the parentalist has sufficient evidence to think that something is better for the subject than achievement of the goals of even her stable projects and the good of pursuing goals her own way. He is more likely to have such evidence if she is incompetent or seriously encumbered, but on occasion he may have it even though she seems competent and amply endowed with self-regarding virtues.

Consequentialist Antiparentalism

The antiparentalistic arguments establish a presumption against any proposed parentalistic act but fail to justify absolute antiparentalism. The counter-arguments identify conditions under which the presumption can be defeated. The position precipitated by this dialectic is an antiparentalism with exceptions, both of which are justified by the consequences of following them. This becomes evident when we consider the decision process which the position generates.

Let us imagine that Alfred thinks Betty is on the verge of doing something that will hurt her badly, or she is about to miss an important opportunity, or she is incapable of caring for herself in some area of her life. Alfred also believes that he can intervene in a way that will effectively alter Betty's harmful action or act on her or in her behalf for her own good. Let us imagine further that compassion, affection, or some social role has established a caring relation between the two people. Alfred's solicitude consequently arouses a strong impulse to intervene in her life. However, Betty's opposition to his meddling, together with his concern for her autonomy and his sense of his own limits, cause him to hesitate long enough to analyze the situation along the lines required by our brand of anti-parentalism. He asks himself these questions before rushing to act:

What is the magnitude of the immediate harms or losses that will ensue for Betty if I do not intervene? How probable are they?

What will be the long-range consequences of her prospective action or condition if I do not intervene? (She may learn from her mistakes and become more self-reliant, or she may suffer a crushing defeat and lose self-confidence.)

What will be the effect of my intervention on her present and future auton-omy? How valuable to her would be the decrements (and any subsequent incre-ments) due to my intervention? (Under this heading, Alfred must determine whether Betty's autonomy is already impaired and whether the intervention will further impair it, leave it unimpaired, or repair it for the future.)

Has Betty explicitly or tacitly consented to the intervention at an earlier time and, if so, was she more rational or speaking more for her "true self" than she is now? Can I bring her to approve of the intervention before I act, or after, by rational means or by any means that would alleviate her hostility and the conflict between us? How important would the various acts of consent or dissent be to her as exercises of autonomy? How important are the good or bad feelings which the parentalistic action will cause?

What will be the effects of the intervention on Betty's other values besides autonomy? What are their magnitudes and probabilities?

Will my action on this occasion reinforce intervention as a habit for me or a practice by others? What is the expected value of the habit or practice—for example, will it be abused on other occasions?

Are there alternatives besides the particular intervention and complete nonintervention? That is, can Betty be rationally dissuaded from her course or persuaded to accept help? Might it not be better to reward her some way for taking care of herself even though she is too foolish to do so on her own and won't listen to rational arguments? or to coerce her or deceive her into doing so?

The foregoing are questions Alfred should ask himself about the objective state of affairs. He must also assess any evidence for the alternatives, their consequences, values, and probabilities. He must ask the following.

How reliable are my judgments compared to those who think that these particular actions should not be taken? Specifically, since Betty does not consent, do I have evidence that her judgment about her interests is less reliable than mine? (At this point Alfred should consider clues to Betty's true needs in her prior consent, generic or specific; her present disposition to consent, actual or hypo-thetically unencumbered; and her likely future attitude.)

Is the evidence I have about what is objectively good for Betty, my knowledge of causal or means-end relationships relevant to promoting her welfare, and my understanding of human nature on the basis of which I am interpreting her needs sufficient to overrule general counsels of caution about parentalistic actions?

What is the resultant of all the vectors pointing toward and away from the parentalistic act? (Alfred must somehow bring to bear all of his measures, rankings, and intuitions on a net judgment leading to an action.) Is the resultant sufficient to defeat or sustain the prima facie prohibition of parentalism?

Only Betty's interests are at issue in this situation. In real cases, there would be the interests of other persons to consider, perhaps Betty's husband and children, her other friends, and Alfred himself.

If anyone conscientiously asks these questions and finds that honest answers dictate parentalistic action, surely the action is justified and praiseworthy. Parentalism is prima facie objectionable, but the subject's welfare may be endangered by her actions or conditions beyond her control. Solicitude demands intervention if the stakes are sufficiently grave. Parentalism should be prohibited for the usual case, but not absolutely. Its prohibition must not countermand the generous impulses of the warm and conscientious heart. The prima facie objection to parentalism demands that the values at risk be analyzed carefully and objectively. The recipient's autonomy must be given heavy weight, but it must be weighed in the same balance as other goods and sometimes it will be outweighed by them.

11

VanDeVeer's Consent-Based Antiparentalism

Donald VanDeVeer's book is the most carefully crafted deontological analysis of parentalism.[1] It deserves a thorough examination.

Dignity and Autonomy

VanDeVeer's theory is a version of justification by consent. He declares that the moralist must choose between principles that refer to the subject's consent and his welfare in evaluating parentalism, and he opts for consent in the name of respect for persons. This leads him to deny that abridgments of a person's autonomy without some form of consent are ever justified. To accommodate intuitively justified cases of parentalism when the need to help someone without his actual consent is urgent, he is forced to appeal implausibly to a form of hypothetical consent.

VanDeVeer says that his analysis is his best shot at deriving the implications of what he calls the Ultimate Theory ("the ultimately complete and rationally justified ethical theory," p. 45). He does not claim to have worked out the Ultimate Theory, but suggests its content by proposing "rather basic principles as rationally defensible, universal guides to deciding fundamental questions about the justifiability of intervention with persons on paternalistic grounds" (p. 8). These purport to illuminate the important but vague notion of human dignity and what is involved in respecting it.

VanDeVeer believes that human dignity requires us to respect competent persons categorically and incompetent ones in a qualified way. Persons of both sorts make decisions affecting their life-direction, so *respecting a person* must involve, in *some* fashion, not undermining that person's decision-making capacities, his decision-process, or rendering the latter impotent to eventuate in chosen outcomes" (p. 5). This treats persons, at least competent ones, as "arbiters of their own lives, as final authorities over the dispensation of their own efforts and time, and as proper adjudicators of their own contrary wants, and intrapersonal conflicts of interests" (p. 60). Human dignity thus is the ground for a fundamental autonomy right: "Each competent person has an equal right to direct the course of his or her

145

life by choosing any alternative within the sphere of acts not wronging others" (p. 59). Moreover, recognizing persons as "final authorities" over behavior that does not wrong others treats their right to autonomy there as absolute (p. 128).

VanDeVeer does not present an account of the nature of moral wrong, but he attempts to clarify it by intuitive examples of presumptively wrong actions that fail to respect persons. They include "the use of force to alter another's choice or action, the use of coercive threats, killing, physically impairing, certain forms of indoctrination and conditioning, and various modes of deception. Such acts, in an important sense, fail to respect persons" (p. 21). The central question of parentalism is whether it is ever permissible to use presumptively wrong measures to interfere with actions of the subject that are not presumptively wrong.

In light of our prior discussions, several features of VanDeVeer's account stand forth. First, his right to autonomy is open-ended: one cannot tell what conduct is required to honor it. He needs a panoply of supplemental rules, and it is hard to see how they could be derived from the vague concept of respect for human dignity or our intuitive preanalytic favorable feelings toward autonomy. Second, VanDeVeer makes no serious effort to show why autonomy should be assigned absolute value, though he refers to both its intrinsic and instrumental value. Our examination of autonomy has shown that its value in both ways is real and important, but it is not absolute. Third, though reluctant to tie his theory to a particular conception of the good, VanDeVeer acknowledges implicitly that what is truly good for a person can be distinguished from what the person thinks is good. VanDeVeer asks us to respect absolutely the individual's pursuit of what he thinks is good even if it entails sacrifice of his objective welfare. This injunction is implausible on the face.

VanDeVeer recognizes that the vagueness of the exhortation, "Respect human dignity!" makes it difficult to apply. (The difficulty is complicated by the appeal of competing, equally vague exhortations, notably, my own to provide for the well-being of those for whom we care.) VanDeVeer tries to resolve the perplexity about respect by a theory of "autonomy respecting paternalism" with two parts, one for competent subjects and the other for incompetent ones.

The difference between competent and incompetent is fundamental because competent persons possess the battery of capabilities required for autonomy, whereas incompetent persons lack some of them. Possession of the capabilities is a necessary condition for the right to direct one's life, so "incompetent persons lack this right" (p. 267). Since the function of consent is to waive the right to autonomy, consent-based justifications for parentalism are appropriate for competent persons. One might expect a different type of justification for incompetent persons, but VanDeVeer manages to introduce consent there too in an attenuated form, as we will see. We will deal with his treatment of competent persons first.

In a summary passage, VanDeVeer characterizes competence as follows:

> The general competence which is of interest is simply: competence to direct one's own life. . . . [I]t is competence to acquire information, to identify alternative courses of action, to employ reason to assess alternatives, to choose among them in such a fashion as to promote what one takes to be the good (which

may be what one finds prudent, what one believes to foster the good of others, or what one believes to be right), and to express one's will in action by taking steps toward achievement of that good. These general capacities require in turn the possession of many more precisely characterizable capabilities, or "competencies," for example the ability to understand, foresee, explain, predict, communicate, count, and evaluate in some moderately successful fashion. (p. 265)

VanDeVeer observes that general competence is accompanied by pockets and episodes of incompetence and incompetence by pockets and episodes of competence. Moreover, the capabilities that compose competence vary in degree, so that performances may be more or less effective and decisions more or less prudent. "Moderately successful" and "reasonably prudent" seem to mean to be successful or prudent in a high percentage of cases, but not necessarily to a high degree.

The capabilities essential to competence for VanDeVeer are primarily intellectual. Notably absent are emotive-conative qualities such as self-control and stable self-identity, which are critical to effective action or autonomy in the fullest sense. VanDeVeer recognizes that rational capacities include "conative" as well as "epistemological" elements, but the conative are intellectual: the rational person strives for what he takes to be good for himself or others. Actions not aimed at any good are evidence that the person is incompetent (pp. 122–123). The epistemological components of rationality include the capabilities involved in learning and processing data with a modicum of logic. Thus VanDeVeer defines rationality procedurally rather than substantively—that is, in terms of what the subject does in pursuit of his goals rather than in terms of those goals, which may be foolish or immoral (p. 116).

In dichotomizing competence and incompetence and tying competence to rationality, VanDeVeer adopts a threshold concept. The capabilities that bestow rationality range in degree along many continua (he recognizes that rationality is a "range concept") and so a point must be selected on each continuum above which the individual is said to reason competently. VanDeVeer selects rather low points. The "rational" or "reasoned" choices of the competent person may be seriously unreasonable due not only to inadequate data but failure to process data effectively, and, I would add, they may be accompanied by an inability to carry out reasoned choices due to defects in character, personality, or self-control.

Parentalism and Its Justification

VanDeVeer's "canonical definition" of parentalism (paternalism) may be paraphrased as follows: P's doing or omitting A toward S is parentalistic if and only if (1) P deliberately does it; (2) P believes that doing it is contrary to S's operative preference, intention, or disposition at the time; and (3) P does it with the primary aim of promoting a benefit or preventing a harm for S, believing that this will not accrue without the act (p. 22). This definition delimits a broad concept of parentalism. P and S range over both individuals and groups. Act A may be either a positive act or an omission. Its aim may be to promote a benefit or prevent a harm. It may employ a variety of measures, including shaping S's preferences and beliefs, physically controlling his behavior, and attaching incentives and disincentives to certain of his options.

VanDeVeer would honor competent choices and honor them absolutely if they injure no one other than the agent. He makes this point in dismissing what he calls the Unreasonable-Harm Prevention Principle, which justifies intervention in a person's life if his actions are seriously unreasonable and threaten to harm him significantly (pp. 124–127). The implausibility of the grounds on which VanDeVeer rejects this principle is apparent in his discussion of autonomy. Since autonomy is a function of rationality, which is a range property, it is also a range property. Thus the strongly autonomous person places "a highly personal stamp on his life" by using his rational capacities to the fullest, thinking through alternatives, setting his own goals, and resisting pressures to conform. The weakly autonomous person "moves in the direction of prevailing currents" by letting others decide his life for him (pp. 129–130). Despite these descriptions, VanDeVeer fails to credit autonomy in its stronger forms with greater value. He simply insists that we should honor people's autonomy at whatever level.

VanDeVeer argues that two kinds of consent, one actual and the other hypothetical, suffice to justify parentalistic interventions in a competent person's life, and no other considerations do so. He begins by distinguishing between consent in the strict sense and acquiescence and approval. He designates strict consent as the "authorization sense" to signify its justificatory role: it authorizes the action to which the subject consents. For a person to authorize another to act in some fashion requires (1) his choice to allow her to act, (2) his possession of a right, a legitimate claim, or legitimate authority to decide whether or not she may act in a given manner, and (3) typically a successful communication of his choice to her (p. 46). VanDeVeer calls the primary kind of strict or authorization consent valid consent. A person's consent to another's doing A is valid if and only if his consent is (1) broadly voluntary and (2) the product of reasoned choice, and if he has (3) a right or legitimate claim to influence the performance of A (p. 48). In the present discussion, "consent" will mean valid consent.

VanDeVeer's criteria of valid consent are rough because he characterizes his key concepts loosely. "Broadly voluntary" means not coerced: "a coercive threat (roughly) involves one party threatening to make another even worse off than the latter already is, at the time the threat has been made, unless the threatened party complies with a demand by the threatening party" (p. 78). "Reasoned choice" is to be understood "weakly and not, for example, synonymously with 'fully rational choice' " (p. 78). As noted above, VanDeVeer clearly does not restrict reasoned choice to choice of what is best for oneself, nor to choice which is totally unencumbered. He observes that choice in a " 'rationally unencumbered manner' is to be construed not as 'fully rational' but as 'a manner approximating the subject's rational best' " (p. 80 n). One's rational best may not be very good by absolute standards.

At the end of his book VanDeVeer summarizes his central claim:

Respect for the right of competent persons to form, revise, and pursue their concept of the good in ways which wrong no others requires deference to their choices — except in the special cases of ascertaining competence or when there is prior valid consent to invasive intervention, or it is *reasonable* to believe that *they, given their basic outlook and values*, would consent to such intervention *when* there is *no* viable opportunity or means to ascertain whether or not they actually and validly consent to such intervention. (p. 438)

He states this formally as the Principle of Autonomy-Respecting Paternalism (PARP): P's parentalistic interference, A, with generally competent subject, S, is morally permissible if and only if (1) A involves no presumptive wrong toward S or others or (2) A does not wrong anyone other than P and S and either (a) S has given currently operative valid consent to A or (b) S would validly consent to A if (i) S were aware of the relevant circumstances and (ii) S's normally capacities for deliberation and choice were not impaired (p. 88).

I shall not discuss provision (1) of PARP other than to remind the reader that there are circumstances under which an agent could use unexceptionable measures (rewards, rational arguments) to induce a subject to do what is best for himself and yet should not intrude. Certainly the subject might resist the intrusion, so it would need justification.

The critical issue is the validity of provision (2). It states alternative conditions sufficient to justify intervention. VanDeVeer explains part (a) in terms of a Restricted Consent Principle (RCP) and part (b) in terms of the Principle of Hypothetical Individuated Consent (PHIC).

RCP

If (1) S has given currently operative consent to A, (2) in S's estimation A is likely to promote a benefit or prevent a harm for S, and (3) A does not wrong anyone other than S or P, then A is permissible (pp. 51–52). VanDeVeer accommodates cases in which it is intuitively right to harm third parties to help S by a doctrine of necessity: it may not be wrong to harm others if it is necessary to help S. Now, surely he does not mean that it is right to inflict any and all harms on third parties necessary to help an individual, but he fails to specify what "necessity" justifies. His framework would not allow him to do it in the obvious way, by weighing benefits for the beneficiary against harms inflicted on the third party, and it is hard to see where respect for persons would lead us.

One is tempted to think that provision (2) in RCP is a misprint since, as VanDeVeer immediately reminds us, S must not think that A will benefit him or else A is nonparentalistic. For the same reason, the "currently operative consent" mentioned in (2)(a) of PARP and (1) of RCP must not take the form of fully informed and rational consent to A. Earlier VanDeVeer describes two forms of consent which "plausibly seem to justify otherwise wrongful acts," prior irrevocable consent and current consent (p. 50). In respect to the second, it is questionable that current consent absolves the parentalist from wrongdoing when A harms S or abets his self-harm. Such actions clearly can be wrong if the consent is irrational or ill-informed, and it is also the case if consent is based on S's settled desire for what is harmful and the parentalist knows that it is harmful.

In respect to the reference to prior consent, it is preferable to stipulate that it be unrevoked consent rather than irrevocable, since a person's foolish or uninformed present wish or dissent is not sufficient in itself to revoke a revocable earlier authorization of action A. VanDeVeer's theory imposes the difficult task of distinguishing between prior consent which has been revoked, which is revocable but not revoked, and which is irrevocable. He does not indicate how this is possible except to suggest that, illustrating by Odysseus' command to his crew, consent is irrevocable if the subject says "proceed no matter what I say" and revocable if he says "unless I change my mind." Such explicit instructions are rare, so VanDeVeer adds that consent may carry an implicit rider that it is revocable. Uncertainty about whether a prior consent carried a rider would leave a prospective parentalist in the dark much of the time about whether the subject had revoked his consent. Presumably, when in doubt she would assume that his current dissent indicates that he has revoked his prior consent and refrain from acting. If this is what VanDeVeer has in mind, his principle is strongly, and I believe illegitimately, biased against intervention.

PHIC

VanDeVeer argues that every generally competent person wants to be able to make his own decisions even at the cost of mistakes: "Life is not in *all* respects unlike a game where there is something valuable, translatable perhaps in terms of self-respect, in *playing one's own* hand as best one knows how, rather than being 'helped' to avoid mistakes by 'benevolent' and controlling fellow persons" (p. 84). Though VanDeVeer seems to recognize that the value of choosing for oneself is limited, he treats it as an absolute right: P is justified in intervening *if and only if* S authorizes the act as a way to pursue S's own goals. I believe that this move is fatal for VanDeVeer's position; but even if it is not, it leads to a morass of problems as he tries to account for intuitively justified cases where intervention does not enjoy actual consent.

VanDeVeer maintains that all such cases are ones in which the person would have consented had he not been uninformed or emotionally disturbed. To capture these cases he proposes PHIC: A is justified if (1) S would validly consent to A if (a) S were aware of the relevant circumstances, (b) S's normal capacities for deliberation and choice were not substantially impaired, and (2) A involves no wrong to those other than S and P (p. 75). VanDeVeer notes that this conception is close to Hodson's concept of hypothetical unencumbered consent, but he argues in relation to specific choices;

> Considerable ignorance is rather common with respect to a large number of consumer purchases. Similarly, choices of careers, mates, divorce, and treatment for injury or disease commonly involve much ignorance and emotional stress. Persons making such decisions often regret them, but to think that invasive paternalistic intervention is thereby legitimate is to be committed to a wide range of, I believe, invidious and unduly meddlesome interventions. . . . My main

reservation about appeal to a hypothetical, unencumbered will of a subject concerns the fact that not all emotional stress and ignorance need be thought of as an encumbrance. Further, some ignorance may be an essential feature of a person's identity. Consider a competent person, L, who is dedicated to finding the Loch Ness "monster." (p. 83 n)

This criticism of Hodson and a similar one of Feinberg follow from VanDe-Veer's notion of general competence, which allows numerous pockets and episodes of incompetence and yet forbids intervention without the subject's consent.

My objections to the status VanDeVeer assigns to hypothetical consent are three. First, since it is not actual consent, how can it waive an actual right? VanDeVeer himself levels this criticism against rational consent:

The expression "fully rational person" refers to no actual person; it is a logical construct as is "frictionless plane." There is no consent given by a fully rational individual, that is, no actual giving of permission to constrain [the actual person] provided by a fully rational person. What PHRC proposes in the final analysis is that it is all right to impose on [the person] constraints or goals which may be foreign to those he does or might autonomously and reasonably choose. (pp. 74–75)

Hypothetical individualized consent is equally a construct and cannot waive an actual right.

Second, VanDeVeer is not able to make the notion of competent choice and hence of hypothetical consent any more precise than Feinberg can make voluntary choice or Hodson unencumbered choice. He promises to when he dismisses the notion of a rational subject as "murky," "indeterminate," and "not entirely transparent" and claims that an individual's hypothetical consent is empirically confirmable. But he (necessarily) characterizes competence so sketchily that one is at a loss to know exactly what evidence at the time of some episode of incompetence of the subject would confirm what the competent subject would consent to. What circumstances would the hypothetical Competent-S be aware of? Not a wide range, for VanDeVeer indicates that the circumstances do not extend to those which provide bases of his fundamental beliefs (for example, facts relevant to belief in God or the Loch Ness monster). How unimpaired need his reason be? Not very, for VanDe-Veer would guarantee the subject the right to make quite irrational decisions as long as these did not destroy his capacity for deliberation and choice.

Moreover, PHIC is based on the assumption that persons have a single set of settled beliefs and desires respecting each area of life for which parentalism might be an issue. Actual persons may have none in particular areas or several which they have adopted at times of varying competence. From his discussion of honoring the prior competent desires of a now incompetent person (p. 402), it is evident that VanDeVeer would think that the last set upon which the person competently settled are the ones that should be honored. Also, he would think that whether the most recent competent consent was meant to be revocable or irrevocable would be decisive in the case of fluctuation between revocable and irrevocable consents (p. 298). It will never be easy and in many cases impossible to determine the person's settled preferences. Yet without secure knowledge of the particular desires that would motivate the subject's hypothetical consent, others are forbidden to help him avoid even irremediable severe harms or take advantage of irretrievable golden opportunities, a consequence which is unacceptable.

This leads to the third point. For VanDeVeer the parentalist is justified in acting in the face of the subject's ignorant or irrational dissent to promote goals which he has adopted at a prior time. But the value to him of her promoting faulty goals is even less than the value of pursuing faulty goals for himself, so this cannot be the justification for appealing to his hypothetical individualized consent. If his dissent is overruled, should not it be for his true interests?

Treatment of Incompetents

VanDeVeer denies the right of autonomy in self-affecting matters to incompetent persons. He proposes the Principle of Individualized Substituted Judgment (PISJ) to justify interventions in their lives: the intervener must imagine the judgment regarding his treatment that the *incompetent person* would make if he were competent.

The strongest competitor of PISJ is the Revised Harm-Prevention Principle (RHPP), which justifies intervention to prevent serious harm to the incompetent person as this is determined by the *intervener's* understanding of that person's interests. Since RHPP is close to the principle which I have proposed for all parentalism, I must deal with VanDeVeer's objections to it.

Our examination of autonomy should make us suspicious of any attempt to divide humanity into sheep and goats, the competent and the incompetent. It is useful to draw competence boundaries for specific tasks on the basis of what VanDeVeer calls "performance-based criteria," but here there are no natural dividing lines. Boundaries must be drawn more or less arbitrarily according to community needs and standards of successful performance (p. 351). There are a fortiori no natural boundaries between general competence and incompetence.

I have maintained that only task-competencies need to be defined in practice. Judgments of general competence and incompetence should be avoided. Dichotomizing humanity encourages society to assume (in VanDeVeer's own terms) that "bright makes right," that the competent have the right to rule the incompetent in a total way. VanDeVeer is anxious to avert this consequence and he takes pains to show that his own position does not sanction it (pp. 348–351). There is a strong possibility, however, that the labeling required to apply his principles would encourage the very attitude he condemns.

My position is more egalitarian on the face. It asks us to treat everyone by the same principle. We should consider the interests of all persons, whether competent or incompetent for particular tasks, as intrinsically valuable. Precisely in recognition of the equal importance of people, we should assign different weights to their autonomous acts according to the degree to which they display important human capabilities, since these variations affect the intrinsic and instrumental value of the acts.

Let us take a brief look at those whom VanDeVeer identifies as incompetent. These include people who suffer from permanent though not necessarily irremediable disabilities in the intellectual capacities which VanDeVeer identifies as necessary for autonomy (p. 347). As a result of disabilities, such people are prone to seriously irrational decisions which make them a threat to themselves and others. VanDeVeer lists several categories, including infants, young children, the severely senile, the severely retarded, psychopaths such as paranoid schizophrenics, and the comatose (p. 86). He suggests that older children, as pre- or protocompetent, must be treated differently than the others, presumably under the principles for competent and less severely incompetent persons (pp. 346, 394).

Two of the ways in which VanDeVeer classifies incompetents which are relevant to our discussion have to do with the extent and history of the incompetence. In reference to retardates, VanDeVeer comments:

> Some, the profoundly retarded, may lack conscious goals and preferences. In that respect they may have no aims by virtue of which they could, if able, direct their lives along some paths as opposed to others. In an important way they are "directionless," even if sentient and, hence, possessing the morally relevant capacity to experience some satisfactions and dissatisfactions. . . . [T]here seems no consent or dissent to take into account, no autonomy or incipient autonomy to consider. In contrast, the mildly retarded clearly have articulable, conscious goals and expressed preferences. (p. 356)

The profoundly retarded share with comatose persons and psychopaths not only an absence of essential components of personhood but permanence in that lack, which leads VanDeVeer to question whether it is proper to refer to them as persons at all (p. 397). Since there is no conceivable way to determine what they would consent to if *per impossible* they were competent, others are forced to fall back on a principle of benevolence in making judgments for them.

VanDeVeer focuses his discussion on "those who were competent but are not now . . . [and] are not comatose. Such cases exhibit two important features: (1) the individual exhibits some history of preferences and beliefs, and (2) no serious claim can be made that such individuals are not persons or that they are lacking in moral standing" (p. 398). For the treatment of such persons, he proposes the Principle of Individualized Substituted Judgement (PISJ), which may be paraphrased: If a person is incompetent with respect to doing B (or choosing with regard to B), then parentalistic intervention A is permissible if (1) A is quite likely to prevent him from causing significant harm to himself by B; (2) if A were omitted it is quite likely that B would harm him; and (3) if he were competent, he would choose that the parentalist do A (pp. 407–408).

The critical provision is (3). VanDeVeer labels a preliminary formulation of PISP the "Infused" version because "[t]he relevant choice is whatever choice would be made by an incompetent imaginatively 'infused' with his prior values, outlook, and capacities for reflection, and relevantly informed vis-à-vis choosing treatment for the incompetent that he actually is" (p. 400). The basis for this exercise of the imagination is data about the subject's prior settled desires and beliefs, specifically those relevant to his present course of action which he formed most recently in the past. Hence, VanDeVeer refers to PISJ as the Historical Version of substitute judgment principles (p. 402).

VanDeVeer points out that PISJ sanctions a different set of parentalistic acts than respect for the subject's current wishes or concern for his objective interests. Permitting him to act on his wishes has some value for him, as it does for competent persons, but it is not a decisive consideration. When the person threatens significant harm to himself by an action or goal (condition (1) of PISJ), this is sufficient to warrant the frustration of the action or goal. VanDeVeer puts this in terms of maximizing utility for the person (pp. 356, 401). On the other hand, to maximize the person's utility in terms of his true interests is not warranted if, when he was competent, he would have chosen different treatment. In VanDeVeer's eyes, to disregard his hypothetical competent desires would be to treat him as a mere utility holder, not an individual person (pp. 393, 411).

In contrast, VanDeVeer claims, PISJ respects his autonomy and is "continuous with" the principle for competent persons (PARP): "PISJ seeks to respect the individual by giving important or decisive weight to that individual's most developed conception of the good, as a creator of choice and/or preference and not merely as one possessing interests" (p. 411). Hence, PISJ is of a piece with PARP in his autonomy-respecting parentalism since it is grounded on respect for persons. Though the incompetent person lacks autonomy rights, others are to treat him according to his rights at his last time of competence.

My criticisms of PISJ should be obvious. First, any inference on the parentalist's part about the judgments which an incompetent person would make if competent is even more a construct than the hypothetical individualized consent of a competent person and shares its deficiencies in comparison to actual consent. A waiver which the incompetent person once might have made but did not does not cancel his present right. If this is not to be a barrier to intervention, VanDeVeer is forced to deny that incompetents have autonomy rights in the first place, which can be justified only by absolutizing incompetence. Second, there has been no autonomous act on the person's part. The parentalist decides for him on the basis of her best guess as to what his "infused" judgment would have been. This judgment has none of the intrinsic, instrumental, or evidential value calculations which an actual act of consent would have. Third, honoring a person's past (competent) desires might be an act of respect in some sense, similar to honoring the wishes of ancestors or deceased friends, there is no connection of this with cherishing autonomy as an ongoing human reality. There is no convincing reason why it should stand in the way of alleviating the present suffering of persons or advancing their current interests.

Criticisms of Good-Promotion

Let us now turn to VanDeVeer's criticisms of the position that most resembles mine and that he treats as his principal rival. It utilizes what he labels a "hedonic" conception, which defines intrinsic good in terms of satisfaction given by such things as knowledge, health, wealth, and friendship; and it advocates "good-promoting principles," which justify actions by their tendency to promote the good of those whom they affect. These conceptions generate the Naive Good-Promotion

Principle (NGPP), which is the rival of PARP for parentalism toward competent persons, and the Revised Harm-Prevention Principle (RHPP), which is the rival of PISJ for incompetent ones. NGPP may be paraphrased: if two people are competent and one's parentalistic performance of A toward the second will result in R and R is for the second's own good, then her doing A is permissible (p. 102). RHPP may be paraphrased: paternalistically doing A to a person and preventing the person from doing B, where the agent is competent and the subject incompetent, is permissible if A will prevent the latter from doing significant harm to himself, omission of A would allow the harm, A leaves him no worse off than if he were to perform B and A is the least harmful means of preventing B (pp. 354–355).

VanDeVeer's criticisms of NCPP are basically two. First, it requires the parentalist to make difficult judgments about the satisfactions which her intervention will bring the subject. While admitting that the subject can be mistaken about his own satisfactions, VanDeVeer observes that he is more likely to know idiosyncratic facts about himself. This I have acknowledged and indeed insisted in requiring the parentalist to have strong evidence that she knows the interests of the subject better than he. Nevertheless, I have pointed out that it is possible for her to know better and to know that she knows better. When the benefit to the recipient is great enough and the parentalist's basis for judgment is strong enough, I would permit her to disregard even his settled desires.

VanDeVeer seems to think that the fact that the subject sometimes has to choose between self-interested and altruistic acts precludes others from choosing goods for him. This would seem to forbid the parentalist not only from promoting the subject's good in the face of his desire to sacrifice himself for some person or cause, but also from challenging him to self-sacrifice, to face up to his obligations, or to put benevolence ahead of self-interest. My position condones such challenges. In fact, it demands that each of us care for others in ways that help them carry their burdens of care. If a person's settled desires or his plan of life plan is devoid of responsibilities—and yet caring for others is a basic value for human beings and hence for him—it must be permissible for the parentalist to urge him not to shirk his responsibilities.

The difficulty of evaluating actions in terms of their consequences—consequences for the agent's own objective well-being and even more for that of other persons—are well known and formidable. One must balance goods and harms, transient goods and lasting ones, goods of different character and quality, the goods and harms of different people, and so on. The best the agent can do is to grope for solutions, utilize available evidence, make comparisons and estimates, counter known sources of bias, and try to learn from experience. Formal techniques of cost/benefit analysis can make judgments more rational, but the intuitive element cannot be entirely eliminated. However, this is only to say that the human condition is one of uncertainty. Respect for autonomy no more eliminates uncertainty about what to do than do the counsels of benevolence. VanDeVeer appears to recognize this. At least he is sensitive to the "epistemological pitfalls for non-omniscient interveners" in applying his principles. This leads him to require only judgments that are in principle confirmable on the basis of empirical data. But even where he succeeds in specifying the conditions of confirmability, he does not show that the judgments of the sort he requires are more reliable than computations of consequences.

This is apparent from the flaws in VanDeVeer's second line of criticism. VanDeVeer notes the obvious, that in deciding what is good for a person, including whether it is better for him to serve others or pursue his own narrow self-interest, the parentalist must act on her conceptions of what is good for him. Thus she must decide whether it is good to honor his choices. Her general conception of value on the basis of which she decides what is good for him may well differ from his, and even a shared conception of good may lead her to differ about specific goods. If she overrules his judgment and infringes on his autonomy to promote her conception of his good rather than his, VanDeVeer claims that she "imposes" her conception of value or "vision of the good" on him and this treats him as a mere "good receptacle" or "utility location." VanDeVeer objects, "persons are not just that. They are arbiters of their own well-being, and not merely sentient, computing, devices to be kept in good repair" (p. 112) and he maintains that when we impose our values on others, we treat them as different from ourselves and not fully as persons.

In criticism of this criticism, I would remind the reader that, whether the parentalist decides to intervene and frustrate the subject's aims or not to intervene and let him pursue them, she can only decide on the basis of what *she* thinks is best and in neither case need she cause him to adopt *her* values. Indeed, it is nearly impossible to impose one's values on another in the invidious sense. Ordinary acts of parentalism alter limited parts of the subject's life by diverting him from particular goals or particular activities; they do not affect his system of values.

How does respect for autonomy dictate that a persons' actual wishes should be sacrificed to his hypothetical more competent ones? That he be allowed to follow paths doomed to frustration with loss of self-respect and self-confidence? That his actual or hypothetical consent waives his right to autonomy or transfers his basic responsibilities to another? These all appear to be implications of the Principle of Autonomy-Respecting Paternalism.

Summa Contra VanDeVeer

To summarize VanDeVeer's position, respect for autonomy dictates adherence to the following principles for categories of people:

1. If a person is generally competent and is currently episodically so, his present wishes should be honored. Another is permitted to intervene in his life if and only if he wants her to.
2. If a person is generally competent, but episodically incompetent, the parentalist should follow the Principle of Autonomy-Respecting Paternalism and intervene only if she has his unrevoked prior or hypothetical individualized consent.
3. If a person is generally incompetent, but has once been competent, the parentalist should follow the Principle of Individualized Substitute

Judgment and act on the judgment he would have made when competent about his treatment now that he is incompetent, given his settled desires at the time of his last competence.

4. If a person is generally incompetent and has never been competent or the parentalist lacks data about his prior competent desires, the parentalist should follow the Revised Harm-Prevention Principle.

As a final statement of my reasons for rejecting this position, let me make the following points. First, moral rights pertaining to autonomy, as VanDeVeer states them and no doubt as they have to be stated, are indeterminate in comparison to codified legal rights. Legal rights legitimate claims of people in given relationships to specific behavior of specific others by a system of statutes and accompanying case law. In contrast, there is an essential vagueness in the concept of the moral right to autonomy due to the great variety of its elements, forms, and degrees. "Autonomy" is a family term rather than an essentialist one for which a simple definition *per genus et differentia* can be given. The claim of persons to "self-direction of their lives" is open-ended. If it is their claim to immunity from interferences which "divert them from their chosen course," it prohibits every intervention contrary to their current preferences. If, on the other hand, it only prohibits interventions that "undermine their decision making capacities, their decision-process, or render the latter impotent to eventuate in chosen outcomes," only the most extreme and global ones have this effect and no one would deny that these are unjustified. VanDeVeer seeks a position that falls between the two extremes but has not found a viable one.

Second, to specify which interventions are permissible and which not under the subject's right to autonomy requires a panoply of supplementary rules. The attempt to derive such rules leads either to consequentialist considerations, which I have endorsed, or quite problematic claims about the importance of autonomy whatever its form, which I have criticized, or appeals to intuitions, many of which I do not share. VanDeVeer takes the last path. He postulates an indeterminate absolute right to autonomy to argue that consent is the only morally relevant fact for the justification of parentalistic interventions. Then he cites his intuitions about what interventions are "too meddlesome" in order to dismiss cases in which intervention without consent might seem justified. It is apparent that the fundamental issues involved cannot be settled by the appeal to intuition.

Third, though VanDeVeer does not undertake to explain in a comprehensive way why autonomy is valuable or how it deserves the extreme respect which he affords it, he concedes that the intrinsic value of pursuing what one desires does not have unlimited value; it has only "considerable value" which should be given "due weight" in deciding what is good for a person (pp. 72–73, 84). If this is where the value of autonomy lies, the individual's claim to autonomy can hardly be absolute.

Fourth, it is noteworthy that VanDeVeer does not tie the value of autonomy to its contribution to bringing the individual other objective goods. Yet the distinction between objective goods and what the individual desires is implicit in his remarks about the right to autonomy in imprudent decisions where the individual is mistaken about his interests (pp. 52, 72, 84). While he does not commit himself to a particular concept of good or what it means to benefit another, he seems sympathetic to the view adopted here, that the prime index of a good is that it brings lasting satisfaction and this is an objective fact independent of the individual's desires.[2] All of this means that it is possible for someone to know better what is good for a person than he does himself. Yet VanDeVeer does not accept that that person is permitted to intervene to provide it.

Finally, VanDeVeer argues that since a necessary condition for autonomy is the absence of both constraints (forcing one to do what he does not want) and restraints (preventing him from doing what he does want), other people are required in the absence of his consent to refrain from constraining him for his objective good. I have criticized this notion at length. Genuine solicitude demands more than that we not encroach on each others' rights. We should try to benefit those in our care and protect them from real harm. Helping them pursue their goals is one major way of benefiting them, but it is a way which must be foregone for other ways. Moreover, it is odd to think that one is permitted, not to say obligated, to help another pursue his goals when she knows that they—ultimately, over the long run, everything considered—will be seriously harmful. It is similarly odd to think that she is not allowed to block his pursuit of such goals if she genuinely cares for him.

The difficulties of VanDeVeer's position are fatal. My alternative is a set of guidelines for what are by necessity crude estimates of the consequences of our efforts for the true welfare of those for whom we care. The guidelines provide a central place for autonomy, but not the only place or always the decisive place.

V

PUBLIC PARENTALISM

12

The State as Parentalist

People take care of others without their consent in two ways. They help them directly, and they support or participate in institutions which in turn serve them. I will refer to the latter form of parentalism as public parentalism, in contrast to the personal parentalism with which we have been occupied to this point.

The last part of this work will be devoted to public parentalism. In this chapter we will examine the activities of legislators and others who decide public policy. In the next we will look at one influential view of legal parentalism, that of Feinberg. In the last chapter, we will consider activities of those who implement social policies and practices by performing publicly defined roles, using the behavior of professionals as representative.

The Need for State Parentalism

We should not assume that justified forms of public parentalism exactly parallel those of personal parentalism.[1] Their contexts differ in significant ways. Agents of the state act at a psychological and often a geographical and temporal distance from those whom they are trying to serve. It is difficult for them to attune their measures to individual differences. They often must treat people by rule under abstract descriptions such as "patient in mental institution," "farmer in need of loans," "family on welfare," and so forth.

Social institutions thus are not well equipped to address the variable needs of individuals. They are better equipped to meet shared needs by measures that are capable of a certain degree of standardization. Some such needs are protection from devastating harm; provision of physical resources for the pursuit of happiness such as medical care, housing, and nutrition; and the guarantee of fundamental liberties such as association, speech, thought, employment, and action. The measures of the state address these needs only externally, by providing facilities and resources for individuals to use their own ways.

The outcome of corporate actions are uncertain because a large number of agents must be engaged to complete them. In the case of an action of the state — for example, protection for fetuses or guarantee of the reproductive rights of women — legislation is only the first step. Further steps must be taken by a large number of others to implement it: administrators, agents, judges, and enforcers who compose the bureaucracy; professionals, guardians, employers, and parents who directly deal with recipients; and members of the public, whose support or acquiescence provides the necessary milieu. At each step the powers of society pass into the hands of new agents. The initiator of the process cannot be sure how these agents will carry the action forward. As a result, the impact of public acts on intended beneficiaries is highly uncertain. The best the public agent can do is observe material results—housing built, entitlements assigned, reduction in use of drugs, occupancy of hospitals, prayers and pledges of allegiance in schools, and so on—and guess at their efficacy in affecting the subjective lives of the benefiaries for the better. The distance between agent and recipient, between initial cause and ultimate effect, make the epistemic element in the justification of public parentalism critical.

The moral to be drawn from all of this is fourfold. First, people acting for a corporate group should restrict their efforts to basic needs that can be served by manipulating external conditions. Second, they should keep in mind that the autonomy of recipients is as important as the particular good—health, freedom of commerce, security or whatever—which is their specific responsibility. Third, the state should encourage the development of institutions that will share burdens with it, and it itself should act at the lowest, most local, or personal level at which it can be effective. Fourth, it should utilize measures that encourage and equip individuals to tend to their own needs wherever possible, rather than thrusting standardized goods on them.

The impersonality and power of large organizations give formal rules a central role in their workings and make it important to guarantee rights of individuals in the public sphere. Indeed, this is the primary home of formal rules and rights. It is always proper for a person to complain of violation of her rights by the state or a large corporation, school, or hospital, whereas it is often officious and contentious when the infringing agent is a private individual who genuinely cares for her.

The rules and actions of the state must enjoy the support of most citizens to be effective. Thus, the members of our society appear to agree that our society should ensure everyone the minimal food, shelter, and clothing necessary for health; a high degree of security from physical assault; assistance in meeting the exigencies of aging, unemployment, accidents, and natural disaster; sufficient education to make a living in a technological world and participate in its political life; an opportunity for gainful employment; and liberty for personal pursuits. This loose congerie of basic goods is generally viewed as the content of welfare rights, and the propriety of public guarantees of such rights is widely recognized.

The widespread support of welfare measures in a democratic society has led moralists with consent-based and other autonomy-respecting theories to argue that they are not parentalistic. In a sense this is correct, and it is important here to explain how it is in order to secure the grounds for evaluating the measures.

Almost everyone consents to there being laws devised by elected or duly appointed officials though she may not welcome particular laws. Does she not thereby consent to the curtailment of their liberty that the laws entail? Are not the actions of society's agents simply the means that members of society have chosen to pursue their objectives? in which case, the actions would seem to be non-parentalistic.

To see that parentalism is pervasive, despite the existence of widespread public support, it is only necessary to remind ourselves of the way legislatures work. A faction—the majority of citizens or frequently a strategic minority, or a majority or minority of lawmakers—decides that certain laws will benefit everyone, but only if almost everyone in the community obeys them. Since more than a few individuals even among those who support the legislation will be tempted to disobey the laws in the hope that the rest will conform, the lawmakers provide coercion to ensure general obedience. Among those coerced may be many who are benefited by the general conformity though they disagree with the laws. They are thus coerced for their own good, and the legislation has a parentalistic dimension, although it also benefits the ruling faction and compliant citizens and so has other dimensions.

The support of the best and most democratic of measures is not by universal, conscious, informed, and expressed acts of consent. In Mill's words, "such phrases as 'self-government,' and 'the power of the people over themselves,' do not express the true state of the case. The 'people' who exercise the power are not always the same people with those over whom it is exercised; and the 'self-government' that is spoken of is not the government of each by himself, but of each by all the rest."[2] However, "consent of the governed" is a useful fiction. It is often rationalized by the myth of social contract according to which all who remain under the jurisdiction of a state—even those who grouse about, scoff at, ignore, or deliberately violate its rules and ways—tacitly consent to its authority.

The myth of contract is a strategm that enables the consent moralist to accomodate intuitively justified welfare measures of the state and still maintain that people must consent for them to be legitimate. However, the fact that a person does not rebel, yields to coercion, and obeys the laws of the community does not mean that he has authorized specific actions. The absence of dissent is not the presence of consent. It does not waive autonomy rights or convert the state into an agent of the passive unresister.

Let us concede, however, that in a weak sense there is generic consent among the populace to having a state and to accepting such laws as are produced by authorized processes. What does this imply for the justification of particular state actions? VanDeVeer and other consent theorists argue that they should be equated to personal acts to which recipients have given prior consent. They cite the example of Odysseus as a paradigm.[3] Odysseus had his crew bind him to the mast of his ship so that he could listen to the song of the sirens without being lured to his death. Knowing that he would demand to be released, he ordered his men to disobey him. That is, at a time of cool rationality he anticipated that he would make an irrational choice and he authorized others to disregard it.

In a similar manner, it is argued, people empower the state to impose restrictions though they know that they will not always welcome the measures their agents choose. The comparison assumes that the action of Odysseus' men was not parentalistic since it was authorized by prior consent. It also maintains that the action was justified because respect for Odysseus' autonomy dictated that his settled values take priority over current wishes transmogrified by the sirens' song. In the same way, the legislature is implementing the settled values of citizens even though it is acting against the temporary preferences of some and it does so with the authorization of all. Hence, its actions are both justified and nonparentalistic.

According to my interpretation of the Odysseus story, however, the crew's action (assuming it was motivated by concern for Odysseus' true welfare and not just obedience to his authority) *was* parentalistic. And it was justified not because Odysseus had commanded it, but because the crew knew that it was better for him to live than to die. The crew acted according to their understanding of his best interests and by Zeus they were right!

Moreover, the cases of Odysseus and the public are dissimilar in a significant respect. Generic consent to a set of laws and their implementing actions by the public is consent to the existence of the set prior to knowledge of what the set will contain. The members of society do not know what they have got themselves into until it unfolds. Odysseus, in contrast, knew exactly what the measures would be which he would later try to countermand. Hence, generic consent does not entail even the kind prior consent that makes measures nonparentalistic according to some schemes, and it counts less toward their justification.

The contemporary state is profoundly parentalistic. This fact is deplored by those who view it as essentially an instrument of domination and hence parentalism as a mask for exploitation. It is equally deplored by those whose sterile concept of liberty would leave individuals to sink or swim in the face of overwhelming natural and social odds. Whatever the evaluation of it, however, state parentalism is a fact of life.

More to the point, it is necessary in face of the exigencies of modern existence. It is one of those things we would eliminate in an ideal society and which we should work to eliminate in our actual society, but which is an unfortunate necessity because of other flaws in the social system. In an age of specialization and technological complexity, the basic needs of the individual are willynilly entrusted to the care of others. In a mass and mobile society these others are often strangers with no personal ties of care with the recipient of care. Moreover, they possess technical knowledge beyond the recipient's ken and expertise that she cannot hope to acquire. At best, education can acquaint her with their specialties sufficiently to enable her to choose experts wisely and hold them accountable for meeting her needs. Unfortunately, few members of society are educated to this minimal level. Most are left to blindly trust technicians to make decisions for them.

The institutions that control the activities of the technicians are massive and interlocked. This puts the individual at the mercy of vagaries of the economy and other parts of the social structure over which she has no influence. Where people were once slaves to the natural environment, they are now tossed about by wars, business cycles, demographic shifts, revolutions in mores, and veers in public policy. At the same time, many individuals are denied traditional sources of physical and emotional security such as an extended family, a local community in which they have deep roots, a traditional moral code and firm religious faith which they can take for granted. They need a sponsor and protector equal to the forces that threaten them. The state tries to meet that need. In respect to many problems, it is the only agency with the power to do so. It is therefore a rational response to modern realities to try to make it work as best it can, while at the same time developing other institutions to take over functions which it discharges poorly.

The question is not whether there should be state care but how to ensure that its actions follow the right path. Unrestrained, even a benevolent institution can stifle autonomy. And benevolent institutions are easily diverted to exploitive uses, with the benevolent facade retained so as to make their exploitation that more pernicious. As we have observed, the most effective restraint on the state and best protection against its parentalistic and exploitive tendencies is a set of personal liberties constitutionally guaranteed and ferociously defended. Nevertheless, some state parentalism is necessary, and some rights in some circumstances must give way to permit it. We will examine the circumstances that warrant—and others that prohibit—parentalistic state actions for four purposes: to protect individual citizens from harm, promote the security of the nation, provide a minimal level of welfare, and inculcate moral virtue.

Protective Legislation

In considering the protective function, we will examine some representative forms of legal parentalism. Dworkin provides a broad classification that suggests its range.[4] Laws that protect people whom they constrain constitute *pure parentalism*. They either directly prohibit self-harmful behavior (*direct parentalism*) or make it difficult to execute (*indirect parentalism*). Indirectly parentalistic laws are *impure parentalism* when they constrain other people in order to make it difficult for a person to perform self-harmful acts. We can make parallel distinctions between laws that provide inducements to the person to perform self-beneficial acts or to others to benefit her.

These distinctions generate three cells: direct parentalism (always pure), indirect pure parentalism, and indirect impure parentalism. A particular aim can be served by any of the kinds of law. For example, if the law imposes penalties on people who fail to wear safety equipment or take precautions in dangerous activities, it is a form of direct parentalism. If it requires manufacturers to incorporate safety features in their products or employers to force employees to wear equipment or if it permits insurance companies to charge those who do not observe these precautions higher rates, it is indirect parentalism. Below are samples of the laws that fall under these rubrics.[5]

1. *Direct parentalism*: prohibition of suicide and self-mutilation; prevention of women, children, or other vulnerable persons from accepting dangerous or arduous work; prohibition of homosexual conduct (when it is considered harmful to practitioners); limitations on gambling and drinking, smoking, and other drugs; restriction of swimming when lifeguards are not on duty; requirement of helmets for motorcycle riders, seat belts for automobile and airplane passengers,

and life belts for boat riders and water skiers; requirement of hard hats, protective goggles, safety belts, and other protective paraphernalia for workers; requirement that sky divers, mountain climbers, skiers, and scuba divers be properly equipped and trained; mandatory schooling to prepare children for adult life; universal military training or public service (when these are viewed as morally beneficial); required prayers, pledges of allegiance, sex and drug training, and moral indoctrination in the schools; mandatory testing for and inoculation against diseases.

2. *Indirect pure parentalism*: exclusion of enforcement of contracts that commit individuals to harmful bargains; denial of assumption of risk as a defense against actions against a person for violation of safety statutes; denial of consent of the victim as a defense against a charge of murder or abuse; exceptions to the right of suit for assault and battery against medical personnel for involuntary blood transfusions, surgery, and other emergency treatment; heavy taxation of tobacco, alcohol, or other harmful drugs (where the costs are passed on to the consumer); honors, bounties, or other incentives for a healthy diet, exercise, or inoculation for a disease; public education and propaganda for healthy activities and warnings and propaganda against unhealthy ones.

3. *Indirect impure parentalism*: requirement of qualifications to be licensed to practice an occupation; forced contribution to a retirement program or medical insurance as a means of maintaining a system; limit on interest that can be charged on loans; prohibition of solicitation for prostitution, homosexual, or extramarital sex and dangerous employment and leisure activities; regulations for humane care of animals; strict guidelines for trustees, guardians, and others in a fiduciary capacity; regulations for the use of public funds for special education or care of the mentally incompetent, drug addicts, or other incapacitated persons; minimum wage levels.

This list is partial, but it indicates the scope of protective legislation. The examples are mixed in two ways. First, many people support the laws, so they are not parentalistic toward them. They are still parentalistic toward ones who do not support them. Second, the laws that constrain some people to protect others are not parentalist toward the former, but they are toward those of the latter who have not asked for the protection. The laws curtail the opportunity of the latter to enter self-harmful relationships.

In light of modern conditions, many of the laws in the list seem legitimate. The limitations that they impose on the liberty of beneficiaries are justified by the benefits they provide, and the limitations they impose on the liberties of third parties are justified by the fact that those liberties are abused. But when the laws are legitimate, we must ask whether the element of parentalism counts for or against their legitimacy.

Consider, for example, laws that require motorcyclists to wear helmets. Are such laws really parentalistic? Some authors who see that they are desirable but have saddled themselves with a categorical condemnation of parentalism attempt to define their parentalism away by tortured appeals to the interests of third parties. For example, they argue that a cyclist who refuses to wear a helmet may end up a gruesome spectacle on the highway or a public charge in a hospital, raising the taxes for citizens and insurance premiums for other cyclists. He can be made to wear a helmet to protect others, hence, the law is not parentalistic. This flirts with absurdity. The magnitude and probability of bystander harms are too slight to justify the curtailment of cyclists' liberty; it is only protection of cyclists that does so. Surely this is the primary motive of actual legislation, as it is with legislation for safety precautions for other activities on the highway, work place, and sports arena. An even more desperate strategm is to defend helmets while prohibiting parentalism is to maintain that the cyclist who prefers riding without a helmet is a changed man after an accident. Hence under the harm principle he may be restrained to protect his future self.[6] The metaphysics of this view entails unacceptable consequences for such practices as contracts and punishment. It thus actually arrives at absurdity.

Helmet legislation is parentalistic, and in my judgment it is justified. However, I recognize that if the state were to attempt to protect its citizens from all dangers, no matter how minor they are or how necessary it is to incur them for important tasks, state intrusion into private life would be intolerable. Moreover, the state would be unable to discharge other functions that are more important. In order not to overload the state or magnify its power until it becomes a threat to those whom it would serve, its protections should be restricted to the gravest dangers and those least voluntarily assumed, and they should utilize the fewest possible constraints.

Thus the magnitude of the danger makes it reasonable to require mountain climbers to be properly equipped, trained, and informed even though they voluntarily assume the risk. On the other hand, pressure of competition for jobs forces people to accept risks at work which they would otherwise avoid. To protect them from these involuntary dangers, it is reasonable to constrain employers to take safety measures. In contrast to these justified forms of parentalism, it seems oppressive for the state to require people to use sunscreen lotion on ocean beaches or prohibit them from using tobacco at least where other people will not be affected, though it seems proper for it to publicize the hazards of sun rays and nicotine.

The guidelines I have proposed for parentalism impose a number of specific obligations on legislators who contemplate safety legislation. First, they should act only after extensive research verifies that there is a need. How many people are injured in a particular form of activity? How seriously? How voluntary is the risk? Second, will the legislation meet the need? In view of the distance between those who design laws and those affected by them, careful research is needed here, too. Laws may be social experiments, not permanent bricks in the social structure. The results of experimental measures must be assessed before leaving them in place, repeating, or expanding them. Third, is there a less coercive way to meet the need? For example, every effort should be made to educate the public to avoid dangerous drugs, an unhealthy diet, and environmental hazards before forcing it to do so by legal sanctions. Coercive legislation is appropriate only if education fails or members of the public refuse to take information to heart. Fourth, where possible, the state should regulate conditions under which activities are conducted rather than banning activities themselves. Thus, safety equipment may be mandated and rules of the road imposed for the use of automobiles, motorcycles, boats, planes, and factory and farm machinery; but the use itself should be permitted. Dog, horse, and human races should be allowed as long as the health of the racers is protected. On the other hand, activities that are harmful per se may be banned, including not only cock, dog, and bull fights, whose combatants have no choice, but also gladiatorial contests, boxing matches, and other lethal spectacles, whose human combatants do have a choice.

The Security State

In the complex and risky environment created by technology, the modern state has a strong obligation to provide for the security of its citizens. We will turn next to national defense. The unquestioned assumption of most members of society is that the primary threat to national life is aggression by other states. It seems necessary to maintain a permanent security system capable of repelling aggressors by force.

Unfortunately, the existence of the system encourages routine use of threat as an instrument of national diplomacy for purposes besides security and sometimes inimical to security. In the last decades, the dreary story of the expansion of military power and its centralization in the hands of a small security establishment has taken a paradoxical turn. The security system itself has become the ultimate threat to security. The drive for military superiority over possible rivals has elicited total weapons whose offensive capabilities exceed all possible defenses. Total war no longer can advance a nation's interests, and limited war is likely to escalate into total. Yet those who manage the security system cannot or will not eschew war as an option. Humanity will not survive this regimen of terror indefinitely. The alternatives seem to be to move to an even higher level of organization for security—to a consortium of nations or perhaps a world government with a monopoly on armed force—or dismantle the war system altogether.

This is not a story to be told here. What is relevant is the way the technologizing of security has transformed it into defense of the many by the very few, placing the mass of society at the bottom of a steep pyramid of command and transmuting defense into a parentalistic enterprise. In democratic societies, the armed forces are ostensibly responsible to elected civilian leaders, who in turn ostensibly carry out the will of the public. The myth is cultivated that the military is merely the arm that wields the sword by which the public defends itself. The reality is that the military-political security establishment has become a corporate whole with interests and a mind of its own. Finding the locus of decision is no easy matter. Who decides what weapons to develop, how to deploy them, the personnel to operate them, when they are used and how—elected or appointed governmental officials? the upper echelons of the officer corps? managers of industrial research and production? No doubt a mixture of these, but in what blend and by what patterns of interaction? The dynamics are not entirely clear. What is clear is that the public at large has little influence over them.[7]

Robert Paul Churchill argues that the U.S. nuclear deterrent is parentalistic through and through:

> Most of the major decisions affecting nuclear deterrence and, hence, our survival, are made in an autocratic fashion by a small group of elite "guardians" who do not seek the consent of the people in making important strategic decisions, and who often withhold information about key policy decisions, or act in complete secrecy. Indeed, since the dawn of the nuclear age, there has been no such thing as a real *public* policy concerning the development or intended use of nuclear weapons.

National survival is in the hands of a nuclear autocracy under the president, who is "a *de facto* dictator concerning the most serious issues of life and death." The dictator and autocracy are shielded from public accounting to the public or Congress.[8]

Churchill argues that the system is parentalistic because it meets these criteria: (1) presumption of knowledge: the autocracy believes that it knows what is best for the public; (2) presumption of acceptability: it persuades itself that the public would approve if the public could only know what it does; (3) the coercive dimension: the autocracy believes that the public would not take prudent measures to defend itself if left to its own resources, hence it must be manipulated to accept the autocracy's program; (4) other-directed motivation: members of the autocracy sincerely intend to benefit the nation.[9] The argument from consent may be advanced to deny that the security system is parentalistic. Churchill responds, "I believe that psychological studies would show that the appearance of general consensus may be a result of apathy, alienation, and the denial and avoidance symptoms of people faced by the nuclear peril."[10] Churchill concludes that nuclear deterrence is illegitimate because it is parentalistic and "contradicts the fundamental principles of democratic order." He takes for granted that this "presents us with the same threat to democracy and individual liberty posed by other forms of paternalism-coercion and the erosion of our capacity to be autonomous." The burden of justification is on the defenders of the present system: "it would be rational to continue to accept the costs of nuclear autocracy only if it succeeds in protecting us from aggression much more effectively than would the security policies resulting from a more open, accessible, and representative decision process."[11] There is clearly no evidence that it does.

I will go further and assert that nuclear deterrence is illegitimate because there is positive evidence that it does not work. It jeopardizes the future not only of those it is designed to protect but also the rest of humanity. It is not just parentalistic, a characteristic with all the bad consequences that Churchill describes; it fails *as* parentalism. It does not provide what it promises—true security in a very dangerous world.

Most citizens of the United States concluded long ago that the issues of national defense are too complex and arcane to understand. At the same time, they have accepted the need for secrecy in weapons development, strategic planning, and diplomatic maneuvers. They have countenanced bluff to intimidate antagonists and been indulgent toward deception of themselves. They have thereby consigned themselves to ignorance about the intentions of their leaders.

In short, they have entrusted their security to decisions made in secret by anonymous functionaries. They are reduced to vague yearnings for peace, generalized apprehensions about the state of the world, and worried suspicions of rival nations. Whenever the security establishment wants to add to its military muscle or flex it in national adventures, it can rouse the public by ritual alarums and ringing calls to patriotism. The public is conditioned to rally behind the flag and accede to demands of the leadership. In the terms of our earlier discussion, consent to national security measures is manufactured. It is far from rational or informed, and so it is not an exercise of autonomy in its higher forms. The very existence of the species and habitability of the planet are in the balance, and yet all that the public is asked to do, or is equipped to do, is trust its leaders. Nagged by suspicions that issues are too complex even for experts and that critical decisions are made to aggrandize the industrial-academic-governmental complex or in terms of ideology and chauvinism rather than sober analysis of the good of humanity, the public has sunk into lethargy. Whether from fatalism, complacency, cynicism, or faith in political celebrity, it has abdicated its autonomy and turned its eyes from the problem of security. Its behavior is a classic case of flight from autonomy, of shrugging off the burdens of self-care, of eager acceptance of dominion by what it hopes to be benevolent masters.

It is hard to see how the business of national security could be conducted in a much different way within the framework of the war-system and the institutions that have been developed to deal with mass society. Someone has to decide these matters, and the public is not able to do so. Individuals may take a stand for or against the establishment, but no one who has not devoted his life to public action can hope to have an impact. He is denied the very data necessary to make his case and a public forum in which to present it. This is not to say, however, that public control could not be enlarged. Institutions could be changed. Decisions about the mechanisms of defense could be made in public. Elected officials besides the president could play a central role. Exposure to the issues could be part of the education of the public. Perhaps it is not vain to urge members of the establishment to reflect on their habits of thought, unconscious assumptions, and inveterate prejudices—to ask themselves whether it would not serve the cause of security and the health of society to seek the rational and informed consent of the public for its efforts. In other words, the security establishment, like any parentalist, could try to change the conditions that make its parentalism necessary.

Welfare Rights

Protective legislation is patently parentalistic since it requires coercion. While coercion is bad per se, it does have the advantage that coercive measures rouse those subject to them to stand on their rights and demand immunity from government interference in their lives. Where the coercion is for their own good, the measures are obviously parentalistic and norms for parentalism immediately come to mind in evaluating them.

Welfare legislation, in contrast, is much less obviously parentalistic. The parentalism may be indirect, imposing restrictions on third parties in order to benefit individuals without their knowledge. Such legislation can often be defended in terms of benefits to those who support the laws rather than unknowing or unconsenting beneficiaries, removing from the public calculation the benefit (and possible harm) to those who do not support the legislation. Yet its parentalistic dimension is relevant, and this is what we will discuss here.

The postulate behind welfare legislation is that everyone needs a minimum level of nourishment, shelter, health care, security, leisure, education, meaningful work, intimate relationships with other people, and other basic goods. The provision of some of these can be left to the individual or to the solicitude of those in her personal circle of intimates and neighbors, but some can only be provided by the state under the conditions of modern society which were sketched above. For these necessities, welfare rights need to be defined and assured.

In a constitutional society, the initial step in defining and meeting welfare rights is legislation. Laws that compel positive actions from people — in contrast to the restrictions on their actions, such as those imposed by protective legislation — pose special problems of classification. It may be argued that the group medical and retirement programs freely chosen by a majority of the electorate or for them by some bargaining unit are not coercive, that contributions are self-exacted, not imposed against the contributors' will, and hence that the legislation is not parentalistic. Thus, many citizens do not trust their own frugality or the stability of the economic system to guarantee the necessities of life for their old age. They realize that voluntary pension plans do not work. In rational self-interest they accede to a compulsory system of saving. Once the system is in place, levies are imposed, whether the individuals who supported them continue to do so and whether new recruits to the system welcome them. Yet the system itself has been freely adopted. Does not this make the legislation nonparentalistic?

Despite this voluntary dimension, welfare measures, like protective ones, have a parentalistic dimension. Those responsible for the legislation (at best a majority of citizens) realize that everyone will benefit only if everyone is constrained to contribute. Prudent persons in the public accept such laws in the interest of the imprudent as well as themselves, though some of them might have taken care of their own interests without the laws.

I believe that the state should vigorously implement the welfare rights of its citizens through legislation. At the same time, I recognize the grave dangers of ill-conceived and ill-effected parentalism due to characteristics of state action. In state parentalism even more than in personal, there is danger that the agent's conception of what is good for the recipient may be badly mistaken. The pervasive power of the state poses the greater danger that an excessive number of parentalistic acts will shrink the autonomy of the recipient to a vanishing point. Worst of all, there is a clear, present, and grave danger that special-interest groups or venal agents of the state will use the mask of parentalism to promote their own self-interested agendas. This is a reason, incidentally, to be more careful with welfare legislation than protective legislation. It is hard to see how anyone but helmet manufacturers could gain from motorcycle legislation, and helmet manufacturers are not likely to have a great deal of influence on the legislature. Provision of health care, on the other hand, affords massive opportunities for profit, and those standing to gain, notably the medical and insurance establishments, have a great deal of clout.

In view of these obvious dangers, it is particularly urgent to impose clear limits on state jurisdiction and hold in readiness antidotes for inevitable abuses in the case of welfare legislation. The prudential question is whether such limits and antidotes can be effective. In endorsing the welfare state—reluctantly, as a necessity in an overcrowded and hypercomplex world, with the proviso that we should be constantly at work to make it better and eventually replace it with something better—I am assuming that there will be a way to ensure that its agents will display a modicum of restraint. I am assuming that it is possible to find leaders who will develop sensible schedules of priorities and make intelligent judgments about the relative importance of goods such as health care and transportation compared to others such as education, affordable housing, and environmental protection. I am assuming that there can be leaders abetted by technical experts who will choose effective means to desirable ends—for example, not perpetuate an insane system of national security based on nuclear terror but seek peace through international order and cooperation, and not support a health system that commits an inordinate portion of the public wealth to medical care and still does not extend excellent care to many of its citizens.

The assumption that it is possible to cultivate rationality and public interest in the leadership of modern mass societies is chancy; but there seems to be no alternative to proceeding on that assumption. Obvious limitations in the wisdom and generosity of actual leaders make it mandatory that we not design a utopian system for managing our affairs, but rather exert every effort to improve the system we have, to choose the most reasonable leaders available, and to reason with them through whatever forums are available and hold them to workable standards of performance.

Having affirmed the importance of the welfare state and welfare legislation, I should ask readers to remind themselves constantly that it is much more desirable for individuals to tend to their own welfare. Also it is much more desirable in the case of such parentalism as is necessary that it be administered by people who know them personally and are tied to them by blood, affection, or special obligations than by public functionaries. Intimates are in a better position to know the individual's true needs, and they are less likely than strangers to use parentalism to mask exploitation and domination.

These considerations mean that the welfare state is the instrument of last resort. Welfare legislation should be enacted only when self-care and personal parentalism fail. To minimize the need for its own impersonal efforts, the state should foster institutions such as the family, school, professions, and economic organizations of such a character as to equip individuals for self-care and encourage care of individuals by intimates.

Legal Moralism

Perhaps the most universally condemned form of welfare legislation is that which attempts to improve the moral character of the citizenry. Thus Mill roundly condemns our predilection for imposing our own morality on others, requiring people to do things "because in the opinion of others, to do so would be wise, or even right." The pairing of moralism with parentalism is decried in early papers on parentalism of Ronald Dworkin, H.L.A. Hart, and C. L. Ten. Their common foe is Patrick Devlin and his advocacy of moralistic legislation.[12]

It is perhaps the way Hart conceives moralism that led others to assume that it and parentalism are mutually exclusive. For Hart, moralistic laws attempt to enforce conventional morality for its own sake independent of whether the prohibited behavior harms others or the agent herself. They produce "mere conforming behavior in abstraction from both motive and consequences." On the other hand, parentalistic laws protect individuals against themselves. This leads Hart to ask, "Is the fact that certain conduct is by common standards immoral sufficient to justify making that conduct punishable by law? Is it morally permissible to enforce morality as such? Ought immorality as such be a crime?"[13] Put in these terms, there should be little dispute about moralism. No reasonable person favors conformity for its own sake.

However, moralism need not be defined in this narrow way. Surely few legislators try to enforce conventional morality *merely* because it is conventional. They assume, consciously or unconsciously, correctly or incorrectly, that conventions have a point and that it is important to live by them, not only for the sake of our neighbors but also for the quality of our own lives. Moreover, the morality that legislators seek to impose is their own as they bring their conscience to bear on the issues, or it is the morality of an interested and vocal minority. They implement their own ideas of right and wrong, or they accede to the clamor of religious groups in respect to abortion, prayer in the schools, homosexuality, and tax benefits for sectarian institutions. The aim in these cases is not conformism to the community's ways, but a reform of them.

Are any instances of legal moralism parentalistic? It is not the content of legislation, but the intent that decides the issue. That is, what makes the difference is not the behavior that is proscribed or prescribed, but the reason it is proscribed or prescribed. A legislature certainly might pass laws against pornography, homosexuality, fornication, miscegenation, nudity, indecent dress, work on the Sabbath, or gambling to protect nonpractitioners, but it might also pass the laws totally or partially to benefit the practitioners. Thus, if the legislature passes a law prohibiting gambling because it thinks that gambling hurts the gambler's family and community, the law is protectionist. If it thinks that gambling is simply wrong, it is moralistic. If it thinks that gambling is wrong and the gambler is hurt by doing wrong, the legislation is both moralistic and parentalistic. The legislature may believe in an Aristotelian way that moral behavior is essential to happiness and that the function of the state is to promote such behavior for the welfare of its citizen themselves.

Note the grounds for legal moralism in the parental analogy. Parents typically hold their children to moral standards in the interest of their development, either because they think that their lives will be more satisfying if they live morally or they will get along better with other people. The aim is not to prevent children from becoming a threat to others. In like manner, the reinforcement of moral behavior among adults can contribute to the quality of their lives. The notion that moralistic legislation is necessarily nonparentalistic seems to be motivated by a narrow concept of welfare. In a broader and more adequate sense, welfare includes an active moral life, not just such passively enjoyed things as health, property, friends, and security.

Moral philosophers from Plato to Dewey emphasize the importance of virtuous habits for the good life and the role of social institutions in inculcating and sustaining such habits. Even Mill provides grounds for justifying some forms of moralism. He points out that the institution of morality would have little use in an ideal society, where there would be no conflicts of interest, but it is indispensable in actual societies. We should therefore recognize the importance of acting by moral principles and appreciate the nobility of those who do so.[14] Moreover, we should recognize that the satisfactions of responsible moral behavior belong among the more obvious "higher" pleasures: "no intelligent human being would consent to be a fool, no instructed person would be an ignoramus, no *person of feeling and conscience* would be selfish and base, even though they should be persuaded that the fool, the dunce, or the rascal is better satisfied with his lot than they are with theirs" (emphasis added).[15]

If a person cares for another, he will want her to enjoy the higher pleasures and he will be concerned about her moral development. However, the issue is just what measures are necessary. In particular, is there a place for laws and other forms of state action? Are there any moralistic functions that the state alone can discharge? Hart and Dworkin criticize two defenses of legal moralism. Devlin's "disintegration thesis" is that society is held together by a seamless web of moral beliefs and immoral acts weaken the web even when they do not injure any individual. James Fitzjames Stephen's "conservative thesis" is that the majority has the right to prevent changes in its moral environment by forcing everyone to act according to its lights. Hart and Dworkin agree that the disintegration thesis is factually ungrounded (society is not likely to collapse because of "immoral" acts that have no victims) and the conservative thesis is normatively ungrounded (the majority, not to mention a minority, has no right to impose its concept of morality on the individual). These justifications of moralism and Hart's and Dworkin's rebuttals are predicated on a conception of moralism as essentially nonparentalistic. Neither addresses the issues raised here.

The position I want to advance is that the moral life of citizens is a legitimate concern of the state. Indeed, it should be a central concern since its raison d'être is the good life for its members and moral action is essential to the good life. Moral action depends on traits of character that spring from natural sentiments such as sympathy and empathy and socially induced habits of behavior implementing what reason decrees to be necessary to make solicitude effective. Among the latter is the habit of deliberating objectively on the basis of available evidence. Moral education involves, therefore, both habituation, prominent in the first years of life, and dialectic or critical reflection as the person matures.

In view of the nature of the moral life, parentalistic moralism, whether practiced on the individual level by parent or teacher or on the state level by legislator and bureaucrat, should rarely take the form of enforcement of specific rules of behavior in the way Devlin proposes and his critics so vigorously condemn. In particular, the remoteness of agents of the state and their inability to take into consideration individual differences mean that their efforts should be indirect. The primary strategy is to create a hospitable environment for institutions whose primary functions include education and whose members are in intimate contact with one another. These include not only the school but also home, church, and local community. Moreover, the state should accept and protect moral pluralism since independent thinking about problematic moral issues is bound to produce wide differences of opinion and depends on differences for its vigor.

Obviously, this implies that agents of the state should be more solicitous than anyone else in the community for freedom of thought, expression, and conscience. It also implies that parents, church worthies, and educators should promote the vigorous discussion of moral issues and the responsibility of personal judgment among those under their care, rather than indoctrinating them in sectarian values or the predominant views of the community.

Moral training is a risky enterprise which should approached with care, but it is essential for the individual's welfare as a social and hence human being. The state stands (in a very limited way) *in loco parentis* toward its members due to the circumstances under which people are forced to live in modern society. The state, therefore, should act like an enlightened parent, aware of its limitations, utilizing restricted and indirect measures, and making every attempt to enlarge the autonomy of its subjects in the conduct of their own lives.

13

Feinberg's Antiparentalism

Joel Feinberg's treatment of legal parentalism is an important contribution to the literature. Having discussed the general issues in the last chapter, it is now appropriate to respond to Feinberg's position, whose implications differ from those of my position.

The Program

Feinberg's discussion is part of a comprehensive study of the moral limits of criminal law. It is obvious that criminal parentalism is unjustified. Not only are the costs of criminalizing self-harmful actions excessive and benefits for the offender dubious, it seems inappropriate to stigmatize him as a criminal. However, the conceptual basis for this judgment is not so obvious, and generalization from it to condemn other forms of parentalism may be unwarranted.

Feinberg announces that his purpose is to develop a liberal position regarding the criminal law.[1] The latter is a paradigm case of coercion and curtailment of liberty. Since liberty is a central good,[2] there is a moral presumption against all liberty-limiting measures. Feinberg distinguishes ten principles that are used to justify restrictions of liberty but they are variants of four main types—Harm, Offense, Paternalist, and Moralist. He accepts two of these as valid, Harm and Offense. His liberalism is less extreme than the libertarians', who acknowledge only the Harm Principle; but with them he takes exception to the Paternalist and Moralist Principles.[3]

Though Feinberg does not claim to provide ultimate moral principles on which to ground the principles of legislation, his intuitions reveal his sympathies, which seem quite similar to VanDeVeer's. Thus, he observes that his argument will be persuasive only to certain persons: "Insofar as readers recognize in themselves the tendency to protest some actual or hypothetical interference in their affairs with such language as 'That's *my* business, not yours,' or 'That's no concern of anyone else,' and insofar as this language is accompanied by genuine feelings of indignation and the sense of usurped prerogatives, to that extent the reader embraces some notion, however vague, of personal autonomy" (HS p.98).[4] The course of his analysis confirms that he has in mind respect for a natural or human right to autonomy in self-affecting matters as a key to the moral limits of legislation. He appears to treat the right as absolute in the legal context. Legal parentalism is thus a violation per se of a basic right.

Of the four positions that Feinberg formulates respecting the relation between the individual's right to self-determination and his personal good, we will consider two, the one he himself adopts (the "soft paternalistic strategy," or SPS) and the one that most resembles mine (the "balancing strategy," or BAS) (HS p. 25–26). He observes that there are a number of conceptions of personal good, including self-fulfillment, pleasure, happiness, and satisfaction. While he does not rule out the others, he defines the two positions of interest in terms of self-fulfillment.

With regard to SPS and its "autonomy respecting rationale," Feinberg observes that personal good and self-determination usually coincide, but

> in those rare cases when they do not, a person's right to self-determination, being so-vereign, takes precedence even over his own good. Interference in these cases is justified only when necessary to determine whether his choice is voluntary, hence truly his, or to protect him from choices that are not truly his; but interference with his informed and genuine choices is not justified to protect him from unwisely incurred or risked harms. He has a sovereign right to choose in a manner we think, plausibly enough, to be foolish, provided only that the choices are truly voluntary. (HS p. 61)

The balancing strategy thinks of autonomy as neither derivative from nor more basic than the possessor's own good, but rather coordinate with it. In the rare cases in which personal good and self-determination do not coincide, "we must balance the person's right against his good and weigh them intuitively" (HS p. 61).

Feinberg accepts the distinction between the individual's objective good and what he desires or prefers. Thus he recognizes that self-fulfillment and autonomy are objective goods, whether or not the individual knows it. My position differs from Feinberg's in that I regard both as components of the individual's personal good. I adopt the balancing strategy because I believe that there are occasions when one must weigh increments of autonomy against self-development and other basic goods and autonomy does not always outweigh them. Hence, under my conception the choice is never between autonomy and personal good but between autonomy and other ingredients of personal good.

Hard Antiparentalism

Most of what Feinberg has to say about "the good of the individual" comes in a discussion of the Harm Principle. He believes that the principle legitimates legislation to protect persons from harms wrongly inflicted by others. The Paternalist Principle, if it were valid, would legitimate legislation to protect people from harm which they inflict on themselves ("single-party cases") or which others inflict with their consent ("two-party cases"). He does not view such harms as wrongly inflicted and hence does not subsume them under the Harm Principle.

To elucidate these concepts, Feinberg introduces a concatenation of definitions (HO pp. 31–36). A person's *interests* are the things in which he has a stake. "These interests, or perhaps more accurately those things these interests are *in*, are distinguishable components of a person's well-being: he flourishes or languishes as they flourish or languish. What promotes them is to his advantage or *in his interest*; what thwarts them is to his detriment or *against his interest*." To *harm* the person is to thwart, set back, or defeat one of his interests or his total self-interest (that is, "the harmonious advancement of all of [his] interests in the plural"). To *wrong* him is to violate one of his rights by unjustifiable and inexcusable conduct. Because of features of rights which we do not need to explore, it is possible to violate a right without harming the person; but "in all but certain very special cases such conduct will also invade the other's interest and thus be harmful to him." Hence, almost all wrongs harm. Many harms (set-backs to interests) on the other hand are not wrongs, notably including those to which the victim gives valid consent.

Two sets of interests are basic. The first set is "minimal and nonultimate goods," which Feinberg labels "welfare interests." They consist

> in the necessary means to [the individual's] more ultimate goals, whatever the latter may be, or later come to be. In this category are the interests in the continuance for a foreseeable interval of one's life, and the interests in one's own physical health and vigor, the integrity and normal functioning of one's body, the absence of absorbing pain and suffering or grotesque disfigurement, minimal intellectual acuity, emotional stability, the absence of groundless anxieties and resentments, the capacity to engage normally in social intercourse and to enjoy and maintain friendships, at least minimal income and financial security, a tolerable social and physical environment, and a certain amount of freedom from interference and coercion. (HO p. 37)

Feinberg remarks, "In one way . . . they are the very most important interests a person has, and cry out for protection, for without their fulfillment, a person is lost." In another way they are trivial because they are only necessary, not sufficient for a good life. They must be supplemented by "ulterior interests," the person's more ultimate aims such as "producing good novels or works of art, solving a crucial scientific problem, achieving high political office, successfully raising a family, achieving leisure for handicraft or sport, building a dream house, advancing a social cause, ameliorating human suffering, achieving spiritual grace" (HO p. 37).

It makes a fundamental difference to the theory of parentalism whether one acknowledges the distinction between what is objectively good and what the person desires. Feinberg does distinguish goods from wants, but in the critical cases he thinks that they are intimately tied together. Welfare interests are generalized means to the advancement of ulterior interests and hence are good whether or not the individual knows it and therefore whether or not he desires them. In the case of his ulterior interests, however, "wants have an essential role to play, for it is difficult at best to explain how a person could have a direct stake in certain developments without recourse to his wants and goal. . . . I seem to have a stake in them because I desire their fulfillment, not the other way round" (HO p. 42). Not all wants for ulterior goods cause the individual to invest a stake in them. Rather, only "a relatively deep-rooted and stable want whose fulfillment . . . can be both reasonably hoped for and (usually) influenced by one's own efforts" creates an interest (HO p. 45). The net consequence of this line of analysis is that to harm a person means to thwart his welfare interests or necessary means for advancing them. This is not the same as to inflict evil, since while frustration of transient desires and the pain and distress that ensue are bad, they generally do not affect his interests. Though this is not a point that Feinberg emphasizes, they also do not necessarily interfere with his pursuit of happiness: a person's success achieving his goals may not bring him contentment or satisfaction since they may be based on an imperfect understanding of life or himself. Likewise, the frustration of his misguided aims may prevent disappointment and dissatisfaction.

Feinberg invokes absolute autonomy rights to argue that it is not just inexpedient for the state to utilize criminal sanctions to protect individuals from themselves, but "morally untenable." He recognizes that the moralist following the BAS strategy can appreciate the value of self-determination and even acknowledge a basic right to it, but she must maintain that autonomy is not always more important than other goods and autonomy rights are defeasible, else "balancing" would not be necessary. Against this view Feinberg poises his hard antiparentalist strategy. Like BAS, SPS addresses the problem of "reconciling our general repugnance for paternalism with the seeming reasonableness of some apparently paternalistic regulations." Its strategy is to show that, appearances to the contrary notwithstanding, parentalistic regulations are not reasonable and reasonable regulations are not really parentalistic:

> One way of accounting for the reasonableness of apparently parentalistic restrictions is to apply what we have called 'the soft paternalistic strategy' to show that there is a rationale for protective interference that gives decisive significance, after all, to respect for *de jure* autonomy. Such an argument would show that the reasonableness of the restriction consists in the protection it provides the actor from dangerous choices that are not truly his own. (HS pp. 98–99)

In saying that SPS gives *decisive* significance to respect for autonomy, Feinberg seems to be saying that autonomy rights are absolute. Thus he asserts that autonomy is "a moral trump card, not to be merely balanced with considerations of harm diminution in cases of conflict, but always and necessarily taking moral precedence over those considerations" (HS p. 26).[5]

The Model of Sovereignty

It is significant that to explicate the moral right to autonomy Feinberg borrows two basic concepts, competence and sovereignty, from law and politics. This is a pattern we have seen in other authors who transport concepts appropriate to public parentalism to deal with private.

In the law, competence is "an all or nothing concept." One is either competent (to stand trial, enter a contract, and so on) or not. Since the capabilities that make one competent in the ordinary sense vary in degree, the law and (according to Feinberg) rational morality must adopt a threshold criterion. Everyone above a very low threshold is "competent." While humans start life below the threshold, most surpass it in a few years and few revert below it (HS pp. 28–29).

The legal model does lead Feinberg to introduce a note of relativism not prominent in VanDeVeer's discussion. Impairments in the abilities needed for competence differ in degree and kind. The law recognizes that a person may be incompetent for certain tasks, even such a large number as to require a guardian, and yet be competent for others. Hence, while denying incompetents certain legal powers (for example, to enter contracts), it allows them others (for example, to make wills). Feinberg imports this notion into the moral sphere. Persons may lack some moral autonomy rights because of particular forms of incompetence while retaining others because of forms of competence. Nevertheless, Feinberg considers the individual either competent or incompetent in each respect, not just competent to some degree.

Feinberg also utilizes a political model to develop his concept of individual autonomy. Under international law states have the sovereign right of self-determination within their territorial limits. Sovereignty is one and undivided, basic and underivative, and it is the ultimate source of authority for the state's actions. Like competence "sovereignty is an all or nothing concept: one is entitled to absolute control of whatever is within one's domain however trivial it may be. . . . Only a nation's own sovereignty (in the guise, say, of 'self-defense') may ever be placed in the scales and weighed against another nation's acknowledged sovereignty, for sovereignty decisively outweighs every other kind of reason for intervention" (HS p. 55). Feinberg bases his opposition to legal parentalism on the "sovereignty" of the individual over his "territory" of personal affairs. While it is difficult to draw territorial boundaries for an individual's personal domain, Feinberg suggests that they include his body, privacy, property, and vital life decisions.

The political model accounts for Feinberg's use of the label *sovereignty* for what he regards the absolute *de jure* autonomy of the individual in self-regarding actions. In a useful discussion, he distinguishes four senses of autonomy: capacity, condition, character ideal, and "sovereign authority to govern oneself." His threshold concept of competence is crucial since he believes that the sovereignty of the competent person prohibits encroachment on his personal domain even though he may be functioning at the threshold and making many self-harmful choices.

> The person whose relevant capacities are just above the bare threshold of competence that qualifies him for *de jure* self-government may rightfully rule himself, but in fact he may rule himself badly, unwisely, only partially. He may in fact have relatively little personal autonomy in the sense of *de facto* condition, but like a badly governed nation, he may retain his sovereign independence nevertheless. A genuinely incompetent being below the threshold is incapable of making even foolish, unwise, reckless, or perverse choices. Jellyfish, magnolia trees, rocks, newborn infants, lunatics, and irrevocably comatose former 'persons' if granted the right to make their own decisions, would be incapable of making even 'stupid' choices. Being stupid, no less than being wise, is the sole prerogative of the threshold-competent. (HS p. 30)

People's autonomy, in the sense of both power and its exercise, vary in form and degree in different people and in the same person at different times. The immense number of forms is suggested by Feinberg's list of traits that enter into ideal autonomy: self-possession, self-identity, self-selection, self-creation, self-legislation, moral authenticity, moral independence, integrity, self-control, self-reliance, initiative, and responsibility for self (HS pp. 44–47). Each of these involves a great variety of capacities and abilities, each of which with many forms, which generates a vast number of combinations and permutations and defines many sorts of autonomy.

Surely anyone who achieves high levels of actual autonomy enjoys a quality of personhood and ability to perform successful actions that are immensely valuable. Surely anyone who cares for another wants to help him approach the ideal as closely as possible and cherishes his actual qualities and respects his actual choices to the extent that they approximate the ideal. What is not obvious is that comparable respect should be afforded lower qualities and degrees of autonomy. Yet Feinberg attributes to every competent person an absolute right to exercise autonomy to whatever degree he can and will. This is reflected in his postulation of actual consent as a necessary condition for intervention in the life of a competent person and hypothetical consent for intervention in the life of an incompetent one.

The Significance of Consent

Feinberg is most interested in consent given by a subject to harmful acts of some third party which the parentalist tries to curtail by legislation. His question is whether such consent absolves the third party of wrong-doing and hence removes the legislation from the domain of the Harm Principle and puts it under the Paternalist Principle. Here we will be concerned with a different question, whether a subject's consent to the intervention is necessary or sufficient to justify it.

Like VanDeVeer, Feinberg distinguishes between valid and invalid consent of competent persons. He remarks, "consent may fail of its normal effect because it is not valid consent, and *invalid consent* is no better than *no consent* at all" (HS p. 188). The "normal effect" of valid consent is to make intervention in a person's self-affecting affairs morally permissible by canceling the agent's standing obligation of noninterference, this prior to consideration of whether the interference is beneficial and therefore warranted. Valid consent is thus necessary, but not sufficient, to warrant intervention.

Feinberg's primary problem is to define boundaries between valid and invalid consent in the face of the recognition of the many forms and degrees of ability and autonomy among competent people. For example, he draws a line between strong and weak consent. One of the strong forms is where a subject requests intervention and one of the weak forms is where he accedes to what the intervener suggests. Such distinctions generate a typology of consent in which each sort bears distinctive values as an autonomous act.

The varying value of different sorts of consent is important for the balancing strategy, but apparently not for Feinberg's hard antiparentalist strategy. At least he remarks, "The common denominator [in strong and weak consent] is a genuine agreement, a deliberate choice, whoever the initiator, whatever the motive, wherever the expected major gain" (HS p. 99). The differences among forms of agreement involving deliberate choice pale in importance in comparison to their main effect, converting the intervener into the subject's agent and authorizing her actions in his sphere of sovereignty as if they were his own.

Feinberg maintains that valid consent entails a voluntary choice. In exploring its ingredients, he deals first with current actual consent. To have its effect, the consent must be expressed; a person's mental state unknown to the intervener could hardly relieve her of the obligation of noninterference in his life: " 'consent' in the sense of mere psychological willingness or passive acquiescence is not *authorization*; it does not transfer responsibility for A's act jointly to B. If the act in question is one which crosses the boundaries of B's autonomy then it requires B's permission if it is to avoid wronging B and thus falling within the range of the harm to others principle" (HS p. 173). What is necessary for authorization is a "linguistic or symbolic performance that brings into existence new moral or legal relations." This performance can take for the form of silence (tacit consent) if the opportunity is available for dissent.

According to Feinberg, valid consent is free and informed; consent given under certain forms of coercion and on the basis of certain forms of defective belief is invalid.[6] No choice is fully informed or completely unconstrained, so consent must only be "sufficiently voluntary" to be valid. Moreover, voluntariness does not require rationality in the sense of ideal reasonableness or proportionate to the subject's degree of reasonableness. Feinberg thus would protect foolish choices as long as they are not coerced or deceived.

If we can take Feinberg's discussion of the role of consent in the legal context as definitive of his concept of its role in the moral context, the validity of the subject's consent is an all-or-nothing matter; it either absolves the intervener of the obligation of noninterference or it does not. Yet the amount of information and freedom from coercion—and the subject's degree of reasonableness insofar as it affects his ability to pursue his interests—are matters of degree. Hence, a line must be drawn—by the legislator for liberty-limiting laws, by the moral agent for personal acts of intervention—to determine when the subject's consent is voluntary enough to allow intervention. In a significant concession to common sense, Feinberg asserts that the line will differ according to the kind of intervention. It is defined by a "sliding marker" on the scale from perfect voluntariness to perfect involuntariness (HS p. 118). For each category of intervention, the subject's autonomy rights require the parentalist to desist from intervention unless the subject either falls below the marker or consents.

Critics complain that Feinberg's criterion of "substantially nonvoluntary" is too vague to permit a precise determination of the rights involved in concrete situations. In my view this is no objection. Any alternative procedure requires judgments as to the amount and quality of the subject's autonomy which will be affected by an intervention. Feinberg's criterion is unacceptable only if one demands a sharp natural dividing line between competence and incompetence and uses the line to determine which subjects have natural rights of nonintervention in their affairs and which lack such rights. Abandon this demand, and Feinberg's position at this juncture is no less reasonable than its competitors.

However, the way that Feinberg suggests for determining where the sliding marker is located does throw into question the foundation of the scheme in respect to autonomy. Feinberg would dispute this. He claims that his "autonomy respecting liberalism" affirms "the importance of our distinction between the *voluntariness* of consent, itself a matter of degree measured on various sliding scales from total involuntariness to the ideal 'full voluntariness', and the *validity* of consent when it is 'voluntary enough' for a given moral or legal purpose" (HS p. 309). One would expect the waiver of a moral right by the subject with a view to serving his own interests to be sufficient to provide the intervener a moral or legal purpose. However, Feinberg does not appeal to respect for the subject's rights or a natural threshold for his competence relative to particular activities to determine where the sliding marker stops. Rather, he suggests that the legislature, if not the individual agent, will consider consequences:

> Validity and invalidity, like guilt and innocence, liability or no liability, are all-or-nothing concepts. . . . How much voluntariness is required for a valid (legally effective) act of consent is at least partly a matter of policy, to be decided by reference to a rule itself justified by the usual legislative reasons of utility and social justice. These rules will specify standards of voluntariness whose stringency varies with the nature of the context (implied warranties in automobile purchases, voluntary research in prisons, plea bargaining before trials) and the particular legal outcome at issue (contractual obligation, criminal liability, assumption of personal risk). (HS p. 261)

Feinberg suggests that the relevant variables are risk to the subject, the irrevocability of the harm to which he is exposing himself, and special circumstances such as the restrictiveness of his environment.

As I have observed, it is not certain that Feinberg is proposing the same grounds for moral decisions as for legislation. If he is, he would seem to be conceding here that the conception of personal sovereignty is inadequate to determine when intervention is permissible. The parentalist might well be justified in setting the sliding marker for voluntary consent high enough to allow her to prevent serious and irrevocable harm to the subject due to what are defined as his "involuntary" choices, whatever his current wishes or desires, consent or dissent, toward the proposed intervention. If this is the implication, Feinberg's position is in danger of collapsing into the one I have adopted. Where the sliding marker stops is determined by questions of utility for the beneficiary, not by his autonomy as a moral trump card.

In the Absence of Consent

SPS (the soft parentalist, hard antiparentalist strategy) attempts to show that reasonable interventions in a person's life are not parentalistic *either* because he has consented to the intervention, hence, it does not contravene any voluntary choices that he does make, *or* because he is incompetent, hence, he has no choices to contravene. Feinberg recognizes that competent subjects have not given current and expressed consent in many intuitively justified cases of intervention. He attempts to accommodate these cases by substitutes for current consent that have the same legal and moral effect, distinguishing them from "counterfeits" which do not. His analysis (HS pp. 118–124) closely parallels VanDeVeer's, and my criticisms are largely the same, so I will only summarize his and my conclusions.

Feinberg notes that six kinds of surrogate consent have been suggested to permit invasion of autonomy to protect a person's on-balance interests when there is no opportunity to get his permission. He himself considers prior and tacit consent to be equivalent to actual. He considers dispositional consent to have the same moral effect as actual when the intervener has sufficient evidence of its existence and the harm to be prevented is substantial. On the other hand, he dismisses the subject's psychological states such as desires and preferences and his subsequent approval and hypothetical rational consent as not adequate to permit intervention. The important thing to note in the various cases is that for Feinberg it is the subject's interests, in the sense of the ulterior goods in which he has chosen to invest a stake, that are decisive in determining what he has or would consent to and hence what is morally permissible in his behalf. Feinberg does not consider the subject's objective good in the sense of what will in fact bring him lasting satisfaction to be decisive, as is the case in my approach.

Justified interventions may not be parentalist not only because the (competent) subject gives his (valid) consent to them, but because the subject is incompetent and cannot consent or dissent in a meaningful sense. In dealing with incompetence, Feinberg has in mind extreme incapacity. He maintains that desires due to incapacity do not produce real choices or express the person's true self. Being incapable of choice, the incompetent person is not capable of voluntarily dissenting to interventions in his life any more than consenting, so interventions cannot be said to be against his will or to violate his right to autonomy. Choices have to be made for him, and a guardian or custodian can sanction interventions by surrogate consent. The proxy's options are to decide in terms of either the true interests of the subject or the consent he would have given if he had been competent. According to Feinberg, respect for the subject's autonomy requires the proxy to do the latter if possible. If the subject had once been competent and the proxy has adequate evidence of what his desires were, she should decide in terms of those desires. Only if he has never been competent or there is insufficient evidence of what he would want in the given case should the proxy decide in terms of his interests. This position is very close to VanDeVeer's, the objections to which I have spelled out in Chapter 11.

14

Professional Parentalism

John Swenson, an aging man dressed in neat overalls, appears at the office of James Saunders, M.D., urologist, at 8:45 A.M. The waiting room is already crowded. Swenson stands before the receptionist's window. A matronly woman busies herself with clerical work. She finally looks up.

"Yes?"

"I have a nine o'clock appointment with Doctor Saunders. I've been having a lot of trouble with . . ."

"Yes, please sign in and take a seat."

Swenson occupies himself with desultory conversation with other patients and with reading old copies of magazines. About 10:15 he returns to the window.

"When do you think the doctor can see me? I had to take off work and I'm due back . . . and I have this pain . . ."

"The doctor is very busy this morning. He'll see you just as soon as he can."

At 11:25 a young woman in a nurse's uniform enters and calls, "John?"

"Here."

"This way, please." She ushers him into an examining room. "Please strip to your shorts, John, and put on this gown. The doctor will be with you in a minute. We need a urine sample. Put a little in this jar—up to here—and the rest in this one."

About 20 minutes later, Dr. Saunders, wearing a white coat, briskly enters the room. He examines Swenson quickly and scrawls out an illegible prescription. "Here, take this, get plenty of rest, and come back to see me next week." He cuts short Swenson's inquiries. "Don't worry. This'll take care of it."

Social Roots of Professional Power

An offensive form of parentalism tinged with self-interest sometimes creeps into professional deportment. We will complete our analysis with an examination of professional parentalism as representative of socially sanctioned role behavior, the second form of public parentalism mentioned in Chapter 12.[1]

Many of a person's decisions are made by virtue of the roles he plays in groups such as family, friendship circle, church, and community. His occupational role is one of the most important in his life. Among modern occupations the professions have come to the fore in several ways. Professionals have a major effect on the welfare of others in their dealings with colleagues, clients, and the customers, competitors, and adversaries of clients. The professional ethic is a model for the work ethic in general, and the way professions are organized is emulated by other occupations in what is called the "professional project."[2]

The professions are part of the environment to which both professional and client must adjust, much like the weather and terrain. People who become doctors, lawyers, engineers, or professors are presented fixed schedules of responsibilities. People who patronize doctors, lawyers, engineers, and professors must accept their ways, since practitioners enjoy a monopoly over services and almost all provide them in the same manner.

This, of course, needs qualification. People face significant choices relating to the professions. They decide whether to enter a profession. Once in, they decide how to fulfill its role expectations. When they reach a position of influence, they decide whether to try to influence its ways or let them be. Likewise, clients choose whom to consult and whether to follow the professional's instructions. Unless they have been involuntarily committed to care, they can always break off the relationship.

The first step in developing guidelines for such choices—here guidelines in respect to parentalism—is to examine the social structures that define them. It is the structure of professions that both empowers and tempts professionals to act more parentalistically than other people. If there are difficulties, they require structural solutions.

The state has important caring responsibilities. Among the measures it uses is the establishment of monopolies of expertise. It gives control over the production of knowledge, who is admitted to the ranks of the profession, and how they practice its art to professional associations and schools.

The niche in society that professions occupy enjoys the vague generic assent of the public, or more accurately its passive indulgence. Most people assume that the organization of the professions is the way things are—the way they must and should be. No alternatives are presented the public, nor is it encouraged to imagine any. Nor has the professional configuration been selected by anyone else on the basis of a careful evaluation of alternatives. It has been assembled piecemeal by occupational elites. Leaders of professionalizing occupations have mobilized their memberships, organized pressure groups, and promoted their cause by ideological appeals and alliances with patrons in the existing power structure of society.

This is not a criticism. Most institutions just grow as groups pursue particular aims and utilize available ideological, political, and organizational resources. Professions are products of historical circumstances and targets of opportunity, not carefully conceived plots. The point here is that their history shows they have evolved without the informed consent of those they claim to serve. To the extent that they benefit the individuals whose freedom of choice they curtail—patients, customers, clients, and employers—rather than those to whom they give power—the professions and professionals—the result is institutional parentalism.

For illustration, let us look at the paradigm profession, medicine. The licensing of physicians and the requirement that drugs be available only by their prescription are archetypical parentalistic measures. Legislation gives physicians control of the approximately 5,000 medicinal drugs now available. This strictly limits the ability of individuals to medicate themselves or obtain medication from unlicensed practitioners, not only potentially many alternative healers such as acupuncturists, homeopaths, and naturopaths, but groups that subscribe to medical orthodoxy such as nurses, chiropractors, and dieticians. Access to medication is a powerful incentive to patronize physicians for the whole range of medical services.

Prescription and licensing laws are typical of legislation that enables self-selecting, self-perpetuating, and self-regulating occupational groups to maintain control over vitally needed services. Some laws explicitly mandate the control by prohibiting practice by anyone outside the group; others permit or support control. In the case of medicine, physicians are given custody of the body of knowledge on which medical treatment is based, educational curricula and qualifying tests by which individuals become certified to practice, access to facilities such as hospitals and clinics, and such discipline as there is over practice. As a result of this corporate autonomy, physicians collectively command the title "medical profession" and individually enjoy autonomy in the "health care team." Nurses, therapists, laboratory technicians, hospital administrators, and others are their aides.

Physicians have most nearly achieved the institutional form specified by the sociological ideal-typical theoretical model of profession. This is hardly surprising since sociologists derive the model from medicine. More important, it is the model that other occupations have mimicked in organizing themselves and winning a near monopoly for their services. Some examples:

1. To practice law one must be admitted to the bar, which is almost impossible without training in a law school accredited by the bar association. In practice, participation in the association is expedient to gain referrals of clients. Participating or not, the attorney must observe disciplinary rules of the American Bar Association in its *Model Rules of Professional Conduct*, which are incorporated in laws of almost all of the states.
2. By law, certain kinds of plans and designs must be "signed off" or "sealed" by a professional engineer. PE's are licensed by state boards staffed by PE's. They pass tests constructed by a professional association. Boards that license engineers also have the power to suspend or revoke the license or publicly reprimand engineers for malpractice. The norms used by many boards are provided by the National Council of Engineering Examiners in its *Model Rules of Conduct*, which comprise the enforceable parts of the National Association of Professional Engineers' *Code of Ethics*.
3. There are less stringent but still significant legal controls on the practice of psychotherapy, counseling and testing, social work, nursing, public school teaching, and business specialties such as accountancy, realty, and

actuarial work. Other occupations enjoy quasi-official recognition as professions without licensure.

Typically, judgments of malpractice are made by the courts on the basis of the profession's standards and the advice of the accused's peers. Disciplinary boards are composed of professionals sponsored by the professional association and apply norms based on the profession's code of ethics. The policing of professionals is in the hands of fellow professionals. It should be observed, however, that discipline is slack. Professional courtesy discourages colleagues from monitoring one another's day-to-day performance. They must work with each other over the long term, they rely on each other for referrals, and they do not have personal connections with one anothers's clients. They are reluctant to expose a colleague's shortcomings since scandal tarnishes the whole profession. They do not so much cover up for one another's mistakes as take precautions not to know about them.

To summarize, society grants the professions a monopoly over services and a great deal of autonomy in providing them. It sets limits for practice by malpractice laws and regulatory agencies, but these controls leave the practitioner a great deal of personal autonomy.

Psychological Bases of Parentalism

Social provisions make professional parentalism possible. The psychological relationship between the professional and the client makes it seductive. It is characterized by need and ignorance on the side of the client. She goes to the professional when something is wrong or lacking in her life: she is ill or emotionally distraught, under legal siege, or needs a structure or tool to do her work. She cannot take care of herself because she lacks knowledge or expertise: she does not know what drug is best; the way out of stress, paranoia, depression, or compulsion; how to draw up a will or make machinery.

The professional is precisely the one who has the knowledge and skill to help her. Professionals in modern societies perform something like the role of the shaman in nonliterate ones.[3] They possess an esoteric lore. They speak a special language and perform mysterious rituals. They obtain results that members of the tribe urgently want by powers that pass their understanding. This role generates what is called the "charism of skill." When a person entrusts a portion of her life to the professional, she wants to believe that the provider knows best. This disposes her to trust him and reinforces psychological dependence.[4] The professional aura is not easily dispelled, and the professional has few incentives to dispel it. His clients want to believe in his infallibility and dedication to their welfare; they are outraged if their faith is misplaced. Incompetence and dereliction are not just harmful, they are a betrayal. If you cannot trust your doctor (lawyer, engineer, professor), whom can you trust? Confronted with the severe consequences of failure, it is no surprise that professionals may resort to mystification to conceal their failures. Concealment is ordinarily an opprobrious act, but it is rationalized in the professional ideology on the ground that it serves the interest of the client. For professionals to do their jobs, the client must seek their services, trust their discretion, and follow their instructions. The professional mystique nurtures this behavior.

In fairness, we should acknowledge that very many professionals resist the temptation to exploit their charisma and either restrict themselves to justified forms of parentalism or shun parentalism so completely as to err at the other extreme. Moreover, the pride of professionals in their expertise is warranted. Pride, however, grows into hubris when authority is unchallenged, and hubris may bring an illusion of infallibility that tolerates no dissent by the client. Or, a professional may simply accept what he is given to believe by his subculture: that he knows best, and clients seldom know anything useful about their conditions. If he should be uneasy about his risks or uncertain of his judgments, the professional may insist on being totally "in charge" and again brook no questions.

We have noted that the history of professions shows that they meet the first requirement of parentalism: they exist without the full consent of those whose welfare is entrusted to them. The history, however, raises a question of whether they meet the second requirement of parentalism: Are they oriented toward the welfare of their clients and the public at large?

The public seems persuaded that the professional is unusually dedicated to its welfare. True, it grouses about high fees, the impersonality of services, and the unintelligibility of jargon. It resents the rapacity, arrogance, and ostentatious consumption of more flamboyant practitioners. Yet, in the end, it respects professionals, calls upon them in times of need, and does not challenge their prerogatives. Their opinions carry authority in social councils. Their position in society is unchallenged.

Moreover, respect for professionals is grounded in personal experience. Most of us have been healed by a physician, utilized noble buildings designed by engineers and architects, and kept out of harm's way with the advice of an attorney. The heroic efforts of intrepid professionals are the stuff of popular legend. However, the professions have not relied on the public's one-on-one experience to ensure their power and privileges. They have waged aggressive campaigns to persuade the public that their services are worth the social cost. Their codes of ethics and professional responsibility are replete with protestations of service. The ideological fantasy is fostered that the professional works to aid clients rather than to receive fees or a salary and that the design of the professions assures service for everyone. Those who can afford it, purchase it on the open market; those who cannot, receive *pro bono* free or cut-rate help. Hence, the professions claim and the public seems to accept that the public good is being well served.

Ideologies are not false per se. Indeed, they must contain an element of truth to be persuasive in this age of public sophistication. It is assuredly the case that many individual professionals are motivated by a strong desire to serve. But it is also the case that many are interested in their own social and material advancement. More to the point, much of the effort of their professional organizations is devoted to improving the occupation's position in society and its ability to serve those who pay the freight—patrons, clients, and employers—rather than the nebulous cause of "public welfare."

How Professional Parentalism Works

I will not attempt to determine the mixture between self-interest, service to clients, and dedication to the general welfare that animates most professional transactions. Rather I will concentrate, as is appropriate for the present study, on those instances when the professional uses his power to act parentalistically.

Whether from hubris, insecurity, complacency, or ideological bias, the professional typically highly values his own autonomy in professional decisions and undervalues that of the client. By training and practice he is geared to act in the client's behalf according to his own best judgment. This may lead him to attribute client reluctance to childish apprehension or lack of trust. This tempts him to keep her in the dark by discreet silence, mystification, or outright deception.

I have suggested that the practitioner is schooled by his culture to think that his encroachments on the client's autonomy are in her interest. His primary duty is to foster her health, safeguard her legal rights, provide a design or product of high quality, teach her what she needs to know, soothe her mind, or adjust her to society. He is not taught that his duty is to preserve or enlarge her autonomy. He is used to justifying his decisions in instrumental terms: to do whatever works to promote the client's assumed need. He encounters obstacles not only in objective conditions but also in the client's attitude, so that attitude must be altered. If necessary, she must be manipulated into accepting what is best for her. The habitual denigration of client autonomy is thus reinforced by a narrow utilitarian ethic that stresses external consequences and hence the harmful effects of client decisions on her welfare and which ignores the intrinsic value of autonomous actions and hence the importance for the client of making life-effecting decisions.

Someone may object that the practitioner may ignore the professional ideology and the client may resist its implications. Many professionals scrupulously confine themselves to advising clients of their options and the probable consequences. Many clients exercise their right to reject advice. Unfortunately, it is also true that many critical professional decisions are not made this way. The professional assumes that he knows the client needs on the basis of objective, standardized, and inadequate signs: the patient needs to be cured, or she would not be in my office, and she needs to be cured of the illness revealed by my technique of diagnosis. The client needs to win this lawsuit or evade this criminal charge or sign this contract because this is what the normal, or stereotypical, client would want. The student should follow this curriculum because it provides what most students need to pursue careers, to function as citizens, or to enjoy rich lives.

Moreover, the professional is prone to magnify the importance of the custodial value of his profession—health, if a physician; legal rights, if an attorney; a safe structure, if an engineer; education, if a professor; "the news," if a journalist; salvation, if a clergyman. The client's autonomy or idiosyncratic values seldom figure in the schedule of objectives, particularly if the custodial value does not occupy the position in her scale which the professional believes it ought. Indeed, the professional often subtly shapes the values of the client so that she will "need," or want, what the professional thinks she ought to have. Tampering with ends is a way of inducing acceptance of means.

Likewise, the professional may shape the ends of the client by the way he presents alternatives and their costs and consequences. Hughes points out that this occurs at the societal as well as individual level. The professions shape the public's conception of its needs by their philosophies of medicine, law, engineering, and so on.[5]

The Justification of Professional Parentalism

Public assistance is necessary when individuals are incapable or unwilling to meet the basic needs of other members of the community. The assistance is parentalistic when it lacks the informed consent of the beneficiaries. The form of parentalism under scrutiny flows from the socially established monopoly over services and right of self-rule of professions and professionals. These arrangements do not enjoy the full consent of those to whom the services are provided. If professional monopoly and autonomy are justified, it is by the benefits that redound to the public.

While our general guidelines provide a justification for some intitutionalized intervention in the lives of individuals, they condemn it when it is concerned with too narrow a range of values and where the context fosters an underestimation of the importance of the beneficiary's autonomy. Such is frequently the case with professional parentalism. A considerable amount of professional parentalism is inescapable, but autonomy-disrespectful professional parentalism is too prevalent.

One of the ways chosen by some moralists to combat professional parentalism has been to postulate a basic human right to autonomy in self-affecting matters.[6] This has led them to condemn professional parentalism categorically. I do not make the concept of rights central to my position, nor do I believe that it is wise to posit an absolute right to autonomy, and I believe that a considerable amount of parentalism is desirable in the professional context. However, I believe that socially defined autonomy rights are essential to maximizing benefits which are likely to accrue from public activities and this applies to professional practices.

The professional/client relationship falls somewhere between the intimacy of the relations between members of a family or close friends and the impersonality of those between government or commercial bureaucrats and the public. In this quasi-public and semi-external relationship, it seems expedient to assign a prominent place to rights on the side of the subordinate party. Some protection of the client's autonomy should be provided by laws of the state and further protection by professional codes of conduct. However, there are limits to what laws and codes can accomplish. It is important to leave a margin of discretion for the knowledgeable caretaker, in this case, the professional. Legal space must be provided to perform caring acts, including those of justified parentalism. It appears that the primary safeguard for client autonomy, then, must rest in the informal mores of the professions and the internalization of these in the consciences of practitioners. The balance between the respect for the client's autonomy and the obligation to provide the custodial values of the profession, regardless of the client's wishes, cannot be reduced to rule or formula. We can, however, derive some guidelines from those that govern parentalism in general.

It is seldom the case that the overall or aggregate autonomy of the individual is compromised when she relinquishes the power of decision in respect to a problem turned over to the professional. The patient who blindly follows her doctor's orders does not thereby relinquish decisions regarding work, family, church, political community, and other important segments of life. Partial or temporary loss of control over her body hardly terminates her status as a moral agent. The same is true of partial and temporary loss of control over other aspects of her life under the ministrations of a lawyer, teacher, minister, counselor, engineer, or other technical expert.

More than ever, people need to be schooled in self-care, both to do as much as they can for themselves and to choose experts wisely. Seen in this context, the limited relinquishment of autonomy in the use of professionals is more than matched by expanded opportunities for autonomy made available to the individual by the growth of professionalism. The proliferation of professions expands her opportunity to become a professional herself and acquire new domains for autonomy to compensate for its diminution as she becomes dependent on professionals. However, an assumption is necessary here: that the opportunity to enter the professions is made available to everyone.

Respect for client autonomy should be made a central provision in the ethical codes of the various professions, and, as a matter of fact, the conspiracy of silence to keep clients in their place is far from total. Many professionals go out of their way to inform clients and involve them in decisions that affect their welfare. Every profession has external critics and internal activists only too anxious to reform its practices. Their efforts should be encouraged.

The public must have the opportunity to educate itself about professions and equip itself to make more informed judgments about the competence and ethics of individual professionals. Education is expanding through the efforts of schools and the media and the prodding of consumer advocates. A professional morality, one of whose central imperatives is to inform clients fully about their condition, prospects, and alternatives, may be emerging. Less evident but equally important is the imperative that clients inform themselves and demand an accounting from those into whose care they entrust themselves. This emphasizes the client's obligation of self-care and the need to equip herself as much as practicable to do for herself what she may now routinely turn over to professionals.

All of this said, we must note that the movement toward greater concern for client autonomy has received little encouragement from professional organizations. Their codes of professional responsibility are weak on the point. These are full of strictures against exploitation of clients and betrayal of employers. They enjoin their members to engage in "fair practices" to take the edge off of competition for employment and assignments. They pay lip service—eloquent or perfunctory—to "service" and the need to "protect the public." But they say almost nothing about client autonomy or the dangers of parentalism.

To the extent that critical ethics as distinguished from moral indoctrination becomes part of the socialization of professionals, discussions such as this may help to inhibit more thoughtless and routine forms of parentalism. Formal professional training unfortunately does not ordinarily provide exposure to the problematics of ethics, and the impact of the reflections of ethicists is limited. Better ways need to be found to communicate guidelines to practitioners during professional socialization and to see that they are observed in the course of professional practice.

The professional usually has more options than either to follow his own judgment without regard to the client's wishes or do exactly what the client wishes. He may be able to convince her rationally that the course he proposes is best. He may at least be able to persuade her to accept a second-best course which will still meet her basic need. In either case, he should weigh the effect on the client's autonomy since he should further her total welfare. He should be particularly careful about taking advantage of his psychological position to browbeat her into submission or deceive or mystify her to manufacture her consent.

This being said, it is still the case that the custodial values of the professions are very important, and the difficulty of the client in providing them for herself or deciding whether they are being provided effectively for her are quite real. It is necessary on occasion for the professional to act without consent or to exploit his position of dominance to bring off his action against her wishes or by manufacturing her consent. This must always be done with caution and regret.

Where parentalism is necessary, encroachments on the client's autonomy should be held to a minimum. Restraint is demanded even at a cost to custodial values. If the professional has reason to think that he will not have the informed consent of the client when the time comes to provide necessary services, he should try to secure the client's prior or generic consent or, failing that, her subsequent approval. Besides the obligation to hold encroachment on autonomy to a minimum and seek informed consent, the professional is obligated to give an account of his actions by submitting them to evaluation by clients and appropriate others.

Respect for the client's autonomy obligates the professional to educate her for self-care in order to reduce the need for future parentalistic interventions. The necessity for specific acts of parentalism is no excuse for perpetuating dependency or allowing parentalism to become chronic or routine. Connected with this is the profession's obligation to educate the public about its work. It should take the lead in equipping the public for self-care and for making critical choices among professionals and critical evaluations of professional services when self-care fails.

Professionals should remember that their acts reinforce professional practices and, given the prestige of their profession, are taken as models by workers in other fields. They should remember that their acts also reinforce their own habits and affect their later acts when they may not be so alert to client rights. Professional acts have ramifications beyond the welfare of the individual client, and the professional should keep the precedent factor in mind.

I have argued that the weight of moral condemnation should be thrown against parentalistic practices to the extent of placing the burden of justification on the shoulders of the would-be parentalist rather than on the abstainer. He must assure himself that the case for parentalism on the particular occasion is strong, rather than automatically opting for the parentalist response. Hubris springing from cognitive prestige and fortified by the professional mind-set may lead him to assume that he knows best. He may routinely assume that he knows better than the client not only the technical means to promote her welfare but also what that welfare comprises. The facts of the situation, however, may ensure just the contrary. The formal character of the relationship means that the professional seldom knows when the values of the individual differ significantly from those of the typical or stereotypical client. If the latter expresses reservations about the professional's actions, he should take this as evidence not that she is defective in rationality, but that her values are atypical—that is, that her real goods and not just her transient and poorly informed wishes differ from those of other clients. The professional should not cavalierly dismiss her wishes as just another case of the lay person's inability to understand technicalities. In the face of the evidence which her wishes provide about her true good, he needs strong counterevidence that he really does know what is good for her before overruling her opinion.

The Model of a Model Professional

Some reservations about the effect of formal rules on the moral life should be appended to the guidelines. Overconcern with "the rules"—casuistry, caviling, quibbling, pettifoggery, legalism, the general importation of the ways and attitudes of a litigious society into personal relationships—freeze the caring heart and maim solicitude. The counsel of wisdom, therefore, is to concentrate on becoming the right kind of person and striving to acquire and act according to moral and intellectual virtues, not to preoccupy oneself with formulas specifying exactly what one ought to do or rationalizing what one wants to do.

I will conclude the discussion with some remarks about the sort of a person a professional should be in order to discharge the social roles that have been assigned to him. I will adapt Michael Bayles's excellent discussion of what he calls ethical models of the professional-client relationship. He derives the models from analogies between the professional-client and other familiar relationships. They are ethical in that they do not describe typical relations, but prescribe desirable ones.

Bayles thinks that ethical norms should be designed for usual rather than unusual situations. "An analysis based on unusual situations is . . . likely to distort normal situations. Professional ethics should be based on the usual sort of contact average clients have with professionals."[7] This allows Bayles to concede that professional parentalism is justified under unusual circumstances (viz., when the client is incompetent) while rejecting the Paternalist Model.

Bayles distinguishes his models according to conceptions of the responsibility and proper authority of the professional to make decisions pertaining to the client's welfare, and hence the models are particularly relevant to our concern for client autonomy. On the basis of the client's relative ignorance and the professional's autonomy as a moral agent, Bayles rejects the Agency Model according to which the professional is a mere functionary who executes decisions of the client. He rejects the Contract and Friendship Models because they assume a parity of authority and interest between the professional and client, the Contract Model representing the relation as instituting limited rights and responsibilities by arm's-length transactions between equals and the Friendship Model representing the relation as a form of intimacy that is lacking in most professional contexts.

Bayles reserves his most extensive criticisms for the Paternalist Model. In it, the professional is charged with the authority and responsibility for making all major decisions for the client. Bayles's conception of parentalism (paternalism) is standard:

> The key element of paternalism derives from the agent, X, acting regardless of the person's, Y's, complete voluntary and informed consent. X's reason is that he or she judges the action to be for Y's well-being regardless of Y's consent to it. Y might be incapable of consent (a young child or psychiatric patient), Y might never have been asked, or Y might have refused to consent to the act.[8]

Bayles makes clear that he has in mind the broadest conception of "acting for the person's well-being" since all sorts of parentalistic acts, promotive as well as protective, may occur in the professional context.

Bayles' reasons for rejecting the Paternalist Model seem valid in the sketchy form in which they are stated,[9] though they are a mixed bag that might not prove to be mutually compatible if they were spelled out. In this respect they exemplify the primary danger of a superficial treatment of parentalism—by condemning the usual cases where it is clearly misguided, we are easily led to reject justified cases.

Bayles's first argument is that reasonable persons would not want others to make judgments for them when they are competent to do so themselves, and, as Bayles takes pains to point out, clients are usually competent to decide whether professional conduct will benefit them when its ramifications are explained properly. At the same time, reasonable persons would allow others to make decisions for them when they lack the capacity to make reasonable judgments. Hence, Bayles seems to be saying, actions for another without her consent when she is not rational are not really parentalistic because she would have relinquished her autonomy if she had been rational. This seems to be a version of the argument from hypothetical or rational consent. If, it fails, because a hypothetical or imaginary agent has no authority to cancel the rights of a real person. However, Bayles's argument may boil down to the innocuous requirement that the agent think as rationally as he can before acting on behalf of another.

The second argument against the Paternalist Model is that professionals are not particularly trained to make value choices and even if they were "they might not know a client's value scheme sufficiently to determine what is best for him or her when everything is considered." Bayles does not explain whether he means by "value scheme" the client's preferences or what is objectively good for her. If he knows what is objectively good for the client and the stakes are high enough, he can well be justified in acting against her preferences—that is, parentalistically. However, this is a big "if," and a conscientious professional would need strong evidence that he does know better than the client.

The third argument against the Paternalist Model rests on the right to autonomy. "To deny clients authority and responsibility by adopting the paternalist model is to deny them the freedom to direct their own lives." As we have noted, this overstates the case. Professional interventions, like other sorts, affect a limited part of clients' lives and fall far short of denying them the freedom to direct their lives. Still, autonomy is a basic good, and any curtailment of it must be balanced by some important gain. Once again, the professional is justified in acting parentalistically on rare occasions but usually should avoid it like the plague.

Bayles's final argument is that professional measures have been empirically shown to be more successful when the client plays an active role in the decision to adopt them. This is true and important, but only in general and admits exceptions, so the door is left open for limited parentalism.

The concept of the professional-client relationship that Bayles does favor is the Fiduciary Model. His formulation is worth quoting at length:

> As a general characterization of what the professional-client relationship should be, one needs a concept in which the professional's superior knowledge is recognized, but the client retains significant authority and responsibility in decision making. The law uses such a conception to characterize most professional-client relationships, namely, that of a fiduciary. In a fiduciary relationship, both parties are responsible and their judgments given equal consideration. Because one party is in a more advantageous position, he or she has special obligations to the other. The weaker party depends on the stronger in ways in which the other does not and so must *trust* the stronger party. . . . The term *consents* (the client consents) rather than *decides* (the client decides) indicates that it is the professional's role to propose courses of action.[10]

Bayles concludes by deriving an important set of obligations of professional to client from the fiduciary role under the headings of honesty, candor, competence, diligence, loyalty, fairness, and discretion.

The ideal professional for Bayles turns out to be close to the ideal caring human being who chances to possess esoteric knowledge and skills that are extremely valuable to people with certain kinds of needs and into whose care some of those people have been entrusted by society. This personal ideal is appealing and can be recommended without reservation. I would only fill it out in two directions, one suggested by Bayles's analysis and the other by my own.

First, it is useful to distinguish between professionals such as many (but not all) doctors, lawyers, teachers, ministers, and counselors who have individuals for clients and professionals such as many (but not all) engineers, accountants, military officers, and journalists who are employed by corporate groups and deal with customers or "the public." The first group should take to heart Bayles's Friendship Model. True friendships can develop between professional and client despite the asymmetry of their relationship. The client is expected to expose private aspects of her life to the professional if he is to be of service. Friendship nurtures the kind of personal solicitude that makes him worthy of her trust. We should remember that a true friend retains the objectivity that is necessary if his solicitude is to follow the right path, that which respects her autonomy and levels with her about her responsibilities, and this is precisely what we should expect of this group of professionals. The second type of professional should take to heart Bayles's Contract Model. He stands at a greater distance from his "client" than a professional of the first type. An apparatus of rules, rights, and obligations such as might be negotiated by strangers at arm's length on the basis of equality is appropriate in order to keep parentalism in check, as well as to obviate exploitation, deception, fraud, and treachery.

Second, I would add to Bayles's list of traits a strong dose of humility. The professional must remind himself that he is human though his role is quasi-divine. He is privileged to care for others and has received the opportunity and training to do so from society as a gift which he must repay. He is able to care for a limited aspect of other people's lives, but he cannot claim general superiority — or intellectual, moral, or political. Moreover, in this complex society, he is dependent on many others to meet his own needs. He, like all of us, relies for authentic human existence on a network of relationships in which he is the recipient as often as the donor of care.

In steering the tricky course between deficient caring from an exaggerated concern for the autonomy of others and excessive intervention, the guidelines and personal qualities of the ideal professional are complementary. The professional faithful to his fiduciary responsibilities will want to follow rational guidelines, and the guidelines will lead him where he wants to go, to genuine service to those whom he is pledged to serve.

To intertwine the strands of thought that we have been drawing out: professions are structurally parentalistic. They are organized to take care of particular aspects of human welfare in ways beyond the capacity of clients to understand fully. Hence, professionals often act in ways that enjoy no more than generic consent of those whom their actions affect and sometimes not even that. They claim to act for the benefit of these individuals and through them society as a whole. They claim also that their advanced technical knowledge cannot be put to effective use in any other way.

The professions have been delegated immense power over the lives of others, they have been exempted from social control so as to enjoy a great deal of autonomy, and their position is sustained by laws and customs for which the professionals themselves rather than an informed public are responsible. The design of a profession is the work of a few ostensibly for the good of the many. It is, in a word, a product of parentalism, and professions are parentalistic institutions. The public passively acquiesces to the professional structure and the professionalization of new occupations.

The last hundred years have seen professions move to the center of the occupational stage. In consequence, modern society has become ever more parentalistic in its basic structures, and there is every reason to expect the trend to continue unless effective barriers in a reformed professional morality can be erected.

15

Conclusion

Mutual solicitude binds people together into genuine communities in which they flourish as human beings. Solicitude, however, may deteriorate into domination that either reduces others to dependency "for their own good" or uses them as means to ulterior ends. Critical reflection is necessary to prevent solicitude from becoming a mask for these degenerate forms.

The analysis in this volume invites readers to reflect on the demands of authentic solicitude. It asks them to recognize their interdependence with special individuals and the vast congerie of persons who compose "society" and "humanity." It urges them to see that the dependence of others imposes a heavy burden of care on them if they are to be true to their nature as human beings. It urges them equally to acknowledge their need for care from others. Mutual care is the primary foundation for authentic existence and genuine community.

Those for whom we care do not always realize that they need our help. We must decide whether to intervene in their lives without their consent, whether to commit the act of parentalism. Sometimes parentalism is justified and even demanded by clear-eyed solicitude. In a world of labyrinthine organizations, intricate technology, and hyperspecialization, the areas in which it is needed are not diminishing. The caring society calls for parentalistic initiatives. At the same time, it calls upon us to maintain a critical attitude toward them lest they be subverted into domination or exploitation. This means that the burden of proof is on the parentalism to justify interventions by valid moral norms.

I have proposed guidelines for decisions about whether to intervene in the lives of people without their consent. We have followed the serpentine path which the guidelines describe through the cluttered and perplexing landscape of human relationships. We have found that they do not generate anything like precise formulas or rigid rules of conduct. However, they do point out factors that should be taken into consideration in conscientious decisions of care. They do not replace good sense and judgment, but they indicate the points on which these should be focused, the points at which moral experience and ethical reflection should be brought to bear so that we will make choices we can justify in living a caring life.

Let me conclude by reviewing the distinctive features of the position I have developed.

1. The postulate of the analysis is that care is the critical factor in relationships that bind people together in true community and enable them to achieve an

authentic existence. The concept of care combines notions of practical love and intelligent choice of means, affection, and obligation with heavy responsibilities and profound gratifications.

2. The analysis labels care for other people as solicitude. It distinguishes the kind of solicitude that helps others achieve authenticity and pursue happiness through carrying their own burdens of care from the kind that takes their proper cares from them and reduces them to dependency and inauthenticity.

3. In caring for the others, the proper aim is to provide what is truly or objectively good for them. While they usually know what is best for themselves, in some cases others know better. Then what is good for them is different from what they desire, and others may have a reason to act contrary to their desires.

4. Justified parentalism is motivated by the better kind of solicitude and implemented by adequate knowledge of what is good for the recipient. Unjustified parentalism is motivated by the bad kind of solicitude or implemented according to misconceptions about what is good for the recipient. Both justified and unjustified parentalism are distinguished from pseudoparentalism, which is intervention in the lives of others to exploit them under the mask of solicitude.

5. Goods for a person are those things (objects, states, activities) that will bring them deep and enduring satisfactions. Each individual's schedule of goods is unique since his or her makeup is unique. But individuals share features as human beings. As inheritors of a common human nature in the human condition they are confronted with similar situations in life. Their schedules of goods overlap, and certain goods are basic for every human being. True solicitude is guided by a knowledge of human nature and its basic human goods supplemented by information about the unique nature of the recipient.

6. It is generally recognized that one of the most important basic goods is autonomy. However, 'autonomy' and related terms such as 'competence' cover a great range of capabilities, each capability with many dimensions, each dimension admitting many degrees. Autonomy, competence, and so on should therefore be treated as relativistic or range properties rather than as threshold concepts. The latter lead moralists seeking to rationalize absolute bans on parentalism into grave conceptual cul de sacs. Threshold concepts are appropriate in special contexts when people must be divided into mutually exclusive categories and treated under rigid rules for practical purposes. They are inappropriate in formulating norms for the treatment of individuals as individuals.

7. The goods associated with the many modes of autonomy are generally more valuable in proportion to the degree to which the person is informed, rational, self-controlled, and equipped with resources. Acting for what one desires has some value; acting rationally for reflective goals has more; acting successfully for what is truly good has most. These differences are sometimes critical in deciding whether autonomy should be sacrificed for competing goods.

8. Autonomy is not the only basic good. Hence, components, conditions, forms, and degrees of autonomy must sometimes be sacrificed for other goods. Despite claims by moralists that autonomy cannot be weighed in the balance with other goods, it constantly is, and clearly this can be done in a better or worse fashion. Thus, it must be done and should be done as well as we can.

9. Autonomy is obviously weighed in the balance when we decide to sacrifice it for other goods. It is likewise weighed when we judge it to be more important than other goods—for example, when we sacrifice wealth, health, or friends for freedom or when we thrust autonomy and responsibility on others at a cost to their complacency or peace of mind. Likewise, we are judging that something is objectively good for others and better than other goods when we decide to refrain from intervention in their lives out of respect for their autonomy. As long as we take account of the well-being of others when we interact with them, we must weigh their autonomy against the other dimensions of their welfare.

10. Parentalism is defined as intervention in the life of others for their own good independent of their will. Following the comparison on which the concept is based—to actions of good parents in the care of children—the definition of parentalism is interpreted in the broadest sense regarding who can act as parentalist, who can be subject to parentalism, the aims parentalists can have, and the measures they can use.

11. The definition covers cases in which subjects dissent from interventions, are ignorant of them, or have their wishes disregarded. It covers acts that parentalists are able to perform because of any kind of power they have over those whom they try to help. Moreover, parentalists can aim at preventing harm or promoting positive goods. And they can use all manner of measures ranging from coercion and deception to urging rational arguments upon averse subjects. The reason for adopting a broad conception of parentalism is that all combinations of aims and measures can confront prospective parentalists as options among which they have to choose, and the same values are at issue in assessing the alternatives.

12. The principle of parentalism is a simple application of the consequentialist principle that we should always aim at the maximum benefits distributed as fairly as possible for all who are affected by our actions. This is a near relative of the principle of utility, but it incorporates concepts of just distribution of benefits; the intrinsic value of autonomous and, in particular, of moral actions; the long-term benefits of being faithful to principles, adhering to practices, and reinforcing traits of character; and other aspects of the moral life emphasized in nonconsequentialist ethical theories. All of these are considered "consequences" of actions in the sense that they must be assessed along with consequences as ordinarily understood.

13. The principle of parentalism requires us to abstain from parentalism unless we have good evidence that intervention will improve the net welfare of the recipient. It is put in this negative form in recognition of the prima facie objection that parentalism always compromises the autonomy of the recipient. The term 'parentalism' retains a mildly pejorative connotation. Labeling an act as parentalistic imposes the onus of justification on one who would perform it rather than on one who would abstain from it.

14. In its concise form, the principle of parentalism says little. Its implications are spelled out in corollaries and guidelines. These direct attention to the specific factors that an agent must consider to determine whether particular acts are justified and indicate limits beyond which even justified actions should not go. Guidelines are not strict rules that can be applied mechanically or algorithmically

to cases. Rather, they point out the variables whose values must be assessed—measured or ranked if possible, intuitively estimated for the most part—to determine whether on balance the act ought to be performed.

15. Caring persons are concerned about the well-being not only of those with whom they are intimately related but also everyone in the community. They find that solicitude requires them to care for other individuals whom they know well, as well as support institutions that nurture care among all members of the community. Moreover, their roles in society entail behavior toward many whom they know less well or not at all. Hence, a distinction must be drawn between personal and public parentalism, and one should expect different applications of the principle of parentalism in the two spheres.

16. The apparatus of rights—conceived as claims to specific performances from specific individuals in specific contexts, authorized by law or moral rules and backed by sanctions—has a more prominent role to play in public than in personal acts. This is because public acts by agents of the state and by people in socially defined roles such as professionals involve the exercise of power over others at a distance with limited knowledge of them as individuals. More protections against abuse and more restrictions on well-intentioned attempts to promote the welfare of unwilling or unknowing individuals are required than in the case of personal acts.

17. While it is useful to guarantee specific forms of autonomy under laws and other forms of autonomy under moral guidelines, the most general moral principles such as that of parentalism should not be formulated in terms of rights. In particular, attempts to specify an absolute right or a lexically first right to autonomy on the basis of respect for autonomy as the foundation for morality fail in general and do not provide plausible or practicable guidelines for parentalism.

18. Connected with the difficulties of rights-based ethical theory are flaws in attempts to formulate principles for parentalism in terms of consent. These take the form of distinguishing forms of consent to intervention in a person's life besides explicit current consent, attempting to specify which forms justify intervention and denying that intervention is justified by any other consideration. I have challenged these views on the basis of an examination of the value of consent.

19. Actual acts of consent are valuable substantively as acts of autonomy, practically in ameliorating the tensions that spring up among people who intervene in one another's lives, and evidentially in suggesting to the intervener where the true interests of the subject lie. They are more valuable as they are better informed, more rational and less encumbered. But in any form they are neither necessary nor sufficient to justify intervention.

20. The disposition to consent—hypothetical consent of the actual person and consent of the hypothetical completely rational person—has none of the value of actual consent and has no more than a heuristic role in justifying parentalistic decisions.

21. With all of the deficiencies of public acts, they are nevertheless necessary in our mass, technologically complex, interdependent society. To ensure necessary measures, welfare rights to minimal levels of basic goods, as well as

autonomy rights, must be guaranteed. The welfare state, parentalistic to the core, is inescapable. This makes guidelines for legitimate public parentalism that much more urgent. While not attempting to provide detailed rules, the present work has sketched the parameters that should be taken into account. It illustrates them by application to parentalistic legislation, the national security system, and the practices of professionals.

Analysis can carry us only so far. After these reflections, each of us must return to the daily decisions of life. With the guidelines for parentalism in hand, we still must take care in our judgments, doing our best to see that the intuitions which determine the application of the guidelines to concrete cases are as informed and as critical as possible. Our primary responsibility is not to *think* about care but to *care*. Thinking is a prelude to action and worthwhile only if it informs action. Our primary responsibility is to take care in our caring and forge ahead in living a caring life and building a caring society.

Appendix: Critical Review of the Literature

Chapter 1. The Life of Care

Heidegger explains *Sorge* in the following terms:

> Man is . . . "thrown" from Being itself into the truth of Being, so that ek-sisting [*Existenz*, rendered *Ek-sistenz*] in this fashion he might guard the truth of Being, in order that beings might appear in the light of Being as the beings they are. Man does not decide whether and how beings appear, whether and how God and the gods or history and nature come forward into the lighting of Being, come to presence and depart. The advent of beings lies in the destiny of Being. But for man it is ever a question of finding what is fitting in his essence which corresponds to such destiny; for in accord with this destiny man as ek-sisting has to guard the truth of Being. Man is the shepherd of Being. ("Letter on Humanism," p. 210)

He goes on to say "It is in this direction alone that *Being and Time* is thinking when ecstatic existence is experienced as 'care'." Thus care, authenticity and other structures are ontological categories, not normative or ethical ones, though Heidegger suggests murkily that when man finds a home in the House of Being he enters a realm of healing which frees him from "the malice of rage."

Whatever this means, it is clearly not how I am using the concept of care. I am talking about care of human beings, not of Being, and the moral obligation to care for them properly.

Chapter 2. Care and Moral Intuition

According to Kohlberg's scheme, individuals pass through six stages of moral thinking:
   A. Preconventional level
      Stage 1: The punishment-obedience orientation
      Stage 2: The instrumental-relativist orientation
   B. Conventional level
      Stage 3: Interpersonal concordance or "good boy–nice girl" orientation
      Stage 4: The "law and order" orientation

    C. Postconventional, autonomous, or principled level
        Stage 5: The social-contract legalistic orientation
        Stage 6: The universal-ethical-principle orientation

Everyone begins life at Stage 1 and reaches his highest stage in adolescence, so the stages are steps toward maturity. One is never mature unless he achieves Level C, and valid moral intuitions occur only there, as is evident from the sense in which the structure is natural, "not in the sense of being innate, but in the sense of being the sequential results of processing moral experience, not derivative from particular teachings or particular moral ideologies or theories" ("Claim to Moral Adequacy," p. 634).

Kohlberg claims that a philosopher's formal moral theory "is an elaboration of certain portions of his 'natural' moral-stage structure." His data are intuitions about hypothetical moral dilemmas that he has solicited from philosophers and the comparison of them with principles which these philosophers advance in their writings (*Philosophy of Moral Development*, pp. 159–166). The two popular families of ethical theories are based on intuitions of the two highest stages. Stage 5 intuitions produce social contract, rule-utilitarian, and natural rights theories, as typified by Mill and Locke. Stage 6 intuitions produce deontological theories, typified by Kant and Rawls ("Claim to Moral Adequacy," pp. 634–635). Kohlberg shows his own Kantian bias when he argues that Stage 6 thinking is superior to Stage 5. Stage 6 people display greater psychological equilibrium in their moral judgments. Their theories better meet metaethical criteria of differentiation, integration, reversibility, universalizability, and consistency (*Philosophy of Moral Development*, pp. 135–136, and ch. 5, "Justice as Reversibility").

Kohlberg maintains that his stages are almost universal across cultures. His theory implies that they *should* be since the developmentally later stages are superior to the earlier ones. Cultures that frustrate the movement of individuals to the higher stages are morally defective. This notion allows Kohlberg to discount evidence contrary to the claim of cultural universality (*Philosophy of Moral Development*, p. 128).

Level C is distinguished by "a clear effort to define moral values and principles that have validity and application apart from the authority of the groups or persons holding these principles and apart from the individual's own identification with these groups" (*Philosophy of Moral Development*, pp. 131–132). Stage 5 defines right action in terms of rights for individuals and standards that have been critically examined and agreed on by society. It sees personal values as relative and emphasizes procedural rules for reaching consensus. The result is a legal and contractual point of view. Stage 6 defines right in terms of a decision of conscience made in accord with principles chosen for oneself on the basis of comprehensiveness, universality, and consistency. These principles are justice, reciprocity and equality of human rights, and respect for the dignity of human beings as individual persons (*Philosophy of Moral Development*, pp. 165–166).

The Heinz dilemma:

> In Europe, a woman was near death from a very bad disease, a special kind of cancer. There was one drug that the doctors thought might save her. It was a

form of radium for which a druggist was charging ten times what the drug cost him to make. The sick woman's husband, Heinz, went to everyone he knew to borrow the money, but he could only get together about half of what it cost. He told the druggist that his wife was dying, and asked him to sell it cheaper or let him pay later. But the druggist said, "No, I discovered the drug and I'm going to make money from it." So Heinz got desperate and broke into the man's store to steal the drug for his wife. ("Claim to Moral Adequacy," p. 638)

Kohlberg explains his hermeneutic phenomenological-cognitive approach in the following terms:

> The first meaning of cognitive for us is that observations of others are made phenomenologically; i.e. by attempting to take the role of the other, to see things from his or her conscious viewpoint. Second, we mean by cognitive the fact that interviewing and scoring are acts of 'interpreting a text' around some shared philosophic categories of meaning. Insofar as each of us has been through the moral stages and has held the viewpoint of each stage, we should be able to put ourselves in the internal framework of a given stage. To understand others, to put oneself in the framework of others, is to be able to generate from their statements other statements that they can or do make from this framework, not because we are imposing upon them a framework to predict future speech acts but rather because we can organize the world as they do; i.e., for the moment we can share their meanings. . . . 'Cognitive', then, means not only (a) phenomenological or imaginative role-taking activity, and (b) the search for logical or inferential relations and transformations, but also (c) the definition of the subject's structure in terms of the *meanings he or she finds in the world*. (Kohlberg et al., *Moral Stages*, pp. 11–12)

Note that in order to understand the views of anyone at any of the stages, the psychologist must progress through all of them. To understand the views of subjects at the highest stage, he must have reached the highest stage himself and be an ethically mature person. Quite a demanding standard!

In groping for an androgynous view, Gilligan treats the perspectives of male and female experience as complementary: "Moral maturity then presumably entails an ability to see in at least two ways and to speak at least two languages, and the relationship between justice and care perspectives or voices becomes a key question for investigation" ("Preface," p. xx).

Chapter 3. Care and Morality

Nielsen distinguishes between what I have called apologetic and reformist normative ethical theories in terms of their approach to ordinary morality:

> Some ethicists are iconoclasts and moral critics like Nietzsche and Camus, and seek to show that at least some of our actual normative ethical ideals are irrational. Some, like Kant and Sidgwick, are concerned to exhibit the rational foundations of common-sense normative ethics; they seek to state the hetero-geneous claims of common-sense morality in some systematic order, to state its fundamental principles, and to show how they can be rationally justified. Some, like Bentham and Dewey, pursue both courses, with emphasis on the latter. ("Problems of Ethics," p. 119)

Mine is the combined approach.

The implications for parentalism of the insistence that morality is composed of categorical imperatives are evident in Gert and Culver. They restrict parentalism to acts that violate one or more moral rules ("Justification of Paternalism," p. 200). In *The Moral Rules* Gert derives what he calls The Moral Rules from the single principle, Do not harm. Not all inflictions of harm are immoral because it is sometimes necessary to violate one rule to honor another. Moreover, moral ideals call on us to prevent harms, and one must sometimes inflict harms to prevent others. Gert defines moral rules and ideals entirely in terms of harms and ignores benefits. He denies that utilitarian ideals, which ask people to promote the good of others, warrant violation of moral rules or ideals. To be moral is to avoid actions of a certain character, not to pursue certain ends.

Most types of parentalism are wrong under this scheme because they violate one of the rules, Do not deprive of freedom, Do not deprive of opportunity, or Do not deceive without adequate reason. The few types of parentalism are justified by moral ideals that override the moral rule that must be broken, for example, when one deceives a person to save his life.

Gert's scheme accommodates intuitions about justified forms of parentalism more adequately than the simplistic theory of absolute rights. Unfortunately, its complexity eliminates its convenience as a decision mechanism. It requires us to consider many imponderables. Is this rule or ideal more important than that in a given situation? Presumably the answer turns on the severity of the harms to be avoided or prevented, but then it must be possible to balance harms against each other. Why not also balance goods against harms, and why then cannot utilitarian ideals override moral rules or ideals?

Gert's reasons for excluding goods from the moral equation may be due to the preconception that principles of morality must be categorical. It is not possible to be *doing* any particular thing at every moment, but it is possible to be *not doing* any number of things. Thus we can obey the commandment, Thou shalt not kill, every second of our lives. Now, if categoricality is part of the definition of morality, why be moral? Intuitively, the provision of a great good for an individual warrants the infliction of a few minor harms. If this be "immoral," one should be immoral. However, it seems better to recognize provision of positive goods in caring relationships as a moral obligation. Allowing avoidance of harm to monopolize the moral domain reflects the false conception of human society as composed of self-interested individuals competing for goods who would be constantly at one another's throats if they are not restrained by a stern morality. Human beings are not to be reduced to this. They are more, and potentially much more. The institutions of morality should bring out the best in them, not settle for stifling the worst.

In discussing the universality of rules, we should distinguish two kinds of "exceptions"—those permitted by explicit exceptive clauses and those that are justified violations of the rules even with their exceptive clauses. On the basis of this distinction, a case can be made that Mill is a strong rule–utilitarian in the sphere of public action. He seems to believe that it is more feasible for society to habituate people to follow rules strictly than to educate them to use their discretion in violating them. However, his remarks in *Utilitarianism* count against this interpretation. To the charge that utilitarianism allows individuals to rationalize violations of rules, for example, against lying, he replies that

> even this rule, sacred as it is, admits of possible exceptions, is acknowledged by all moralists. . . . But in order that the exception may not extend itself beyond the need, and may have the least possible effect in weakening reliance on veracity, it ought to be recognized, and, if possible its limits defined; and if the principle of utility is good for anything, it must be good for weighing these conflicting utilities against one another, and marking out the region within which one or the other preponderates. (p. 223)

Mill goes on to suggest that discretionary violations are justified even when all major exceptive clauses have been built into the rules: "It is not the fault of any creed, but of the complicated nature of human affairs, that rules of conduct cannot be so framed as to require no exceptions [i.e., violations]. . . . There is no ethical creed which does not temper the rigidity of its laws, by giving a certain latitude, under the moral responsibility of the agent, for accommodation to peculiarities of circumstances" (p. 225).

Mill proposes rules for the purpose of promoting utility in particular sorts of circumstances. They may not be appropriate to others. Thus his strictures against parentalism are not absolute. He stipulates exceptions and rejects others on the basis of utility in the context of the concrete conditions that confronted him in Britain and elsewhere when he wrote *On Liberty*. He permits the individual to violate even correct rules *cum* exceptive clauses if exceptional utilities require it. We may assume that he would favor different rules were conditions to change.

Mill advances his contextual theory of rights in blocking out the area of peoples' lives where the principle of liberty should hold sway, what are now called "self-regarding" actions. Mill distinguishes two sorts:

> As soon as any part of a person's conduct affects prejudicially the interests of others, society has jurisdiction over it, and the question whether the general welfare will or will not be promoted by interfering with it, becomes open to discussion. But there is no room for entertaining any such question when a person's conduct affects the interests of no persons besides himself, or needs not affect them unless they like (all persons being of full age, and the ordinary amount of understanding). In all such cases, there should be perfect freedom, legal and social, to do the action and stand the consequences. (*On Liberty*, p. 276)

All actions have *some* effect on others. To delimit a domain for the protection of liberty, Mill maintains that society has jurisdiction only over actions that *directly* affect others without their consent. The distinction between actions that directly affect others and those that do not causes problems. I shall adopt J.C. Rees's interpretation to resolve them ("A Re-Reading of Mill on Liberty"). The central passage from Mill is this:

> [T]he fact of living in society renders it indispensable that each should be bound to observe a certain line of conduct toward the rest. This conduct consists, first, in not injuring the interests of one another; or rather certain interests, which, either by express legal provision or by tacit understanding, ought to be consid-

ered as rights; and secondly, in each person's bearing his share (to be fixed on some equitable principle) of the labours and sacrifices incurred for defending the society or its members from injury and molestation. These conditions society is justified in enforcing, at all costs to those who endeavour to withhold fulfillment. Nor is this all that society may do. The acts of an individual may be hurtful to others or wanting in due consideration for their welfare, without going the length of violating their constituted rights. The offender may then be justly punished by opinion, though not by law. (*On Liberty*, p. 276)

Certain goods are so vital to the individual's welfare that they should be guaranteed whether or not he desires them. They should be declared rights, and infringements should be subject to the sanctions against illegal and immoral conduct. We may refer to the basic interests that ought to be assured by society through the institution of morality as moral rights and those that ought to be assured by positive law as legal rights. What Mill maintains is that if the actions of an individual directly injure the basic interests of another, they violate the latter's moral rights and are candidates for control by society. If they do not affect others or affect their interests only indirectly or if they voluntarily submit to them, the actions are self-regarding and should be protected against interference. Such actions may affect others by frustrating their wish for everyone to live like they do, but the actions do not harm anyone's basic interests and hence cannot be curtailed on that ground.

Assuming that it is possible to draw a line between self-regarding and other-regarding actions, exactly what kind of protection from interference does Mill advocate, and what is the force of the appeal to rights? Recognition of differences in what individuals need for happiness and in the concrete circumstances and resources of particular societies focuses attention on the particularity of rights. Different rights will be guaranteed in different historical situations. This historical relativity of rights does not preclude a recognition of common human needs and hence a core of basic rights common to all situations, and Mill is not reluctant to generalize about human nature and the conditions for human happiness. Nevertheless, his empiricism and relativism make it impossible for him to cull a neat list of inalienable rights and order them lexically. Indeed, talk of rights is not his style. The concept is not essential to the foundations of his sort of moral theory though the theory sanctions the introduction of rights as a tool of morality.

Chapter 5. Parentalism Defined

The term *paternalism* was coined to combat the use of the paternal analogy by elites to justify their privileges. Throughout vagaries of usage it has retained a pejorative connotation. We are conditioned to react negatively toward any act labeled paternalism. The message is that it is a Bad Thing, not to be practiced except in unusual circumstances. Generalization of the concept of parentalism to include intuitively justified actions loosens the pejorative connotations. Edward Sankowski suggests that anxiety to condemn state parentalism has led authors to neglect other contexts in which parentalism is more justified (" 'Paternalism' and

Social Policy"). This may explain why sponsors of an absolute right to autonomy resist generalization. Under a narrow concept, the offensiveness of core cases permeates the entire category. The vehement antiparentalist fears that association of offensive with inoffensive ones will weaken resistance to the offensive ones.

This is also the key to McDonald's puzzle: he wonders why so many moralists first condemn parentalism wholesale and immediately introduce exceptions ("Autarchy and Interest"). The reason is that their strategy imposes the burden of proof on the would-be agent to show that his case is exceptional.

The effect of generalization is not always to soften the term—seeing some actions as parentalistic may cause us to make negative judgments about the actions rather than to wonder whether parentalism is so bad after all. Nevertheless, the broader the category, the less clean-cut our judgments of the undesirability of instances and more our second thoughts about knee-jerk condemnation of them. As Sankowski says about the evolution of his own feelings,

> Especially in the light of the fact that such a variety of policies can plausibly be called "paternalistic," and so many of them have a title to be considered morally justifiable, it is doubtful that there is even a strong *prima facie* case that any instance of "paternalism" is objectionable *just as such*. Many instances of paternalism may be *prima facie* objectionable on other grounds, e.g., as instances of coercion. Or we might say that the objectionable features of paternalism enumerated earlier support some sort of mild *prima facie* suspicion, at least for some classes of cases. But this is very mild. It is not the sort of *prima facie* objectionableness that would properly oblige us to presume the paternalistic policy to be wrong in the absence of a well-argued defense. (" 'Paternalism' and Social Policy," pp. 10–11)

I agree that it is fairer to say that parentalism is prima facie suspicious rather than that it is prima facie wrong.

We can imagine an opposite approach. One could mandate parentalism wherever people are in need and treat unjustified cases as exceptions. This would put the burden of proof on the one who would refrain from helping his neighbor. The approach is tempting for the philosophy of care. Why then persist in characterizing parentalism in pejorative terms? An agent who thinks in these terms will believe that only a few, clearly specified types of parentalism are justified; if an action does not belong to one of these types, he dismisses it without further thought. An agent who adopts the alternative approach becomes a routine parentalist and is inhibited by circumstances spelled out as exceptions. The two approaches, while logically sorting out cases the same way, cause reflection to come to rest at different points and turn different sets of actions over to unreflective habit. The difference between the two approaches affects behavior despite their logical convergence.

The very ideal of a caring society makes caution about parentalism important. If we were to surrender to the idea that society is an aggregate of atomically independent self-interested agents, there would be no need to worry about parentalism. Brakes are necessary precisely where institutions encourage people to be solicitous toward others, involve themselves in their lives, and establish organic ties with them through mutual care. In such an atmosphere, special precautions are needed to ensure that solicitude assumes the proper form.

Criticisms of parentalism have shaped the popular consciousness to the extent that 'paternalism' is firmly entrenched as a tag of disapproval. Even the practices of fathers come under review. Perhaps, it is suggested, even children should not be treated as children, that is, as children have traditionally been treated. Thus, Amy Gutmann argues that the state has the right (perhaps the parentalistic duty) to limit the indoctrination of children in the parent's religion if the parent wants to deny the child the opportunity to attend public schools and obtain a liberal—that is, pluralistic and liberating—education ("Children, Paternalism and Education").

Locke argues the impropriety of comparing the king to a father in the First Treatise and chapter 6, "Of Paternal Power," in the Second Treatise (*Two Treatises of Government*). Interestingly, his argument anticipates the later attempt to incorporate women's moral experience in the empirical base for moral reflection. He points out a fault of "words and names that have obtained in the World." The phrase paternal power "seems so to place the Power of Parents over their Children wholly in the *Father*, as if the *Mother* had no share in it, whereas if we consult Reason or Revelation, we shall find that she hath an equal Title. This may give one reason to ask, Whether this might not be more properly called Parental *Power*." He then observes that this locutionary reform would discomfit his adversaries, for who would ascribe absolute power over her children to a mother?

> [I]t will but very ill serve the turn of those Men who contend so much for the Absolute Power and Authority of the *Fatherhood*, as they call it, that the *Mother* should have any share in it. And it would have but ill supported the *Monarchy* they contend for, when by the very name it appeared that that Fundamental Authority from whence they would derive their Government of a single Person only, was not plac'd in one, but two Persons joyntly. (Second Treatise, p. 322)

The major part of Locke's argument is devoted to attacking the parental analogy by discussing at length respects in which sovereign and father differ. Sovereigns are not usually much wiser and more selfless than their subjects, nor are subjects as ignorant, helpless, or incapable of self-rule as children.

VanDeVeer's definition of paternalism is informative. Its points of agreement with my definition of parentalism make some of his arguments for it relevant to the defense of mine. They also make it illuminating to play it against Gert and Culver's definition, which is, as VanDeVeer observes, clear, explicit, and the product of a careful analysis, but conceptually flawed.

VanDeVeer's "canonical definition" is that P's doing A (act or omission) toward S is parentalistic behavior if and only if (a) P deliberately does A; (b) P believes that his doing A is contrary to S's operative preference, intention, or disposition at the time [or when A affects S—or would have affected S if A had been done]; and (c) P does A with the primary or sole aim of promoting a benefit for S [a benefit which, P believes, would not accrue to S in the absence of A's doing (or omitting) A] or preventing a harm to S [a harm which, P believes, would accrue to S in the absence of P's doing (or omitting) A] (*Paternalistic Intervention*, p. 22; the qualifications in brackets are VanDeVeer's).

Gert and Culver's definition is as follows: P is acting parentalistically toward S if and only if P's behavior indicates correctly that P believes that (a) his action is for S's good; (b) he is qualified to act on S's behalf; (c) his action violates a moral rule with regard to S; (d) he is justified in acting on S's behalf independently of S's past, present, or immediately forthcoming free and informed consent; and (e) S believes that he generally knows what is for his own good ("Paternalistic Behavior," pp. 49–50).

This introduces an irrelevant requirement—that P's behavior indicates correctly (to some other observer or to P himself?) that he has relevant beliefs. Whether P believes his action will contribute to S's welfare does not depend on whether anyone knows that he so believes. Either he is or is not trying to help S. Parentalism is in the action of the parentalist, not the eye of the beholder.

P's state of mind must include not merely beliefs but an intention to act on them. P might believe all that the definition specifies and still not be acting parentalistically. Thus my definition specifies that P not only must believe that A will benefit S, but perform A in order to benefit S. Likewise, VanDeVeer's definition requires P to perform A with the "primary or sole aim of securing a benefit for S."

While provision (d) in the Gert and Culver definition properly stipulates that P's decision is independent of whether S consents to A, which is preferable to stipulating that it be against S's will as VanDeVeer does, the requirement that P believe he is justified in performing A is too restrictive. P may impulsively or emotionally perform it without reflecting on its justification or in the face of an intellectual judgment that it is not justified. Nor is there any need to specify, as does provision (b), that P believes he is qualified to act on S's behalf. If "qualified" merely means that P thinks he is able to protect or benefit S, in most cases he does or he would not act. Even if we ignore the rare cases in which P acts without such confidence, it is not necessary for him to make a reflective judgment about his qualifications to believe that he is able to help. If, on the other hand, Gert and Culver mean by being qualified that P has received a formal charge or credential to act in S's behalf—for example, as a physician, representative or trustee—the requirement is too restrictive. It would exclude many informal acts that are similar to the ones Gert and Culver discuss.

The point of provision (e), that S believes he generally knows what is for his own good, is seen by Hodson to exclude from the category of parentalism the care of newborn babies, comatose people, and animals. Perhaps Hodson wishes to exclude the cases because the care involved is obviously justified. According to my definition, the only thing required is that P does not allow S's wishes to affect his decision. S may not agree that A is for his good, may not have any wishes relevant to A, or may even desire A.

Provision (c), that P believe he is violating a moral rule in helping S, attempts to build into the definition the prima facie objection that should be raised against any action when it is identified as parentalistic. However, as I suggest for 'parentalism' and VanDeVeer argues for 'paternalism' (*Paternalistic Intervention*, pp. 16–18) the definition should be value-neutral, though mild negative connotations may be allowed to hover over the term. VanDeVeer cites cases of interference in the lives of others, which are similar to acknowledged cases of parentalism but which do not violate generally accepted moral rules. The Gert and Culver definition could be defended by defining all actions that violate its other provisions as ipso facto immoral, but this question-begging procedure would frustrate the aim of the definition, to collect cases prior to evaluating them. Gert proposes a narrow conception of morality according to which all moral rules are negative, every normal person is familiar with them, and nonviolation makes an action morally permissible. Even if we were to accept this, it would not necessary for P to be conscious of violating a moral rule for his action to be a parentalistic intervention. We do all sorts of things without calling to mind moral rules or asking ourselves whether we are violating them.

My term 'intervention' and VanDeVeer's 'interference' share the defect of implying a positive act on P's part. Some forms of parentalism involve the omission of something that one routinely would do—for instance, Sarah refuses to lend her car to friend Tipple when he is drunk or she "forgets" to bring home the ice cream for her obese husband, Lard. VanDeVeer repairs this omission by including awkward repetitions of 'does (or omits)'. I prefer to use 'intervention' in the definition and to introduce clarifications in the subsequent discussion.

Another definition that is concordant with mine but too brief to be illuminating is Kleinig's: P acts parentalistically in regard to S to the extent that P, in order to secure S's good as an end, imposes on S (*Paternalism*, p. 13). ("Imposes" presumably means something like intervenes without S's consent.)

Dworkin's characterization of parentalism as "interference with a person's liberty of action justified by reasons referring exclusively to the welfare, good, happiness, needs, interests or values of the person being coerced" ("Paternalism," p. 144) introduces a feature of parentalistic actions that is out of place in a definition, namely, their justification. He clearly does not mean to assert that only justified acts, or only acts the agent attempts to justify, are parentalistic. He may intend to say that an action is parentalistic only when the agent would appeal to the recipient's welfare if asked to justify it.

Authors concentrating on protective parentalism include Hart, who is concerned only with the protection of individuals against themselves, and Ten, Allen Buchanan, Hodson, and Wikler, who also deal with protection against others. A number of treatments of parentalism besides Brock's take note of the equivalence of protective and beneficent parentalism. Feinberg distinguishes between the two types in legal parentalism: "to protect individuals from self-inflicted harm . . . [and] to guide them, whether they like it or not, toward their own good ("Legal Paternalism," p. 105). Beauchamp refers to "protective or beneficent reasons" for paternalism ("Paternalism and Biobehavioral Control," p. 67), and Carter speaks of the "protection or promotion of a subject's welfare" ("Justifying Paternalism," p. 133). Laurence Houlgate, Bayles, Regan, and Kleinig also take the broad view.

The parental analogy sets no limits to the goods a parentalist may promote; parents are characteristically concerned about every aspect of their children's welfare. Some interests, however, have proved to be particularly relevant to justifying parentalistic acts. They are distinguished by their importance to the subject, the agent's ability to promote them, and the subject's inability to enjoy them without the agent's help. It is standard practice to divide intrinsic goods into basic or primary and derivative or secondary. Thus Murphy, following Rawls, characterizes liberty, self-respect, and security as "things that every rational man is presumed to want. These goods normally have a use whatever a person's rational plan of life" ("Incompetence and Paternalism," p. 481). Primary goods are critical because parentalism encroaches on some of them (liberty, self-respect) and can be justified in Murphy's eyes only by the furtherance of other primary goods.

In dealing with both parentalism and moralism, Hart focuses on measures that deter disobedience to the law by the threat of death, pain, or deprivation of liberty. Schrag, Carter, and T.M. Reed and Patricia Johnson simply identify parentalism with interference with actions which the subject desires to perform. Some later authors, such as Hodson, equate intervention with coercion or, like Douglas Husak, acknowledge other forms but confine their discussion to coercion. Among authors who insist that noncoercive measures need to be evaluated against coercion are Smiley, Sankowski, and Hobson. Hobson, for instance, notes that "paternalism need not always be seen as involving coercion or deprivation of liberty but may on occasion involve actions more accurately described as deception, breaking of promises, restricting opportunities for pleasures, amongst others." He suggests that the choice of measures should be evaluated primarily in terms of the extent to which they violate the subject's rights, especially to liberty, and the long-term repercussions for his life ("Another Look at Paternalism," p. 294). In a recent essay, Dworkin recognizes that parentalism can occur whenever anyone alters the way another arrives at decisions: "It is not as if rational argument cannot be paternalistic while brute force must be. Some people may want to make their decisions impulsively, without rational deliberation; insisting that they hear arguments (for their own good) is paternalism. On the other hand, brute force used to prevent someone from crossing a washed-out bridge need not be paternalism" ("Paternalism: Some Second Thoughts," p. 107).

Buchanan points out that it is possible to interfere with a person's decision process by forcing information upon her. For example, a physician overrides a patient's request that she not be given certain information about her condition when she wishes to make her decision about treatment without taking the information into account or wishes not to make the decision at all ("Medical Paternalism," p. 62). Dworkin decides not to exclude any category of action from parentalism as long as it "constitutes an attempt to substitute one person's judgment for another's, to promote the latter's benefit." Douglas in his classification of measures typically used by parents in the care of children observes that the parental analogy suggests the broadest conception of "intervention" for parentalism: "parents obviously engage in the full gamut of behavior commonly referred to as paternalism, ranging from the 'weak paternalism' of attempts to influence behavior indirectly, through direct attempts to control behavior noncoercively and attempts to interfere with liberty of action, to the very 'strong paternalism' of severely coercive actions" ("Cooperative Paternalism versus Conflictful Paternalism," p. 173). It is the burden of my argument to show that the indirect measures of weak parentalism include persuasion and rewards.

Chapter 6. The Evaluation of Parentalism

My form of consequentialism spills over the boundary that Regan draws between theories in the "dialectic of paternalism." He attributes to utilitarians the view that pleasure is all that counts and argues that they ignore the intrinsic value of free choice. Since he values freedom over pleasure, he rejects consequentialism ("Paternalism, Freedom, Identity, and Commitment," p. 114). My position, however, is that satisfaction is what counts, and acting autonomously brings its peculiar satisfactions. These satisfactions are real, but they must be weighed against other sorts of goods that can be achieved by an action. To adopt conse-quentialism, therefore, is not to deny the value of freedom and autonomy. It is to refuse to absolutize it.

It is useful to compare my position with Brock's, which is also consequential-ist. Brock utilizes a different conception of goods and harms. He espouses what he calls "desire theory," according to which individual good consists in the satisfaction of one's desires. My theory is an example of what he calls "ideal theory," which says that components of a person's good exist independently of whether he desires them; this includes the development of certain uniquely human capacities, possession of knowledge, and participation in nonexploitive personal relations. In the version of ideal theory presented here, the index of goods is the satisfactions they bring, and it is an objective fact that a particular individual will achieve satisfaction through the possession of certain objects and performance of certain deeds. He may or may not know that they are good for him, and one who cares for him may know that they are good for him independent of his views.

Arneson distinguishes between "welfarist" and "perfectionist" views. The welfarist believes that he should optimize the good of the other as determined by the welfarist's own values and preferences. The perfectionist believes he knows what is objectively good for the person. Thus far, the perfectionist is on solid ground. But Arneson goes further to maintain that the perfectionist believes that if "the limit of ideal deliberation about one's good was approached, all persons would converge in agreeing on a certain conception of human flourishing, which constitutes the good for humanity" and that "the view converged upon would be substantially the same as what the perfectionist now upholds" ("Paternalism, Utility and Fairness," p. 431). My position does not require the parentalist to assume that the subject's objective good "constitutes the good of humanity"—that is, is the same as the objective good of other persons—so my position is not perfectionist. This does not drive me to the welfarist position since I maintain that the parentalist must determine what is good for the subject, which may differ from what is good for the parentalist or other people.

In Brock's categories my position is a "mixed ideal theory" rather than a "pure ideal theory." It contains both universal and personal elements. That is, it recognizes that while objective goods are the same in outline for individuals (the universal element), they vary in detail and order of priority (the personal element). If one wants to help a person, the extent to which she resembles other human beings and hence her goods resemble theirs and the extent to which she differs from them and hence her goods are unique are empirical questions. If we should perform and promote those actions which are objectively best, we should take into account *all* of the person's values, both universal and personal.

Desire theories are based on the insight that two objective goods that are *necessarily* connected with the person's desires are the active pursuit of what she desires and success in gaining it. What must be done by another to promote these goods for a person is essentially determined by that person's desires. It makes no sense to talk of overruling her desires to promote them, as it does in order to promote other goods for her. Thus, consistent consequentialism requires the ideal theory of value. There is no reason to adopt the desire theory.

While agreeing with Brock on many points, I disagree on one important one. His desire theory incorporates an ideal element that is fatal to its coherence. He endorses Rawls's view that we human beings have "a highest-order interest in our status as moral agents, able and free to form, revise, and rationally pursue our plans of life over time." Brock thinks that autonomy is essential to the status in which everyone has a highest order interest, that of moral agent, and that autonomy is expressed in activities whose goals are not specifiable independent of the means employed: "the end or purpose of engaging in the activity is, at least in part, the exercise of one's own judgment and abilities in the activity, as defective or imperfect as they may be" ("Paternalism and Promoting the Good," pp. 150, 157). Goals of this sort cannot be achieved for a person by parentalistic acts; he can only achieve them for himself. Since achieving such goals is supremely important, parentalistic care should not stand in its way. Now Brock recognizes that many people do not particularly value their autonomy. Hence, in asserting that others should respect it, he urges them to act contrary to such persons' desires. Their objective good overrules their desires. The logic of the desire theory itself should force Brock to acknowledge a second objective good: benevolence requires us to help others fulfill their desires in self-regarding matters. This implies that fulfilling desires, whatever those desires may be and whatever is entailed in fulfilling them, is good for a person. Autonomy is conceived in desire theory to consist in acting so as to pursue the goals one desires. Thus two elements in a subject's autonomy should be valued by the parentalist—the exercise of judgment in forming desires and the activity of pursuing what she comes to desire. These are distinct. While pursuit of goals requires the subject to use her abilities, she may not need to use them to the fullest. Likewise, her abilities may not equip her to pursue her goals in the optimal way.

Thus, in contradiction to his desire theory, Brock should acknowledge two objective goods. These may conflict, so that one who would care for another may have to choose between them for her. He would have to weigh their value for her independent of the particular goals she desires. To acknowledge that more than one good is objective and require the parentalist to judge which is the more important for someone for whom he cares in a particular situation presupposes that there is some way to know what is objectively good for a person and compare its goodness against her other goods. The primary evidence of the value of anything (action, state, possession) lies in the depth of the satisfactions that it brings. The test of satisfaction reveals that there are many more than two objective goods. Important and distinctive satisfactions are brought by fulfilled love, rest after hard work, and knowing about something. In the enjoyment of some of these, the exercise of autonomy is minimal, and in others it is not solely autonomy that makes them gratifying. What reason, therefore, is there to restrict the effort to benefit others to just one or two objective goods and precisely those that are connected with their autonomy?

As a consequentialist, Brock is not willing to rank autonomy as the highest good, much less declare it the only good. Yet he treats it as the only one relevant to judging parentalism. Otherwise the parentalist should only consider what the subject desires or thinks is good for her. This position requires a deontological base that locates objective goodness only in actions in their conformity to some formal standard. If one believes that conformity to the standard is what defines autonomy, one can argue that autonomy is the only objective good or at least that it is always more important than goods that are the byproducts or extrinsic consequences of actions and goods bestowed on the subject by external agencies.

A complex act of empathy is crucial to deciding whether to engage in parentalism. Parentalism is justified by the benefits it brings the recipient. To assess this, it is not enough to imagine oneself in his shoes; one must imagine oneself as him in his shoes. Quentin Gibson makes this point in discussing the role of sympathetic understanding (*Verstehen*) in social inquiry. It is the task of the inquirer to determine what situations and actions mean to the parties involved. For this she must identify herself with each actor:

> If I were simply to put myself in Napoleon's place, I would imagine myself reacting in ways very different from those in which I know he did. In order to correct this I would have to draw on my already acquired knowledge of Napoleon's character. This is why the metaphor of identifying myself with another person is more adequate than that of putting myself in another's place. The thing is not merely to imagine myself in another *situation*, but to imagine myself being another *person*. This requires as evidence not merely information about how I feel and act in situations of that type, but also information about how he has acted in a great variety of other circumstances. (*Logic of Social Enquiry*, p. 53)

Identification with others is hard and problematic, hence, the method of *Verstehen* provides no shortcut to certainty for the social scientist. The same is clearly the case with the moral intuitions of the parentalist agent: she must try to view her prospective act from the perspective of the recipient, taking into account the latter's sense of his needs. These needs may not be identical with those which she would have if she were in his place. Her grasp of his needs is bound to be shaky to the extent he differs from her.

In the case of Harry, I am assuming that there is something to the cry-for-help concept of suicide. Battin explores this concept and points out that it often dictates hard parentalism. That is, the parentalistic does not confine herself to judging whether the other's reason is impaired and hence needs therapeutic aid in pursuing what he unconsciously wants (the medical model), but tries to persuade him to change what he wants (the cry-for-help model). Battin seems to prefer the former model of parentalism rather than the latter because of its hard parentalism. She goes on, however, to make the controversial claim that even soft parentalism sometimes requires one to facilitate another's suicide and, on the social level, makes rational suicide acceptable.

Chapter 7. The Anatomy of Intervention

Dworkin cites one "noncontingent" or deontological argument in Mill:

> When Mill states that "there is a part of the life of every person who has come to years of discretion, within which the individuality of that person ought to reign uncontrolled either by any other person or the public collectively," he is saying something about what it means to be a person, an autonomous agent. It is because coercing a person for his own good denies this status as an independent entity that Mill objects to it so strongly and in such absolute terms. ("Paternalism," p. 151)

As evidence of this line of reasoning, Dworkin then cites Mill's argument against enforcing contracts in which people sell themselves into slavery (Mill says, "it is not freedom to be allowed to alienate his freedom"). Dworkin does not use these isolated passages as an excuse to make Mill an absolutist, however; it merely suggests to him, with his different premises, that parentalism is justified only to promote or preserve a person's future freedom—for example, by blocking activities that would reduce his future autonomy such as developing a drug dependency, putting himself in the hands of a loan shark, or commiting suicide. In thus maintaining that a person's future autonomy can justify curtailing his present, Dworkin recognizes that autonomy is additive. What merits respect is the aggregate of autonomous acts throughout the person's existence. It is myopic to pitch decisions solely in terms of the effect on his present acts or hypostatize his instantaneous self and ignore his perdurance through time.

What I take to be a strength in Dworkin's analysis is precisely what is wrong with it for Arneson:

> A difficulty attaches to the project of measuring freedom in order to apply the freedom-maximizing principle. Why not ban cigarettes and fried foods on the ground that these shorten the individual's life span and thereby shrink the range of his freedom? Perhaps one could avert this repressive consequence by stipulating that various freedoms must be weighted by their importance to the agent, so that a man who loves fried food may lose more by the denial of the freedom to enjoy a greasy diet than he would gain by the freedom to enjoy a longer, fat-free existence. But this gambit threatens to collapse freedom-maximization into utility-maximization. ("Mill versus Paternalism," p. 474)

This criticism betrays the aspiration of the absolutist to find clean-cut criteria that precipitate categorical judgments. Dworkin sensibly takes account of a fact which makes such simple judgments impossible.

That forestallment of particular acts need not entail a lack of respect for a subject's autonomy is clear when it is done to determine his true wishes or his rationality. This fact is exploited by Beauchamp to concede intuitively justified cases of intervention while defending a strong antiparentalism. First, he restricts his attention to coercive parentalism, proposing this general principle: P justifiably coerces S by intervention A if (but not only if) (a) A protects S against himself; (b) there are indications that S either (i) does not know his own best interest and this is knowable by P or (ii) does know his best interest but is insufficiently motivated to pursue it unless legally required to do so; (c) A achieves a wider range of freedom for S; (d) it avoids an extreme, manifestly unreasonable risk for S; (e) it avoids serious evils which S might cause himself through decisions that are far-reaching, potentially dangerous, and irreversible, where no rational alternative is more highly valued by him; and (f) the general presumption against coercion is outweighed by the significance of the above conditions, which also must outweigh other principles (for example, confidentiality or privacy) that restrict intervention ("Paternalism and Biobehavioral Control," pp. 69–70).

Beauchamp's argument for this complex principle is based on a qualified respect for autonomy (p. 66). When he applies the principle to parentalism, he denies that control of anyone's "mentation" is justified, but he allows some intuitively justified control of their actions by restricting parentalism to coercion and declaring that intervention in substantially nonvoluntary acts is not coercive. He handles all such cases by "Mill's proviso," arguing that it is not an infringement on a subject's liberty to delay him long enough to inform him of dangers or ascertain whether he knows about them. The officer prevents the pedestrian from doing something (such as stepping onto a collapsible bridge and being drowned) but not what he wants to do (cross the river) since this intention is doomed to frustration anyway. Thus Beauchamp believes that Mill's harm principle and the proviso are sufficient to prohibit all parentalism. Justified interventions that block involuntary acts are not parentalistic since they are not coercive. Interventions that block the voluntary actions for the subject's own good are unjustified.

To turn now to criticisms, unless Beauchamp restricts voluntary actions to fully rational ones, the interventions that he allows are limitations of liberty. The subject is prevented from attempting an action and taking the consequences. The fact that the consequences may be different from those that he anticipates does not gainsay that he has been prevented from carrying out his decision. The pedestrian is prevented from stepping onto the bridge and attempting to cross the river, which is all he could undertake in any case. If it is the mere process of deciding and trying to act that is valued in autonomy and not success in reaching one's goals, then frustration of the first steps ensuing on a decision is an infringement on autonomy and prima facie wrong. There is no reason to deny that the infringement is parentalistic. Regardless of what we call such interventions, we need principles of the sort Beauchamp would avoid, ones that balance goods against harms, to decide whether the interventions are justified.

The exclusion of acts that are not adequately informed from those whose obstruction constitutes parentalism severely contracts the scope of antiparentalist rules since the intervener can reasonably set high standards for a subject to be "adequately informed." This is especially true in an age where so many decisions involve an extensive body of specialized knowledge and technical experts are available to make them for other people.

Beauchamp weakens his principle further by extending the category of involuntary to a wide range of actions, including "those performed under behavior control devices such as subliminal advertising, and drug therapy, or in circumstances involving alcoholic stimulation, mob-inspired enthusiasm, retardation, and psychotic compulsion" (p. 75). Thus he limits the ban on parentalism to interventions when the subject is rational in many respects and allows intervention when he is nonrational in any of several. He does limit intervention to the time required to bring the subject into a state of full rationality, but since the standard for full rationality is high, the provision could justify the indefinite protraction of restraints. In general he comes the long way around to toleration of most of the forms of intervention which a straightforward consideration of consequences would dictate.

Among those who point out the serious consequences of the dichotomous concept of competence for the incompetent is Murphy. He recognizes that autonomy is a matter of degree. At the upper end of the continuum is the fully rational person, "an ideal norm, the model of a fully competent agent as one who acquaints himself with all available relevant evidence, who is unmoved by emotional bias or internal or external compulsion, and who has all his rational faculties intact. No existing person conforms completely to this model, and all of us have some areas in which we blatantly fail to conform—e.g. assessing the beauty of our own children." At the lower end of the continuum lie total incompetents, who "blatantly fail to conform to this model in areas . . . so basic and important to human life that failures in these areas are likely to be irreversibly self-destructive" ("Incompetence and Paternalism," p. 478). To make headway toward distinguishing people between those who fall so far short of rationality as to require extensive care and the large majority who are less than fully rational but competent and to specify restrictions on parentalism toward the latter, some way to assess competence must be adopted. The hard cases lie in the vicinity of the boundary between incompetence and bare competence. As Murphy remarks, the most important question is, "When in doubt, which way should we err—on the side of safety or on the side of liberty?" The intuition of most authors is that we should err on the side of liberty in view of the dire consequences for those who are judged and treated as incompetent. The valuable point is that levels of autonomy have different values, and increments and decrements at different levels should not be assigned equal importance when autonomy has to be weighed against other goods, such as life, health, possessions, and moral development. This, together with the fact that the lines demarking various levels of competence are blurred, precludes rigid rules for sharply delimited categories of parentalistic behavior.

Authors who have written about parentalism provide little in the way of analysis of autonomy. Benn is one who has something to say, primarily by way of a discussion of defects. He classifies lack of self-control under three headings: (1) defects of practical rationality in compulsive behavior such as kleptomania: the person "does not choose—he is impelled by inner drives"; (2) defects of epistemic rationality in paranoia, where the person's belief-structure "is so disordered that his choices are made from mere phantasy-options"; (3) defects of psychic continuity, either as a believer, for example, the schizophrenic who "lacks consciousness of himself as originating changes in the world," or as an agent, for example, the dissociated person "where facets of the subject's personality split into multiple consciousnesses" ("Freedom, Autonomy and the Concept of a Person," pp. 113–115). Other authors recognize that states not considered pathological curtail autonomy, for example, enslavement to custom and overpowering temptation, fear, anger, or love.

Practical implications of Benn's distinctions are explored by Fred D'Agostino in the psychiatric context. He specifies four categories of human beings: (a) those who lack the biologically based potentiality for freedom (rational choice) by virtue of congenital defects, injury, or irreversible mental illness; (b) those who have the potential but are not realizing it (normal infants and some mentally ill); (c) autarchic persons, who are capable of rational choice but do not exercise it (habitual conformists and some eccentrics, political dissidents, neurotics, psychopaths, rational would-be suicides, and cult members); and (d) autonomous persons, who habitually exercise rational choice. The mark of rationality is the way the agent reacts to the consequences that ensue from his decisions. He behaves irrationally "if, given the opportunity, he fails to revise or abandon the false belief he holds, and on which he may act, or if he fails to revise or abandon the unattainable end which he pursues" ("Mill, Paternalism and Psychiatry," p. 325). Development is movement from potential personhood through autarchy to autonomy. D'Agostino observes that people sometimes engage in activities that undermine their development and asserts that parentalistic intervention is generally necessary for the development of autarchy, but intervention in the affairs of an autarchic agent generally undermines his opportunity to become autonomous. The aim of psychiatric treatment is to foster the patient's development. Only in the case of those who lack the biological potential for autonomy should it be relief from suffering. D'Agostino observes, "A humanistically acceptable principle of psychiatric paternalism holds . . . that *coercive psychiatric intervention may be appropriate for those persons who irreversibly lack a biologically-based potential for freedom, and is warranted for those who, by reason of mental illness, are currently non-autarchic, and can be restored to autarchy by the treatment proposed*" (p. 328). He thus would prohibit coercive psychiatric intervention in the lives of potentially autarchic persons if it would not be effective in restoring them to autarchy and altogether in the lives of autarchic persons. He thus does not envisage attempts to promote goods other than autonomy for autarchic and autonomous persons.

D'Agostino's strictures on coercive psychiatric parentalism illegitimately move from the generalization that parentalism usually retards the development of autonomy to an absolute ban on such measures. He neglects the availability of less coercive parentalistic measures, and he implicitly denies that other values, such as the life of the potential suicide, may overrule a patient's interest in development and justify psychiatric intervention.

Discussions in the literature of the role of rational persuasion in intervention are rare. Benn makes a point similar to Mill's about cases in which a person changes another's desires by instructing him about the objective limits of his resources or the opportunity costs of actions, thereby discouraging him from attempting difficult or impossible tasks. He distinguishes this from frustrating the person's wishes:

> "Frustrating" includes creating conditions in which, as in deterrence situations, Alf is supplied with a reason he did not have for not doing what he might otherwise have done; it does not include informing him of what reasons there already are. For to tell Alf what he *cannot* do is not to prevent his doing it. And if the information does not show that he *cannot* do it, but only that the course is less attractive than he thought, then he is still at liberty to do it if he wishes. ("Freedom, Autonomy and the Concept of a Person," p. 110)

This, however, is not all there is to it. A situation of action is a function of both objective and subjective factors. By adding to a subject's knowledge of probable consequences, one alters her perception of possibilities and the conditions of her choice.

A number of authors treat natural and permanent impairments as equivalent to occasional and transient ones, but it is important to distinguish the two. Ten remarks that legislation providing long-term control of groups of people should be reserved for those with gross deficiencies and in need of permanent care ("Paternalism and Morality," p. 60). This is because of the difficulty of changing laws and the crudity of the distinctions which the law is able to make.

Chapter 8. The Value of Autonomy

How should we respond to Feinberg's ascription of absolute rights to human beings on the basis of "an inviolate dignity, which includes the negative rights not to be brainwashed, not to be made a docile instrument for the purposes of others, and not to be converted into a domesticated animal"? In describing candidates for absolute rights, Feinberg does not propose autonomy. His candidates are positive welfare rights (a minimal share in basic goods that are not unlimited by nature) and negative passive rights (not to be tortured, treated inhumanely, or exploited and degraded). He does suggest that the right to dignity or respect is absolute in some sense, and his list of the kinds of treatment incompatible with dignity suggests that it presupposes autonomy; but the list likewise suggests that impositions of limitations on a person's autonomy are not categorically prohibited by his dignity. He observes that dignity precludes only actions that would reduce the subject's autonomy to the level of the animal. Inviolate dignity entails the negative right not to be brainwashed, not to be made a docile instrument for the purposes of others and not to be converted into a domesticated animal. This set of rights is probably the only one that is human in the strongest sense—that is, unalterable, "absolute" (exceptionless and nonconflictive), and universally and peculiarly human (*Rights, Justice, and the Bounds of Liberty*, p. 32).

The right not to be brainwashed might justify intervention to prevent a person from voluntarily submitting to that sort of treatment, for example, rescuing him from a religious cult and "deprogramming" him. If this is so, respect for dignity does not imply a categorical prohibition of parentalistic actions. More generally, when we ask whether various forms of parentalism infringe on rights, we must also consider the possibility that some forms may be required by them. If, for example, people have the positive right to enjoy a certain level of well-being, other people – those to whose care they are assigned by virtue of a social role such as legislator, custodian, guardian, or physician – have the duty to provide benefits even without the consent of the right-holder. More generally, if there are positive as well as negative rights, we need to formulate rules for parentalism that balance the two sorts of rights against one another.

We are surely profoundly repelled by the thought of human beings reduced to the level of domesticated animals, and we would deem a society that practiced genetic engineering or systematic brainwashing grotesquely deformed. The slippery slope down to the Brave New World makes us suspicious of milder forms of thought-control and indoctrination. Yet consider a boundary situation. A society is plagued by severe overpopulation, poverty, disease, and malnutrition. Its ancient traditions prevent any solution without wholesale reindoctrination of its members. Human dignity should be respected, but which shows the less respect – abandoning people to cruel and inhuman conditions, or imposing something like brainwashing on them? Values such as life, health, and shelter – which are taken for granted in ordinary life – become critical when threatened, and then talk of "dignity" becomes problematic.

The only discussion in the literature that complains about the vagueness of the concepts of a respect and autonomy is Kasachoff's. The vagueness explains the disputes that arise when authors base their positions on respect for autonomy. VanDeVeer rejects the Autonomy Preservation Principle, which he ascribes to Dworkin, because it sanctions intervention to preserve or enhance a person's autonomy in face of his desire to relinquish it (*Paternalistic Intervention*, pp. 134–135). He answers the questions about respect for autonomy in such a way as to fit principles to his particular set of intuitions. ("Intuitions," "counterintuitions," "what seems reasonable," and so on occur more than a dozen times in each of his key chapters.) These intuitions are disparate with mine, as well as with those of other autonomy-oriented philosophers. In the end, VanDeVeer fails to clarify what is involved in respect despite an industrious effort.

Chapter 9. The Role of Consent

Carter maintains that the subject's disposition to consent to an intervention waives his right to autonomy even if he never actually expresses consent ("Justifying Paternalism," pp. 134–135). The first form of disposition which she mentions, of the subject to say "yes" when asked if he wants to be helped, can carry weight similar to actual consent if the helper has grounds for believing that the disposition is present, though it is easy to imagine many cases in which she would not have such grounds and hence perforce be acting without consideration of the recipient's wishes.

Carter's second disposition, to consent upon receipt of a relevant piece of information, is problematic. She presumably has in mind relatively minor pieces of information ("He would surely approve if he knew a little more about what I am doing"), but her principle could be extended to almost any intervention by the enthusiastic parentalist ("I could get his approval if I could just talk to him for a while," where a while is an hour, a day, a year, or a lifetime). Even where minor information would win consent, the value of the unexercised disposition is unclear. How could it compensate for the consequences of active dissent?

Carter adds another condition that takes her theory further down the road of implausibility. The dispositions that she accepts as waiving the right to autonomy may develop only after the interventions they justify. The subject's approval at time t_3 retroactively alienates his right to autonomy at t_2. Combining this with the notion of waiver by disposition, the theory implies that a subsequent disposition to approve alienates the right even if the disposition is never activated, for instance, if the subject dies without being asked or receiving information that would have caused her to approve. Let us see what lures Carter into the untenable thesis of post facto justification. She recognizes that there are permanent incompetents who are never able to give informed consent, but need parentalistic care: "[They] are unable to understand or practice satisfactorily the basic requirements of survival, and so their lives would be at worst in constant peril, and at best grossly unhappy, if it were not for intervention on the part of others" (p. 144). To salvage the thesis that the right to autonomy is absolute, Carter is tempted to assert that incompetents have no action rights because they lack the ability to deliberate, hence they have nothing to waive. She recognizes, however, that this would saddle her theory with the untoward consequence that "for certain actions, *temporary* incompetents too will have either weakened or no action rights" (p. 144) and would open the door to far more parentalism than she wants. To maintain the absolute right to autonomy for ordinary persons, Carter denies that action rights are negated by temporary incompetence. She asserts that he can alienate his rights by approving their abridgement retroactively. If he is incompetent and opposes an action at t_2, but regains competence and approves of it at t_3, he alienates his rights at t_2 and Carter thinks that this makes the action permissible. Even if the person never regains competence, the approval that he would have given if he had regained competence does likewise. Thus she comes to the thesis of retroactive waiving of rights.

Chapter 10. Varieties of Antiparentalism

Kleinig argues that an individual flourishes—develops traits and expresses them in action in a way that gives him a distinctively human existence—only through interaction with others who flourish in the same way. Moreover, he flourishes only if he helps others do so. This observation might provide the germ for a conception of care and solicitude. However, consider the ways of contributing to others: by being an inspiration, an instrument for their endeavors, a partner in collective enterprises, and an alter ego with whom they can identify (*Paternalism*, pp. 41–44). These contributions tend to be returned in kind and give each person a stake in the flourishing of others. Help provided in the spirit of self-interest is hardly solicitude in our sense.

Schrag refers to the absolute position that human freedom is an inviolable right as the "customary view" and maintains that it implies absolute antiparentalism: "in a just society paternalism (the coercion of people in their own interest) is virtually absent. . . . [T]he human right to freedom extends to any person at any time" ("Child in the Moral Order," pp. 168–169). When he attributes the customary view to "us," Schrag would seem to include himself, but the difficulties he exposes suggest that he does not. In any event, his primary purpose is to point out problems that beset one ingredient of the "liberal tradition": it improperly classifies children as subhuman in order to justify abridgements of their freedom while giving lip service to a human right to autonomy. The same maneuver in dealing with retardates and others consigned to custodial care allows liberal society to maintain a facade of categorical opposition to parentalism toward full human beings while sanctioning widespread parentalistic practices.

Schrag's point is that the line that society draws between humans and subhumans is arbitrary and that the practical effect of categorizing large groups of the species as less than fully human is intolerable. His position may be that all biological humans are endowed with an absolute right to autonomy whatever their capacities, but his reasons for doing this are not clear. Alternatively, he may be conceding just the opposite—that the right of anyone to autonomy is contingent and can be overruled by considerations of welfare.

Another hint of absolute rights is found in Buchanan's reference to two types of argument against medical parentalism. He advances a utilitarian argument—that parentalistic physicians often fail to help patients in the way they intend—because he thinks this meets physicians on their own ground; but he prefers arguments based on moral rights rooted in a conception of personal autonomy. He finds such arguments more interesting and thinks they provide the strongest arguments against parentalism ("Medical Paternalism," p. 370).

Pollock's analysis proceeds as follows. First, he stipulates that genuine moral oughts are categorical and overriding. He defines what is moral by the freedom principle: "each person ought to grant to other persons an equal right to be free. . . . Thus, interactions between myself and others should be based on mutual consent" (*Freedom Principle*, p. 13). Morality thus is negative: it tells us only that we must not infringe on the freedom of others. It sanctions infliction of pain and distress as long as they do not abridge the victim's freedom. On the other hand, it does not sanction abridgement to provide goods.

Pollock does not claim that it is intuitively evident that autonomy is the highest good, but rather that this status explains our intuition about how we should treat other persons. He thinks of autonomy as pursuit of what one values. It requires the ability to anticipate the future, to act in the light of values and thereby give meaning to one's life. A person is a being with these abilities. Freedom is necessary to exercise autonomy. All and only persons, therefore, are covered by the freedom principle. Pollock thinks of freedom in the negative and external sense of absence of interference by force, threat, and deception. These induce one to pursue what he does not (otherwise) value or most value. Pollock recognizes that not all persons use their autonomy to the fullest:

> There are a number of reasons why a person may fail to act in accordance with his own values. A person might be under the influence of a strong emotion such as anger or fear. His rationality might be impaired by the use of a drug. He might act contrary to his values out of ignorance (e.g., he doesn't know that the bridge he is crossing will collapse). Loss of consciousness may render him unable to act at all. (p. 28)

Such a person lacks "integrity." Autonomy is valuable to its possessor, but he deserves credit only for autonomy with integrity. Similarly, Pollock defines "authenticity" as the pursuit of values which one gets from his own experience and reflection. Presumably Pollock believes also that authenticity deserves respect and unauthentic autonomy does not.

Pollock does not specify the degree of emotion or impairment that makes interferences by others not a violation of the freedom principle. Everyone suffers these in some degree. If the freedom principle did not apply where there is slight emotion or impairment, it would debar practically no interferences in people's lives. This is not what Pollock has in mind, but he does not make clear what he does have in mind.

Pollock defines parentalism and provides a principle for its justification in the same passage:

> A paternalistic act is one in which concern for the welfare of another person is the primary reason for interfering with that person. In other words, paternalism is interfering with that person for that person's *own* good. Paternalistic acts do not violate the freedom principle when the interference causes the person to behave in accordance with his own values. In this case, the agent is not denying the recipient an equal right to pursue his own good; instead the agent is helping the latter to behave in accordance with his own values. (p. 27)

Some parentalistic acts are permissible, but they cannot be obligatory since the parentalist is helping the subject achieve other values rather than respecting her liberty.

To assess this position, we need to examine what Pollock means by a person's values. His account suffers from the ambiguity that besets others who assign extreme value to autonomy. Are a person's values what she does value, or what she ought to and would value if she knew all there is to know? Are her values what seems good to her at the moment or only in times of reflection? Pollock implies the objectivity of values when he remarks, "Value is discovered, not conferred [by the valuer]. Persons find in their experience that certain things are valuable" (p. 112). If this is true, there are all sorts of values of a person which she has not discovered and even her most reflective wants may not be her true values. People seldom pursue exactly what is best for them, and if it is a person's pursuit of true values that others must not interrupt, a wide range of parentalism is allowed. Parentalists only need know better than their recipient what is truly good for her or, even more permissively, they only need to have good reason to think they know better. This would seem to be an untoward implication for Pollock, and in one passage he implies that autonomy in any form, whether in pursuit of what seems good to the agent or what truly is, is the supreme good:

> You may know that a person's life would be better (according to his own values) if he *chooses* to do X. However, it does not follow that his life would be better if he is *compelled* to do X. For one thing, he may resent being coerced, and this resentment may prevent him from understanding that the coercion is (supposedly) for his own good. And this resentment has a reasonable basis. In order to *live* a good life, one must be responsible for one's acts. If the good things in a person's life are the result of coercion, then he cannot take credit for the goodness of his life. A person must be self-directing for *his* life to be good. (p. 30)

This says that nothing is good for a person unless she acquires it by her own efforts, and so no one should interfere with her autonomy no matter how low its level. The claim is absurd, and perhaps one should not take Pollock strictly at his word. In view of his acceptance of some parentalism, he might concede that autonomy at its lower levels is not worth more than many of the goods that others can provide.

However, there is a deeper problem. I understand Pollock to say that the parentalism *is* justified if it promotes the recipient's true values though the subject herself is not pursuing them. But the parentalist can only act on what he believes those values to be, and Pollock does not require that the parentalist's beliefs constitute knowledge. He only asks (quite sensibly) that the parentalist have good reason to think his judgment of it is better than his beneficiary's. Yet in most instances another person will have better evidence about a subject's settled preferences than about her true good. In Pollock's illustrations of permissible interference, he implies that a parentalist is justified in promoting the subject's settled preferences in face of her transient wants, and he takes for granted that the parentalist is then promoting her true values. This vacillation about what is meant by the subject's "own values" leaves unsettled what the parentalist is to do if he has reason to think that he knows the subject's true interests and these differ from her settled preferences.

Pollock's failure to resolve the ambiguity leaves his judgments about particular forms of parentalism hanging in air. In particular, he fails to show how the freedom principle entails categorical condemnation of governmental parentalism in such measures as social security, occupational licensure, and control of drugs. The ambiguity of his concept of autonomy allows him to use the freedom principle to ratify his prejudices against "big brother" (what more sympathetic critics would call the supportive state) while avoiding espousal of the most egregiously heartless measures.

In "Mill versus Paternalism," Arneson advances an extreme form of anti-parentalism in the course of criticizing exceptions to the bans on intervention allowed by Dworkin and Feinberg. Feinberg permits a weak form of legal parentalism: "the state has the right to prevent self-regarding harmful conduct only when it is substantially nonvoluntary or when temporary intervention is necessary to establish whether it is voluntary or not" ("Legal Paternalism," p. 113). Actions are fully voluntary when they are informed, uncoerced, and deliberate and when they express settled values. Arneson complains that " 'Fully voluntary' has here become almost equivalent to 'fully rational' " ("Mill versus Paternalism," p. 484) and restriction of the ban on parentalism to interference with fully rational actions would reduce it to triviality. Few human actions are fully rational, and these few are not the kind with which anyone would be tempted to interfere. Feinberg recognizes this danger and extends his ban on interference to "almost-but-not-fully voluntary choices as well, and probably to some substantially non-voluntary ones" ("Legal Paternalism," pp. 111–112). Nevertheless, his focus on voluntary choices reflects a recognition that a large part of the value of autonomy lies in its rationality or potential rationality, not in the process of choosing itself. From his opposition to Feinberg, one infers that Arneson posits an absolute right of the individual to choice per se at whatever level of rationality.

The intuition that it is rational choice in the end that is truly precious informs Dworkin's position and is the target of Arneson's criticism. The curtailments of present autonomy that Dworkin authorizes because they enhance future autonomy are precisely the ones that interfere with less rational choices to make room for more rational ones. Whether or not fully rational choice is a supreme value and should be guaranteed as an inviolable right, it is obvious that the value of substantially nonrational choices is less than absolute. There is no intuitive justification for putting lower grade autonomy in lexical position ahead of other goods that would suffer through a strong ban on paternalism. Yet that is exactly what Arneson does in criticism of Dworkin. He urges absolute respect for minimal autonomy. He would ban interference with substantially nonvoluntary and nonrational acts even to promote future more rational ones.

This decision to pitch the concept of autonomy low leads Arneson to focus attention on forms of autonomy that can be viewed as a social benefit ("something that institutional arrangements might secure for individuals") rather than as a character ideal ("something that persons might achieve [for themselves]") ("Mill versus Paternalism," p. 475). It is possible to provide social autonomy by agreeing not to interfere in one another's lives, but this does not assure personal autonomy at the ideal or a high level. Personal autonomy consists in acting according to principles the agent has developed for herself. Some people with a great deal of liberty lack the capability of governing themselves, and some people who achieve a high level of personal autonomy exercise it in prison or in other circumstances where they enjoy little social autonomy. Hence, personal autonomy does not require protection against parentalism, whereas social autonomy does require and deserve it. Exactly what is the social benefit that Arneson would guarantee? – "[A] person lives autonomously to the extent that he is not forcibly prevented from acting on his voluntary self-regarding choices except when his prior commitments bind him to accept such forcible prevention" (p. 475). And what is voluntary? – "[A] person acts voluntarily if and only if his choice of the act (a) would not be abandoned if he were apprised of all the act's unforeseeable consequences, (b) does not proceed from an emotional state so troubled as to preclude the full use of the reasoning faculty, and (c) does not occur under conditions of external coercion or compulsion" (p. 482). These definitions undercut the protection Arneson wants to provide against many forms of parentalism. Which of our actions would we not have altered in *some* way if we had been apprized of *all* their consequences? Which are not chosen in emotional states that preclude *full* use of reasoning faculties? Which are totally uncoerced in the sense that costs are not weighted in *some* way by the actions of others? What actions then are protected?

Arneson's intention is clear. He wants to protect a wide range of actions from interference. Individuals who do not foresee some of the consequences of their behavior, neglect to deliberate, or succumb to mild pressure should be allowed to act as they choose. Agreeing with what he takes to be Mill's view, he says "in the sphere of self-regarding action people have the right to make their own mistakes and suffer the consequences, without interference from society. . . . [P]ersons have a right to choose even stupid and degrading life courses without leaving themselves liable to legitimate restrictions of their freedom by others" (p. 485). Arneson thus would guarantee the right to autonomy. What this means is obscure because he characterizes autonomy in terms of only some of its dimensions. His minimalist conception, together with his preconception that autonomy deserves absolute respect, prevents him from seeing the justification of many kinds of parentalism that is obvious to others. In assessing his position, we must ask ourselves whether what we intuitively respect in autonomy is a low level of self-management and whether our respect for it is strong enough to place minimal autonomy first in our constellation of values.

Moreover, Arneson's distinction between autonomy as a social benefit and a personal achievement underestimates the role of society in the latter. While a person must actively engage in the processes that develop personal autonomy and a strong person can exercise it in the face of hostile conditions, society plays an important role throughout: it provides the education that cultivates the ability to make rational and informed choices, and it provides the options that make the ability valuable to its possessor. Parentalistic care is essential to both helping many individuals achieve personal autonomy and providing them favorable conditions in which to exercise it. By casting his discussion in terms of a static dichotomy between personal achievement and social benefit, Arneson conceals the social contribution to the personal achievement and the parentalistic element in that contribution.

Arneson attempts to establish credentials for his position by the implausible thesis that Mill espouses it. His line of argument seems to be that Mill categorically opposes parentalism and hence must presuppose the absolute value of autonomy, though he carelessly neglects to say so. This interpretation puts Arneson in the company of those described by Douglas Husak: "the prospects of formulating a general utilitarian case against paternalism appear so remote that many philosophers who combine sympathy for Mill with an anti-paternalistic bias are prepared to read much of *On Liberty* as a curious departure from utilitarianism" ("Paternalism and Autonomy," p. 27).

Arneson ascribes to Mill his own view that humans possess an inviolable right to autonomy in self-affecting matters regardless of circumstances, and hence the immorality of parentalism follows deductively, independent of the consequences of the particular act. In his later essay Arneson persists in the opinion that Mill's antiparentalism is absolute: "One implication of the liberty principle is *anti-paternalism*: restriction of a person's liberty to carry out a voluntarily chosen course of conduct should never be imposed for the purpose of benefitting either that person herself or others who voluntarily consent to be affected by that conduct" ("Paternalism, Utility, and Fairness," p. 409). Now, there is no question that Mill's initial statement of his Principle of Liberty is bald and uncompromising and, apart from context, countenances extreme antipaternalism. However, as Sankowski notes, Mill speaks only of public parentalism in which "society" (through government and public opinion) limits the liberty of the individual by "compulsion and control" (coercion). At most we can impute absolute antiparentalism to him in this narrow area.

Should we impute even this? Uncertainty about what Mill is getting at is reflected in Marvin Glass's reference to his "quasi-absolute opposition to paternalism" ("Not Going to Hell on One's Own," p. 471. How can "absolute" be "quasi"?). Arneson repeatedly refers to Mill's ban on paternalism as "absolute." Mill himself uses the word sparingly: he asserts that his "one very simple principle" is entitled to "govern absolutely" the use of compulsion and control. He maintains that in that part of a person's conduct which concerns himself "his independence is, of right, absolute." He declares that no society is completely free where liberties of consciousness, taste, and association do not exist "absolute and unqualified" (*On Liberty*, pp. 223ff). These passages occur in the vicinity of the statement of his principle. The larger context and overall argument suggest that Mill is speaking loosely and hyperbolically in order to introduce his claims in a dramatic way. He is saying emphatically that parentalism is prima facie undesirable and should be categorically banned in some areas (of people, societies, times and places, which he does not clearly circumscribe) in view of social conditions there. And that it must be vigorously combated when it is wrong because of its beneficent appearance.

Neither Mill's premises nor the implications that Mill draws provide support for Arneson's criticisms. The latter asserts, "when Mill says 'paternalism sometimes' in chapter 4 he is retracting the robust assertion of 'paternalism never!' in chapter 1" ("Mill versus Paternalism," p. 473). Not only does Arneson imply that Mill could not remember by chapter 4 what he wrote in chapter 1, despite his testimony that he rewrote *On Liberty* several times with the help of Harriet Taylor, he ignores the structure of Mill's argument. What he sees as Mill's "retractions" are merely progressive qualifications of a principle that is stated simply and categorically at the outset for dramatic effect. Thus, immediately after he states his principle, Mill explicitly restricts it to civilized societies and particularly the democracies of Europe and America threatened by tyranny of the majority. He concedes that ancient commonwealths surrounded by enemies were wise to restrict private conduct. Later he explains that his principle does not apply to children or civilized adults who are "delirious, or in some state of excitement or absorption incompatible with the full use of the reflecting faculty" (p. 294). His list of exceptions is substantial and open-ended. His ban is thus anything but absolute.

Even if we did not have Mill's expressions of commitment to utilitarianism in other works, we have his firm statement in *On Liberty* that in trying to raise a barrier of moral conviction against antilibertarian tendencies of his age, "I forego any advantage which could be derived to my argument from the idea of abstract right, as a thing independent of utility" (p. 224). One important barrier that he might want to raise is a socially defined system of rights, but rights as utilitarian tools have a different character from rights deduced from an abstract principle.

The one passage in *On Liberty* that hints at a deontological conception occurs when Mill argues that society should not enforce contracts in which people sell themselves into bondage:

> The reason for not interfering, unless for the sake of others, with a person's voluntary acts, is consideration for his liberty. His voluntary choice is evidence that what he so chooses is desirable, or at the least endurable, to him, and his good is on the whole best provided for by allowing him to take his own means of pursuing it. But by selling himself for a slave, he abdicates his liberty; he foregoes any future use of it beyond the single act. . . . The principle of freedom cannot require that he should be free not to be free. It is not freedom, to be allowed to alienate his freedom. (pp. 299–300)

This is (in Arneson's terms) a "wayward" passage for my interpretation of Mill. In defense of putting it aside, I will point out the following. First, it is obscure exactly what Mill is getting at. Second, it would be strange if he were to introduce an entirely new, deontological, and nonutilitarian ground for his principle in his last chapter, "Applications." Third, his practical proposal is that society not enforce contracts of slavery rather than that individuals be prevented from entering into them. If he were intent on forcing autonomy on individuals on absolutist grounds, he would have urged that additional step. Fourth, it is palpably false that it is not a free act to agree to forego future freedom, so Mill either mispeaks himself or puts his point in a misleading way because he is enamored of a snappy phrase. Finally, there are ample utilitarian grounds for forbidding the enforcement of slavery contracts, so he does not need other reasons to condemn what his intuitions tell him is atrocious.

Arneson admits that there is no evidence that Mill puts autonomy in first position among human values, and he observes,

> It would seem that nothing short of a lexicographic ordering of values placing autonomy first would suffice to guarantee that one's condemnation of paternalism will not admit of exceptions. Short of this extreme weighting, one can say that the more one values autonomy, the less Mill's espousal of libertarianism is subject to contingency. My last suggestion is that insofar as Mill relies on firm contingency his position is secure. Perhaps we could summarize Mill so: given that autonomy is a great value, paternalistic restrictions will never (or hardly ever) advance the interests of the individuals they are intended to benefit. ("Mill versus Paternalism," p. 481)

"Absolute," then, does not mean absolute, noncontingent, or even universal. Yet Arneson still refers to the ban on parentalism, which he imputes to Mill, as "exceptionless." If it were, Mill would have to think this was due to a marvelous accident: no exceptions can be found in the contingencies of human life in all of the historical eras he examines. In logical form, Mill's ban on parentalism can only be conditional, not categorical, within the framework of his ethical and social principles.

One author of absolutist bent who does not judge that autonomy is essential to happiness is Regan: "witness the case of nuns, soldiers, and others who manage to be happy inside of total institutions" ("Paternalism, Freedom, Identity, and Commitment," p. 114). He can detach autonomy from happiness because he identifies the latter with pleasure per se. But happiness is more; it involves satisfactions only provided by autonomous acts. Moreover, nuns and the others do not cede all their freedom. Hence, Regan's attempt to establish freedom as a value independent of happiness is misconceived.

Kleinig does not state his own position in a formal way, but he does argue that deontological arguments do not suffice for the rejection of strong parentalism and by criticizing them he is attempting to "create some moral space" for parentalism (*Paternalism*, p. 74). His criticisms bespeak some form of consequentialism. Concern with consequences is also evident, though not consistently, in the limitations that Kleinig proposes for (justified) parentalism: (1) the parentalist should choose the means for achieving the benefit sought for the subject which involves the least restrictions on her freedom; (2) he should act on the presumption that she knows her own good and try to further her goals rather than what he thinks is objectively best for her; and (3) he should adopt measures with the greatest likelihood of achieving the goal without harmful side effects for her or third parties (pp. 74–77).

Taken at face value, (2) is incompatible with consequentialism and opposed to the position which I have proposed. Kleinig himself points out a difficulty with the maxim: "Generally it requires that we do not interfere with what people voluntarily desire for themselves. But this is based on the rebuttable presumption that even if people's self-regarding decisions are not (in some 'objective' sense) the best decisions they might make, at least they are *their best* decisions. However, our frailties are such that this is not always the case" (p. 75).

Rather than drawing the obvious conclusion, that the parentalist should promote the beneficiary's objective good regardless of her decisions, Kleinig proposes a set of restrictions that maximize the probability that his acts will accord with what would be her decisions were she not irrational or encumbered. Kleinig believes that the parentalist should honor her settled wishes and the decisions that best reflect her persona even if these are not directed toward her objective welfare. If this is Kleinig's position, the consequences of actions are *not* what is crucial for him. The person's right to autonomy or her "basic freedom" to carry out her plan of life should be honored even if it is disastrous.

Moreover, Kleinig confesses that he is impressed by the deontologist's respect for moral agency, and he advances wholesale criticisms of consequentialism. In a puzzling remark, he says,

> We might, in conclusion, question whether consequentialist attempts at justification are really concerned with paternalism. . . . [I]mpositions are paternalistic to the extent that they are designed to secure a person's good, as an end. But it is not someone's good, as an end, that constitutes the focus of much

consequentialism. It is a more general, impersonal end, such as happiness or freedom which is the end, and to which a particular person's good is the means or in which it at best is an ingredient. . . . Of course, consequentialism may be individualized, so that the happiness or freedom which it is proposed to maximize is the happiness or freedom of the individual who is imposed on. But in such cases we may wonder about the 'purity' of the consequentialism. (p. 55)

It is not clear to what consequentialist theories the first quotation refers. In any case, my position belongs among the second. What counts is the objective good of the recipient. Of course, a parentalistic act may harm third parties and be unjustified, so the standard of general happiness fairly shared is relevant to the concrete act, but it is the subject's good that is relevant to evaluating it qua parentalistic.

Hobson provides a short and neat strong antiparentalism in an article that can be viewed as an overview of the deontological perspective. He endorses the Gert and Culver definition of parentalism with its provision that a parentalistic act violates a moral rule. For Hobson that means parentalism per se involves a violation of the right of the subject to liberty or freedom. He believes that it does so even when the subject is functioning at a low level of autonomy, so he apparently believes that all human beings have an absolute right to autonomy. However, Hobson is not an absolutist in regard to parentalism. He recognizes that freedom, and presumably autonomy, varies in value according to the individual's level of rationality. Thus, he announces, "I will be treating freedom as an important but not an absolute value and one that may on occasion be overriden for the sake of overall beneficial effects for the subject of the paternalistically required action" ("Another Look at Paternalism," p. 295). Implicit here is the notion that diminutions in autonomy can intelligibly be weighed against other goods and harms. Hobson proposes the following as "jointly necessary and together sufficient" for overriding liberty: (1) the subject is not able to make a rational decision about his best interests by virtue of some special feature that prevents rational deliberation, or he is ignorant of relevant facts, and (2) the paternalistic interference is necessary to avoid serious harm befalling the subject which outweighs any harm (loss of liberty, for example) brought about by the interference (p. 297). Hobson contends that these criteria "get to the heart of the matter by bringing out the two central features relevant to justifying paternalism, namely the sort of person we are dealing with and the beneficial consequences to be brought about. They essentially capture our common sense intuitions of those factors which are involved in acceptable interference with others for their own sake" (p. 301). In criticism, I see no reason to restrict overriding benefits to protection from harms and exclude provision of positive goods.

Hobson requires the parentalistic act to be necessary to meet a threat to the subject's basic needs. He distinguishes three sorts of such needs (pp. 297-299). The first category is physical—"those things necessary for a minimum level of physical well-being." The second category is psychological—"those factors that are necessary to the maintenance of a minimum level of mental stability and emotional well-being" without which the person "would be seriously hindered in regard to almost any goal he wished to attain." These two sets of goods appear to be objective in the sense I have defined. They are "minimally necessary to . . . a worthwhile level of survival" whether or not the subject realizes it. Hobson seems to condone judgments about what is best for the subject even when the subject does not desire it. Hobson's third category of basic needs are personal—"such things as fundamental religious beliefs, career aspirations, or personal possessions." He may be thinking of these in the objective sense also since they can include "things [the subject] does not necessarily see the importance of at the time," but he immediately observes that the most diverse things such as great wealth, popularity, and success in a sport "could conceivably come under the heading of basic needs if they happened to become of overriding importance to a particular person." Surely not all of these qualify as objectively necessary for worthwhile survival. Thus many personal goods seem to be subjective.

That there is confusion at this point in Hobson's analysis is revealed by his account of his first criterion, that the subject be unable to make rational decisions about his own best interests. By the ability to make rational decisions Hobson might mean capabilities and information necessary to know what is best for himself—that is, what is objectively good. However, he has a much more restricted concept of rationality: "being able to decide what are one's goals or where one's interests lie, knowing the means towards achieving these goals or realizing these interests, and knowing how to act accordingly given one's own particular capacities" (p. 297). A person could possess all of these and still aim at what would be harmful to a worthwhile level of survival for himself. Hence, Hobson is attributing the right to liberty to people with the most self-harmful goals and plans. This interpretation is borne out by his catalogue of the classes of individuals who do not meet the conditions of rational choice and hence may be subjected to parentalistic care: those "(a) too young to understand the issues involved; (b) suffering from mental illness or temporary mental disturbance as a result of shock, terror, drunkenness etc., or (c) mentally deficient as a result of congenital retardation, accident or senility" (p. 298).

The implications of Hobson's premises, the ascription of an important though not absolute right to liberty to everyone including incompetents and the requirement that the individual's basic needs as conceived by the individual must be threatened to override the right, lead him to condemn many of the acts of parentalism which my principle sanctions. According to him, parentalism is seldom justified when the parentalist knows the subject intimately. It is almost never justified when, as in the case of legal parentalism, the parentalist does not know the subjects. These conclusions violate my intuitive sense of cases.

Moreover, Hobson's account for the difference between the two contexts, personal and public parentalism, is fundamentally misconceived. He traces it to what the parentalist can know about what the subject wants or would want if she is minimally informed and rational, not in the parentalist's ability to provide what is objectively good for her. Knowledge of the subject's wants is clearly more accessible in the case of personal parentalism; the ability to provide her objective good is not always greater there than in public parentalism.

Chapter 11. VanDeVeer's Consent-Based Antiparentalism

Kleinig reviews five arguments for justification by consent and notes that they have varying import. Appeals to a subject's prior consent and real will "endeavor to show how, by virtue of their being consented to, some acts of paternalism involve impositions that do not violate or override a person's basic freedoms. This is because the restrictions are seen, in effect, as self-prescribed" (*Paternalism*, p. 59). On the other hand, the subject does not participate in the restriction if the agent appeals to a subject's subsequent approval or her hypothetical rational consent. Such an appeal, nevertheless, "figures as a normative explanation of what are believed to be justified impositions." This is not a perspicuous division of the arguments. The various ways in which subjects consent to actions enter their justification in the complex way surveyed in Chapter 9. They are not amenable to a simplistic account couched exclusively in terms of autonomy.

To appreciate the role of consent in the justification of parentalism, it is necessary to view it in two ways, both of which are reflected by elements in our guidelines. What counts in favor of an intervention in a person's life is the probability that it will promote the person's objective good and the strength of the agent's evidence that his judgments are sound. Correlatively, the agent needs to evaluate the subject's consent or dissent two ways: for its value as an exercise of autonomy and part of her objective welfare and for its value as evidence of her objective good. Both considerations are relevant to evaluating all types of consent. All of the consent-based arguments are, therefore (in Kleinig's words), "normative explanations of what are believed to be justifiable impositions."

VanDeVeer maintains that his definition of paternalism is normatively neutral (*Paternalistic Intervention*, pp. 4, and 16–23). He refers to interventions collectively as "interferences" and claims that, since 'to interfere' is sometimes used neutrally ("the storm interfered with parade"), the term is not pejorative. This is mistaken: human interferences with parades *are* condemned, and the word is pejorative in this context. VanDeVeer concedes that the term 'paternalism' has negative connotations. He explains this fact by the offensiveness of most of the measures which the parentalist uses. Hence, interferences are presumptively wrong, and this is what gives parentalism a bad odor.

Chapter 12. The State as Parentalist

Sankowski notes that many people object to state parentalism not because it is parentalistic, but because it enlarges the powers of the state. Yet parentalism is not the primary reason for the concentration of power; it is rather protection of citizens against each other and foreign enemies (" 'Paternalism' and Social Policy," p. 9). However, once power is concentrated, there is good reason to circumscribe the areas in which it can be legitimately exercised, and parentalism seems a good place to begin.

In regard to the impersonal character of state action, Arneson remarks that Mill's problem is to design a social policy for "the restriction of liberty that will be optimific for actual conditions expected in modern societies, rather than for an imaginary ideal case" ("Paternalism, Utility and Fairness," pp. 420). Hence, he needs

> a rule regarding the treatment of paternalistic proposals that is to guide a policymaking public authority that must make decisions with limited and imperfect information about the impact the policies it is considering would have on the welfare of individual citizens. Moreover, the cost of tailoring a policy of interference to the individual case would be prohibitive even if perfect information were available. Any feasible policy must make broad rough classifications. (p. 411)

As Smiley notes, this means that the government agent must utilize general conceptions of what is good for people rather than search out their individual differences. He maintains that in a democratic society those conceptions are derived from "communal standards" or "social norms," so state parentalism inevitably imposes these on individuals ("Paternalism and Democracy," pp. 305–308). Hodson makes this his central point in condemning state parentalism. The only parentalism he condones occurs when the parentalist knows better the personal values of the subject than the subject does in some state of irrationality or ignorance. Agents of the state are never in a position to know this.

In regard to the use of public conceptions of good in the justification of public parentalism, Smiley charges that many authors, including Feinberg, Dworkin, and Hodson, smuggle them into their criteria of rationality. In their hard antiparentalism they maintain that society should protect individuals against serious harm and provide them primary goods only if they are irrational; they define harms and goods in terms of what representatives of the public would conceive; and they take the failure to value basic goods as prima facie evidence of irrationality.

Smiley's apprehensions toward parentalism have to do with a harm that it may inflict: curtailment of democracy. Arneson's apprehensions about antiparentalism have to with an alternative harm which *it* may inflict: a certain injustice. Smiley objects that state parentalism presupposes and perpetuates inequality and domination of government agents over individuals with incapacities (poverty, incompetence, and handicap, among others). This transforms bureaucrats from servants into "expert protectors," and it stunts the development of the needy. Smiley observes, however, that conditions for collective life include parentalistic restrictions on liberty. His solution of the "liberal dilemma" faced by those who are attached to Mill's principle but unwilling to let individuals seriously harm themselves is to make the restrictions nonparentalistic by requiring them to be adopted democratically. This solution is inadequate because it is not possible to provide the protections without parentalistic treatment of some individuals. Majority sanction of legislation does not mean that those who benefit are not being treated parentalistically. Moreover, Smiley's objections to parentalistic legislation are directed against a straw man. Such legislation need not stigmatize those who receive aid as "deviants." Indeed, the apparatus of welfare rights that bestows aid on individuals only when they are entitled to it should have the opposite effect. As for the claim that state parentalism stunts the growth of its recipients, this is an empirical claim for which there is little evidence. As Sankowski observes, many of the objections to such parentalism "amount to empirical guesses and/or requests for empirical study." All that can be said at this point is that "empirical scientific work would be welcome on the characteristic differences there are between various sorts of paternalistic and non-paternalistic regulation, differences in detail of operations and consequences" (" 'Paternalism' and Social Policy," p. 9). What is valid are Smiley's apprehensions about an elite parentalism burgeoning among government protectors and a further resort to deception to camouflage vested interests. He is right that the protective and welfare activities of the state should be as open and democratic as possible and it should encourage independence or at least not consign citizens to permanent dependency.

In a later article Arneson eases the stout antiparentalism of his earlier one. He still maintains that Mill is an absolute antiparentalist in regard to state action, but he now criticizes him for being too strict. Arneson's "worry" is that adherence to Mill's principle disproportionately benefits those with rational values and extensive knowledge. People deficient in these are hurt by inhibition of state parentalism because they make more self-harmful choices: "A ban on paternalism in effect gives to the haves and takes from the have-nots" ("Paternalism, Utility and Fairness," p. 412). The assumptions behind this convoluted argument are obscure. According to what principle of distributive justice is the failure of an agent to act preferential to some people and unfair to others? Perhaps the point is that agents of the state have the positive obligation to commandeer certain social goods and distribute them to needy members of society. This is the assumption behind the notion of minimal welfare rights and the distribution principle that greater benefits should be provided those who are worse off. The idea is that the representatives of a caring society should do their best to rectify the natural and social disadvantages that people suffer through no fault of their own.

Regan resorts to an even more extreme stratagem to justify protective legislation. He soberly argues that the cyclist who prefers the comfort of riding without a helmet is not the same person as the crash victim who regrets his rashness. He is a changed man after the accident. The man who is the rider is legitimately restrained to protect a possible later self, the accident victim. The justification of helmet legislation thus is the harm principle rather than the principle of parentalism. Regan admits that this denial of personal identity over time "opens a can of worms" in regard to responsibility ("Justifications for Paternalism," p. 203). He does not spell out his own conception of personal identity, but it would seem that any conception that would allow him to deny that the cyclist is the same person before and after an accident would entail unacceptable consequences for matters as promising and punishing. How can a person be rightfully held to a promise or punished for a crime if he is not the same person who promised or committed the crime? If the self is a momentary event, holding people to promises and punishing them for crimes should be abandoned. Since such consequences are intolerable, it reduces Regan's views on parentalism to absurdity.

Chapter 13. Feinberg's Antiparentalism

Feinberg's treatment of parentalism is geared to lay foundations for his treatment of the criminal law. His argument that criminal legislation is legitimated only by the Harm and Offense Principles, and not by the Paternalism Principle are persuasive. I believe, however, that the reason lies in the nature of criminal law, not in objections to parentalism based on *de jure* personal sovereignty. Criminal law should not be used for parentalistic purposes because it does not work. Other forms of legal parentalism and certainly other forms of parentalism do work, utilize less oppressive means, and hence may be legitimate.

Let us consider briefly the nature of criminal law. Feinberg concentrates on penal statutes that "describe a kind of conduct, place it under an interdiction, and threaten punishments for engaging in it" (*Harm to Others*, p. 19). These directly prohibit reprehensible conduct. Feinberg describes the harms that criminal sanctions inflict: "The typical criminal sanction is imprisonment, which is not only a severe deprivation of liberty in all its important dimensions, but also a brand of censure and condemnation that leaves one, in effect, in permanent disgrace." The difference in mode of coercion from other laws is "so significant that it amounts to a difference in kind as well as degree," and this makes plausible the view that "criminal sanctions are special enough to require their own liberty-limiting principles, and among all the common techniques of official coercion, are opposed initially by the strongest presumptive case" (p. 24).

The narrow concept of parentalism as coercion might lead one to think that legislation to protect the individual from himself or prevent others from enabling him to hurt himself is parentalistic whenever it is coercive. The criminal law is coercive by nature. This raises the question of whether there is anything about its sanctions that makes it nonparentalistic even when its aim is to help the criminal by reforming his character or motivating him to adjust to society.

Criminal penalties for failure to wear seat belts in automobiles or hard hats at work would be intuitively repugnant. Such intuitions lead authors to exclude the criminal law as a tool of parentalism in principle; they feel that the definition of parentalism should be formulated to exclude its use. One line of argument is that punishment is appropriate only for actions that are culpable. Criminal laws are justified only if they deter agents from doing wrong, whether or not they protect anyone from harm. Harming oneself is not morally wrong, and so punishment cannot be legitimately used to deter it. Some such notion leads Bayles to deny parentalism as a reason for criminal legislation. Reasons for legislation are "principles" in a special sense: "A principle for criminal legislation presents a characteristic of actions which constitutes a reason, but neither a necessary nor a sufficient one, for legally prohibiting them. . . . Collectively, all acceptable principles for and against provide a standard for good criminal legislation" ("Criminal Paternalism," p. 175). The three principles that Bayles recognizes for legislation are the Paternalist, Moralist, and Harm Principles. He utilizes these concepts to deny that some of Dworkin's examples are really parentalistic. For example, laws that deny the victim's consent as a defense for a person charged with assault are not parentalistic because they punish the assaulter for harming the victim, not the victim for harming himself, which presumably is his right. This is a plausible analysis of some cases, but it fails for others, for example, the battered wife who invites or tolerates abuse from her husband. Forcibly denying him contact with her clearly curtails her liberty of association against her will and makes the action parentalistic.

Bayles maintains the self-inflicted and freely accepted harms in such acts as suicide, submission to euthanasia, drug use, jay walking, neglecting to wear motorcycle helmets or seat belts, and participation in harmful entertainments should not be criminalized. This is certainly true for most of the actions, but the reason is found in considerations of efficacy, not conceptual incoherence in the idea of punishment for self-harm. Consider again the argument to the contrary: sanctions *qua* criminal are punishments for wrongdoing, not just negative rein-forcements of bad conduct. One who harms only himself is not guilty of wrongdoing. Hence, criminal sanctions are not appropriate to deter him. The counterargument depends on the principle that the wrongness of acts lies in their consequences. It *is* morally wrong to harm oneself if there are no compensating benefits for oneself or others. Persistent acts of self-harm, for example on the part of the drug addict, alcoholic, exhibitionist, or compulsive gambler, may reflect character defects and an incapacity to participate in the moral life of the community. Punishment may be appropriate if it will deter the agent and help reform his character.

If all of this is correct, the reason not to criminalize self-harmful actions is not logical, but pragmatic. Criminalization is an extreme form of coercion. It imposes a stigma better reserved for harms that are both serious and effectively deterred by this means. Most forms of self-harm are either not serious (the damage one does to one's liver by moderate use of alcohol) or not likely (injury from refusal to wear seat-belts) or not affected by criminal sanctions (improvi-dence) or more effectively dealt with under the medical model (drug addiction). The state should not waste its limited criminal sanctions on such actions.

This is not to say, however, that society cannot legitimately add to the negative consequences of risky and harmful activities to discourage them. Other penalties besides criminal—such as taxing an activity or making it inconvenient or difficult—may dissuade people who are indifferent to the risk in the activity. There is no reason for the state not to take the initiative in these measures. The reason to hold them to a minimum is practical. There usually are other ways to induce people to care for their own welfare. As Mill remarks, "disinterested benevolence can find other instruments to persuade people to their own good, than whips and scourges, either of the literal or the metaphorical sort" (*On Liberty*, p. 277). The other instruments that Mill has in mind are education and rational persuasion, but erecting obstacles to self-harmful conduct and providing positive inducements to avoid risks are likewise better than whips and scourges.

Consider the criminalization of suicide. Though the act puts the perpetrator beyond the sanctions of law, criminalization may have a deterrent effect. Persons contemplating suicide may have a strong respect for the law. They may be concerned about the stigma for the survivors. They might not want their estate to pay penalties. They may be influenced by a denial of burial privileges. However, criminalization of suicides is a particularly bad idea. Its deterrent effect is problematic. Suicide is a rational and morally permissible course in some circumstances. To apply suicide laws justly, a tribunal would have to decide the motives of one charged with violating them, and the notion of a trial of the deceased is grotesque. The right to decide whether to live or die is central to autonomy. We can imagine conditions in which society ought to restrain the individual from exercising this option, but surely compassion would be the justification. It would be grossly inappropriate to stigmatize the act as a crime; it would dislocate ordinary moral categories and apply them by alien criteria. Hence, while the harm to be prevented is great, the chance of preventing it by legislation is slight, and the cost of trying to do so is excessive.

Not only does the cost to the subject not outweigh any benefit that might be obtained for him by criminalizing self-harmful conduct, but the opportunity for abuse, to exploit or take vengeance on him in the name of his own good, is great. Moreover, this use of criminal sanctions would confuse and weaken its primary use, to protect persons from others. Feinberg states this point effectively, though for a different purpose: the presumption against limitations of liberty

> is not only supported by moral and utilitarian considerations of a general kind; it is also likely to be buttressed in particular cases by appeal to the practical costs, direct and collateral, of criminalization. A new crime on the books might put a strain on court facilities, divert police resources from more serious responsibilities, crowd prisons, and provide markets for the monopolistic and criminogenic enterprises of organized crime. (*Harm to Others*, p. 10)

In view of these pragmatic considerations, it is unnecessary to invoke the notion of autonomy rights to reject criminal parentalism. It may be useful to do so in the way I have suggested since liberty is valuable and coercion has built in harms.

Feinberg declares his fealty to liberalism, but he does not undertake to defend it in *The Moral Limits of the Criminal Law*. He undertakes to explain what it entails for criminal law. He does impose on himself the requirement that his analysis rationalize basic liberal intuitions, which is a step toward a defense. Thus he remarks that his principles must be clarified, tested tentatively against hypothetical possibilities, rendered compatible with "our more confident intuitions" and harmonious with one another. Feinberg acknowledges that the intuitions at his disposal are his own, but he anticipates that they will be shared by the reader:

> If the argument is successful, it shows to the person addressed that the judgment it supports coheres more smoothly than its rivals with the network of convictions he already possesses, so that if he rejects it, then he will have to abandon other judgments that he would be loath to relinquish. The argument may attempt to demonstrate to the addressee that the denial of the judgment to be provided would logically entail other propositions which he could not himself embrace without embarrassment. (*Harm to Others*, p. 18)

He labels this the "*ad hominem* method" and cites Santayana's observation that all philosophical argumentation comes down to this.

A major obstacle to interpreting Feinberg, one of the most lucid of writers, is his reluctance to commit himself on moral first principles. He confesses that he utilizes concepts from a variety of moral traditions, and he disavows any intention to specify which concepts are most basic: "Progress on penultimate questions need not wait for solutions to the ultimate ones." Unfortunately, considered convictions and penultimate principles may reflect socially indoctrinated prejudices. Feinberg recognizes that this is a fundamental problem with the *ad hominem* method, but he provides no antidote.

Sankowski complains that Feinberg's criterion of voluntariness "seems susceptible of use to justify morally unacceptable interventions, depending on how the self-avowedly artful term 'voluntary' is used. And the moral obscurities about when paternalism is justifiable would simply be pushed back a step further, in specifying an account of the voluntary-non-voluntary distinction" (" 'Paternalism' and Social Policy," p. 6). Smiley charges that Feinberg smuggles community values into his criterion by having us judge the voluntariness of the behavior affected by intervention in terms of its rationality and building into rationality a desire to avoid what the community views as extremely harmful consequences.

Hart deals with parentalism incidentally as a foil in demonstrating the illegitimacy of legal moralism. He suggests that parentalistic legislation is justified because there has been "a general decline in the belief that individuals know their own interests best, and . . . an increased awareness of a great range of factors which diminish the significance to be attached to an apparently free choice or to consent" (*Law, Liberty and Morality*, pp. 32–33). His point, however, is not to defend parentalistic laws, but to argue that whatever justification they have is lacking for moralistic legislation. He also displays an awareness that moralistic legislation can have a parentalistic aim when he mentions "the classical thesis" that moral training for the benefit of the individual is a primary purpose of law ("Social Solidarity and the Enforcement of Morality," p. 1).

Ronald Dworkin dismisses the view "that the state has a role to play as moral tutor and the criminal law as its proper tutorial technique" as eccentric ("Lord Devlin and the Enforcement of Morals," p. 988). Ten is the only author to take the possibility seriously. On the basis of the definition of moral harm as "corruption and degradation of people's character," he observes that persons can harm themselves by immoral acts and habits ("Paternalism and Morality," p. 58). However, he does not address the question of whether interference with their liberty to prevent this harm is justified. His point is only that it is difficult to distinguish between this kind of legislation and the moralism that is clearly offensive. Ten is tolerant of legal parentalism while at the same time vigorously rejecting legal moralism:

A restricted policy of paternalism will . . . result in a sparing and highly discriminating appeal to the criminal law. In this respect its spirit is fundamentally different from that of the enforcement of morality. . . . Paternalism focuses attention constantly on the interests of the agent, and not on conformity to the shared morality of society. The enforcement of morality is only too likely to surrender these interests to the probably unreasoning and unreasonable anger and hatred of the community. (p. 66)

Chapter 14. Professional Parentalism

Among those raising the specter of technocracy is Jethro Lieberman, who charges that "[p]rofessionals are dividing the world into spheres of influence and erecting large signs saying 'experts at work here, do not proceed farther.' . . . Professionals frequently say one thing and do another and assert that the layman's inability to find consistency between talk and action is caused by his inherent lack of insight into the professional mysteries." He suggests that the public supinely tolerates mystification in the face of the complexities of technological society. The professions exploit its passivity to usurp functions of government, thereby subverting democracy, so that "the public is losing its power to shape its destiny" (*Tyranny of the Experts*, p. 3).

Lieberman thinks that the dominant motive of the expert is self-aggrandizement. Ivan Illich and his colleagues, on the other hand, see a strong admixture of parentalism, but believe that the consequences are no less pernicious. They liken the institutionalization of professions to the establishment of a state church:

> The professional as teacher of the currently accepted brand of scientific ortho-doxy acts as theologian. As moral entrepreneur and as creator of the need for his services, he acts the role of priest. As crusading helper, he acts the part of missioner and hunts down the under-privileged. As inquisitor, he outlaws the unorthodox: he imposes his solutions on the recalcitrant who refuses to recognize that he is a problem.

The proliferation of professions is sapping the ability of the average person to make decisions not only about means to his ends but about ends themselves. What Illich labels the Age of the Disabling Professions marks the end of the individual's autonomy in major areas of his life and the community's autonomy over public policy:

> In any area where a human need can be imagined these new professions, dominant, authoritative, monopolistic, legalized—and at the same time, debilitating and effectively disabling the individual—have become exclusive experts of the public good. . . . Public affairs pass from the layperson's elected peers into the hands of a self-accrediting elite. (*Disabling Professions*, pp. 19–20)

It is not clear whether Lieberman and Illich hope that their strident alarms will elicit fundamental reforms or are only expressing despair at what they see before them.

Goldman makes a strong case against medical parentalism on the basis of the patient's right to autonomy, but he concedes that parentalism is sometimes justified in other contexts. It is instructive to see how he defends the right to autonomy, yet draws up short of absolute antiparentalism. The problems with his position are illustrative of the difficulties of rights-centered ethical theories in coming to grips with cases.

Goldman begins with a characterization:

> Rights express interests of individuals important enough to be protected against additions of lesser interests across other persons. When they are exercised, the resultant claims to goods or freedoms are to be honored even at the expense of the

aggregate collective welfare. The number of people with opposing lesser interests becomes irrelevant when a right is at stake. Rights themselves are ordered nonaggregatively. (*Moral Foundations of Professional Ethics*, pp. 24–25)

Goldman is talking about moral rights because so much of his critique is directed toward professional codes of ethics. That he has *human* rights in mind—that is, moral rights possessed equally and inalienably by all human beings—is more problematic, but he does not limit his remarks to specific categories of humans. He seems persuaded that all humans have the potential for autonomy and their autonomy is equally deserving of respect.

Goldman conceives of rights (perhaps just some) as absolute in a sense that is not easy to determine. He posits the "absolute priority of rights over utilities." He excludes the notion of trivial rights: rights "express interests vital to the integrity of the individual." Yet he describes some rights as "very important" and "more central," implying that others are less so. He says that rights are ordered nonaggregatively and any right outweighs every aggregate of lesser interests or utilities no matter how numerous these may be for an individual or how numerous the people who have them. Putting all of this together, I infer that Goldman is asserting that interests may be ranked, that interests at the basis of rights rank above those of utilities, and that rights themselves are ranked into higher and lower. He is claiming that it is never morally permissible to sacrifice a right to a lower right or to a utility. It is not permissible either to sacrifice a right of an individual for one of his lesser interests or to sacrifice any of his rights to serve the interests of other people. In the scheme, if there is one right that heads the list, it should never be sacrificed for anything whatsoever. It is unconditional and absolute in the strong sense: the rules defining respect of it are universal and no exceptions are allowed. Each right below the top is conditional, but absolute in the weak sense: the rules for each are universal, but they incorporate systematic exceptions for situations in which the right conflicts with higher rights.

If rights are ordered but not in this tight way, we might have to say that none is truly absolute for either of two reasons: it might be found at a level which is occupied by other rights and sometimes conflict with them, or, even if the rights of a person are perfectly ordered, honoring a right for some persons could require its violation for another person. Presumably Goldman has this in mind when he acknowledges that "[n]umbers do count, but only when the interests on opposing sides are of equal importance, only when rights are opposed by others of the same type, or when it is a matter of mere utilities" (p. 26).

Goldman pushes toward the position that rights are ordered perfectly with the right to autonomy at the top, but he is stopped short by certain considerations. No proposal of a rights-centered morality can be taken seriously unless its author specifies the order of human interests or values. The nature of interests in Goldman's system must be inferred from his remarks about preferences and wants. The task is complicated by the fact that at points he talks about the preferences of actual people and at others the preferences of "the rational person."

On the one hand, in defense of the claim that there is a hierarchy among interests he appeals to the unwillingness of actual people to sacrifice rights for utilities or less vital rights, and he asserts that "[a] person is harmed when a state of affairs below a certain level on his preference scale is realized rather than one higher up" (p. 173). If to harm means to damage true interests, this means that what one prefers is always in one's interest.

On the other hand, in arguing that a patient's irrationality is a reason for the physician to disregard her wishes, he advances the divergence of the patient's preferences from value-orderings "uncontroversially that of any rational person" as a criterion for irrationality (p. 179). Also he advances as a reason for leaving decisions to individuals in matters vital to their interests "the presumption of their being the best judge of their own interests, which may depend upon personal value orderings known only to them" (p. 159). The reference to "presumption" recognizes that she can be mistaken. Her true interests may not be identical with what she wants either in the short or the long term. The rational person is one who knows her true interests and objective good. If we wed this notion with that of care, we can conclude that people who care for others should promote their good as measured by the desires of the rational person. Care does not require that they always accede to the preferences of cared-for persons.

The evidence that the absolute position is the one Goldman accepts is found in his discussion of "perfectionist or ideal-regarding" ethical systems, which contradict utilitarianism in positing goals that override the satisfaction of desires: "One framework might recognize independent value to allowing moral autonomy and freedom of choice, beyond the extent to which these are desired by agents; another might not." In keeping with the objectivism we observed in other parts of his discussion, he endorses the first framework:

> [V]alues originate in the distinct valuations of persons with goals and desires. If it is in relation to such freely valuing individuals and their central projects that other goods acquire their value or utility, then it makes sense that the preconditions for the exercise of creative individuality and valuation should take absolute precedence. . . . There is therefore an ideal-regarding source of the priority of personal rights independent of the strength of desires in particular individuals to retain them. (pp. 27–28)

This says that autonomy is supremely valuable regardless of whether its possessor recognizes it, and others are obligated to respect his autonomy whether or not he demands it. Goldman purports to find support for the ideal-regarding framework in what he calls "factual relativism." This is the proposition that "there may be two or more self-consistent but mutually incompatible sets of values, such that any preference for one set over the others would presuppose values contained in the first but not in the others. In this situation there could be no value-neutral reasons for preferring one of these systems over the others" (p. 10). The objective goods of no two people are ordered the same way. Differences in their constitution and situation would assure this even if they were to be entirely rational and fully informed. In their actual irrationality and ignorance, their schedules of preference differ radically. Goldman presents relativism as a factual, value-neutral thesis. One cannot deduce from it, for example, that we should be tolerant of other people's preferences. The principle of tolerance is normative and requires intolerance of intolerance. Relativism neither requires or excludes either blanket tolerance or intolerance of intolerance. Goldman simply announces that he opts for tolerance and pitches his arguments to those who do so too.

So far, so good, but at this point his argument becomes confusing. The fact of relativism seems to exclude the general ranking of rights as a way of determining how to treat people: "Moral differences are where we find them. . . . For this reason it is impossible to state any interesting general and absolute priorities among types of rights. . . . Even more specific priorities among particular rights have exceptions at the borders as threats to the interests being represented become extreme" (p. 30). This seems to mean that rules defining rights must have exceptive clauses, and even then moral intuition will dictate the violation of some because not all exceptions can be incorporated in them. It may mean more than this—that individual differences are such that there is no single hierarchy of rights for everyone even under an ideal system of rules that takes account of their true interests.

Goldman does not honor these implications of his relativism. He is not reluctant to generalize about human rights. Thus he maintains that some rights "express interests vital to the integrity of the individual," among these, "basic material needs, security in expectations, opportunities, freedom from unwarranted interference, and self-respect" and "rights to autonomy and equality are fundamental." Why they are fundamental is suggested by this comment: "What unifies the vital interests in the list above is not merely the intensity of desire associated with them, but their relation to the ability of individuals to formulate and pursue their own plans of life. The truth of relativism suggests that values originate in the distinct valuations of persons with goals and desires" (p. 27). Despite his relativism and indeed on the basis of it, Goldman makes a fundamental value judgment. He asserts a single universal and absolute right of human beings based on their true interests *qua* human, whatever their differences and preferences. Some people may foolishly not desire the conditions for personal development and creativity, but Goldman judges these to be absolutely important for them.

In summary, Goldman maintains both that there can be no single ordering of rights and that the right to autonomy has absolute priority. He would have to adhere to the second proposition to advocate absolute antiparentalism, but he sensibly rejects this stance. Yet the extreme relativism which is the other horn of his dilemma cuts the ground from the attempt to base moral judgments on a clean schedule of rights. This puts us back to square one in regard to parentalism. Where it is necessary to choose between two of the vital interests listed by Goldman—basic material needs, self-respect, security in expectations, and freedom from interference—which should take priority? Labeling them "rights" does not settle the matter.

It is difficult to pinpoint the flaw in Goldman's position because he does not make clear the ground on which he stands. On the one hand, he acknowledges no basis for demonstrating the superiority of one ethical theory over another. He claims that moral systems differ about the broadest or most basic principles and notes that his own rights-based framework requires a commitment to toleration which is external to the framework. Consequently, he concedes, "[t]he frame-work itself is only one possible social outcome and has no objective warrant over more purely aggregative or collectivist moralities" (p. 29). On the other hand, Goldman refers to our common moral framework. On what is that framework founded and how is it "ours" and "common"?

Even if Goldman is right about the way many people think, why should we follow the reasoning of either philosophers or ordinary people if it does not rationalize our own intuitions? Goldman falls back on a sort of intuitionist-inductivist method when he maintains that "we" (he may mean either ordinary normal persons or reflective philosophers) agree in our moral judgments on concrete cases and the principles behind them. This method for resolving moral disagreements is to reason from cases and principles generalized from cases on which there is agreement to positions on the controversial issues most consistent with this body of accepted data. Our common moral framework presumably comprises the principles that this method has turned up. If the framework is more than a compendium of shared prejudices, however, it must be because "we" descry basic facts about human nature and welfare in the cases on which we agree. In other words, Goldman's position is tenable only if there is an objective basis for moral theory after all.

Notes

Chapter 1

1. Kant, *Foundations of the Metaphysics of Morals*, pp. 252–253. I accept Kant's distinction but not his conclusion about the moral irrelevance of pathological love.
2. Translations from *New English Bible*, I John 4:9, Deuteronomy 6:5, and Leviticus 19:18.
3. Plato, *Symposium*, 202D.
4. Ibid., 206B.
5. Matthew 22:36–40.
6. See Philip S. Watson, "Translator's Preface," in Anders Nygren, *Agape and Eros*, pp. viii–ix.
7. Plato, *Symposium*, 206A.
8. I will be aping Heidegger's exploitation of cognates of the German term *Sorge* in *Being and Time*, but I do not accept his reduction of care to man's role as a "clearing" for Being.
9. Aristotle, *Nicomachean Ethics*, Bk. X, Ch. 4–5.
10. Heidegger, *Being and Time*, pp. 158–159. I adopt Heidegger's distinction, but not his use of it. For him it is ontological; for me it is moral. He professes to be neutral toward the two forms of solicitude; I applaud the second form and condemn the first.
11. Plato, *Republic*, 505D.
12. I hope the reader will find my account of the encounter with the other more sober than Sartre's melodramatic metaphors of a robbery of the world from us and a hemorrhage in which the world flows away toward him. Sartre, *Being and Nothingness*, p. 255.
13. MacIntyre, *After Virtue*, pp. 31–32.
14. Lucretius, *Nature of the Universe*, Bk. II, p. 60.

Chapter 2

1. Feinberg, "Legal Paternalism," pp. 105, 106.
2. Soble, "Paternalism, Liberal Theory, and Suicide," p. 336.
3. Beauchamp, "Paternalism and Biobehavioral Control," p. 77.
4. I have in mind something like the considered judgments of competent moral judges described by John Rawls in "A Decision Procedure for Ethics."
5. Pollock, *Freedom Principle*, p. 28.
6. MacIntyre, *After Virtue*, p. 69.
7. Gert and Culver, "Paternalistic Behavior," p. 46.
8. Kohlberg, *Philosophy of Moral Development*, pp. 118–122, 147–168.

9. Ibid., pp. 131–132.

10. Kohlberg, "Claim to Moral Adequacy of a Highest Stage of Moral Development," p. 634.

11. Gilligan reviews the neglect of females in developmental studies and theories in *In a Different Voice*, pp. 6–13, 151–153. She speaks of the "developmental litany" that intones male values as marks of maturity, p. 23.

12. Ibid., pp. 6, 16.

13. Kohlberg et al., *Moral Stages*, pp. 69–71.

14. Gilligan, *In a Different Voice*, p. 173. Gilligan refers to the male and female "voices" repeatedly, e.g. on pp. 1 and in "Preface" pp. ii, xvii, and xix and in "Remapping the Moral Domain" on p. 8. She discusses the distinctive female moral language in *In a Different Voice*, pp. 49, 70, 73.

15. Ibid., pp. 37–38.

16. Ibid., pp. 159, 160–161, 164.

17. Ibid., p. 100.

18. Ibid., p. 63.

Chapter 3

1. See Richard Brandt, "Some Merits of One Form of Rule Utilitarianism," p. 48.

2. See Kai Nielsen, "Problems of Ethics," pp. 118–119.

3. E.g., Alan Gewirth sets himself the task of demonstrating "categorically obligatory requirements for action." *Reason and Morality*, p. 1.

4. The analysis here follows Joel Feinberg in *Social Philosophy* and S. I. Benn and R. S. Peters in *Principles of Political Thought*. I use these authors because their accounts of rights are standard and Feinberg and Benn have published important articles on parentalism.

5. Benn and Peters, *Principles of Political Thought*, p. 114, and Feinberg, *Social Philosophy*, p. 67.

6. Feinberg discusses absolute and human rights in *Social Philosophy*, pp. 85–86. Benn and Peters discuss them in *Principles of Political Thought*, pp. 109–120.

7. Feinberg, *Social Philosophy*, p. 86.

8. Ibid., p. 86.

9. Brandt, "Toward a Credible Form of Utilitarianism," p. 124.

10. Feinberg, *Social Philosophy*, pp. 58–59.

Chapter 4

1. Fotion, "Paternalism," p. 193.

2. Douglas, "Cooperative Paternalism versus Conflictful Paternalism," p. 172, and Kleinig, *Paternalism*, p. 3.

3. J. B. Thompson and H. O. Thompson, *Ethics in Nursing*, pp. 250–251; A. J. Davis and M. A. Aroskar, *Ethical Dilemmas and Nursing Practice*, p. 171; and Susan G. Taylor, "Rights and Responsibilities," p. 12.

4. The three quotations are from Fromm, *Art of Loving*, pp. 34–37.

5. The two quotations are from Douglas, "Cooperative Paternalism versus Conflictful Paternalism," pp. 173–174.

6. Fromm, *Art of Loving*, pp. 35, 36.

7. "Paternalism is justified only to preserve a wider range of freedom for the individual in question." Dworkin, "Paternalism," p. 152.

8. Morris, "Paternalistic Theory of Punishment," pp. 141, 144–146.

9. Douglas, "Cooperative Paternalism versus Conflictful Paternalism," p. 174.

10. Ibid., pp. 197–198.

11. Ibid., p. 191.

Chapter 5

1. The first illustrations in the Oxford English Dictionary are references to the absence of paternalism from a certain law (1881), a relationship between certain employers and workers (1882), and Martin Luther's concept of government (1898).

2. These are restrictions to prevent harm to others, prevent offense to others, benefit others, punish sin, and—the two paternalistic forms—benefit the persons who are restricted by the laws and prevent harm to them. Feinberg, *Social Philosophy*, p. 33.

3. Hart, *Law, Liberty and Morality*, p. 31.

4. VanDeVeer develops his definition in *Paternalistic Intervention*, p. 22.

5. Gert and Culver's definition is in "Paternalistic Behavior," pp. 49–50, and idem, "Justification of Paternalism," p. 199.

6. VanDeVeer, *Paternalistic Intervention*, pp. 16–17.

7. He uses a related term only once, and there casually, when he refers to practices "which belong to the system of despotic, or what is called paternal, government." Mill, *On Liberty*, p. 235.

8. The material that follows is taken from ibid., pp. 223–225.

9. Ibid., pp. 219, 224, 301.

10. In Ronald Munson's terms in *Intervention and Reflection*, p. 170.

11. Gert and Culver, "Paternalistic Behavior," p. 45.

12. Kleinig, *Paternalism*, p. 7.

13. Childress, "Paternalism and Health Care," p. 23.

14. Scarre, "Children and Paternalism," p. 119. See Schrag, "Child in the Moral Order."

15. Brock, "Paternalism and Promoting the Good," p. 242.

16. Beauchamp, "Paternalism and Biobehavioral Control," pp. 65–66.

17. Ibid., p. 66.

18. Dworkin, "Paternalism," p. 145.

Chapter 6

1. Brock, "Paternalism and Promoting the Good," p. 257.

2. Rawls, *A Theory of Justice*, pp. 48–51.

3. Arneson, "Paternalism, Utility and Fairness," p. 414. I would amend this to include justice under welfare in the broadest sense.

4. Weirich, "Utility Tempered with Equality."

5. Bok, *Lying*, p. 30.

6. Margaret Pabst Battin describes the Van Dusen, Proctor, and Roman cases in *Ethical Issues in Suicide*, pp. 58, 159, 171, citing stories in the *New York Times* of February 26, 1975, December 11, 1977, and June 17, 1979. She exposits the "cry-for-help" model for understanding suicide attempts on pp. 8–9 and 115, having borrowed the term and analysis from Norman L. Farberow and Edwin S. Schneidman in *The Cry for Help*.

Chapter 7

1. Following Daniel Wikler, "Paternalism and the Mildly Retarded," and Dan Brock, "Paternalism and Promoting the Good," respectively.
2. Brock, "Paternalism and Promoting the Good," p. 241.
3. Benn, "Freedom, Autonomy and the Concept of a Person," pp. 113, 116–117.
4. Ibid., p. 113.
5. The account in this paragraph is a summary of ibid., pp. 117–121.
6. Ibid., p. 125. See pp. 128–129. Benn's analysis of autonomy and autarchy is on pp. 124–129.
7. Ibid., p. 122.
8. Mill, *On Liberty*, pp. 299–300.
9. Benn, "Freedom, Autonomy and the Concept of a Person," pp. 111–112; Murphy, "Incompetence and Paternalism," p. 470 n.11.
10. Beauchamp, "Paternalism and Biobehavioral Control," p. 66; Gert and Culver, "Paternalistic Behavior," p. 48.
11. Feinberg, "Legal Paternalism," p. 111.
12. Mill, *Principles of Political Economy*, vol. 2, p. 459, quoted by Gerald Dworkin, "Paternalism," p. 150.
13. Wikler, "Paternalism and the Mildly Retarded"; Schrag, "Child in the Moral Order."
14. McDonald, "Autarchy and Interest," pp. 109, 112.
15. Benn, "Freedom, Autonomy and the Concept of a Person," p. 124.

Chapter 8

1. Mill, *Utilitarianism*, p. 212.
2. Arneson, "Mill versus Paternalism," pp. 479ff.
3. Mill, *On Liberty*, p. 266.
4. Ibid., p. 263.
5. Ibid., p. 282.
6. Ibid., pp. 298ff.
7. Ibid., pp. 262, 270.
8. Ibid., pp. 277, 283.
9. McDonald, "Autarchy and Interest," p. 109.
10. VanDeVeer, *Paternalistic Intervention*, pp. 112, 113.
11. Feinberg *Social Philosophy*, p. 97.
12. Feinberg, *Rights, Justice, and the Bounds of Liberty*, p. 32.

Chapter 9

1. VanDeVeer, "Paternalism and Subsequent Consent," p. 631.
2. Dworkin, "Paternalism," and Carter, "Justifying Paternalism."
3. Feinberg, "Legal Paternalism," pp. 113–114.
4. Beauchamp, "Paternalism and Biobehavioral Control," p. 67.
5. VanDeVeer, "Paternalism and Subsequent Consent," p. 639.
6. Carter, "Justifying Paternalism."
7. Hodson, "The Principle of Paternalism," pp. 65–66.
8. Dworkin, "Paternalism," p. 154.

Chapter 10

1. See Kleinig, *Paternalism*, p. 3, and Marion Smiley, "Paternalism and Democracy," p. 309.

2. Dworkin, "Paternalism: Some Second Thoughts," p. 107. Some authors use "strong" and "weak" for "hard" and "soft."

3. Pollock, *The Freedom Principle*, p. 13.

4. Kleinig, *Paternalism*, p. 36.

5. Mill, *On Liberty*, p. 227.

6. Ibid., p. 226.

7. Kleinig presents the arguments in chapter 2 and the counterarguments in chapter 3 of *Paternalism*.

8. Ibid., p. 39.

Chapter 11

1. All of the references to VanDeVeer in this chapter are to his *Paternalistic Intervention: The Moral Limits of Benevolence*. Kleinig's *Paternalism* is equally rich, but more eclectic and hence less useful as a foil. I have taken the liberty of paraphrasing a number of VanDeVeer's formulations and simplifying some so as not to have to explain refinements which are not relevant to our discussion.

2. He discusses a number of conceptions of good and parallel conceptions of what it means to benefit a person (pp. 102–105, 121–123); he expresses sympathy the satisfaction conception (p. 122); and he implies that what brings satisfaction to an individual is an objective fact (p. 100).

Chapter 12

1. As Tziporah Kasachoff notes about inferences in the reverse direction, from the public to the private sphere, in "Paternalistic Solicitude and Paternalistic Behavior," p. 80. Cf. Peter Hobson, "Another Look at Paternalism," p. 296.

2. Mill, *On Liberty*, p. 219.

3. VanDeVeer, *Paternalistic Intervention*, pp. 295–300.

4. Dworkin, "Paternalism," pp. 144–146. See Feinberg, *Harm to Self*, pp. 8–11.

5. These are borrowed from Dworkin ("Paternalism") and VanDeVeer's (*Paternalistic Intervention*) lists and the discussions of Kleinig (*Paternalism*) and Feinberg ("Legal Paternalism").

6. This position is proposed by Donald Regan, "Justification for Paternalism," pp. 203–205.

7. See Richard Barnet, *The Roots of War*, part I.

8. Churchill, "Nuclear Deterrence and Nuclear Paternalism," pp. 192–196.

9. Ibid., pp. 196–200.

10. Ibid., p. 192. He cites the account of nuclear "numbing" in Robert Jay Lifton and Richard Falk, *Indefensible Weapons* (New York: Basic Books, 1982), pp. 100–110.

11. Ibid., pp. 192, 200.

12. Dworkin, "Lord Devlin and the Enforcement of Morals"; Hart, "Social Solidarity and the Enforcement of Morality"; Ten, "Paternalism and Morality"; Devlin, *Enforcement of Morals*.

13. Hart, *Law, Liberty and Morality*, p. 4.
14. Mill, *Utilitarianism*, pp. 217–218.
15. Ibid., p. 211.

Chapter 13

1. My references will be to volume 1, *Harm to Others* [HO] and volume 3, *Harm to Self* [HS] in *The Moral Limits of the Criminal Law*. Feinberg explains his intentions and methods for the entire work in the General Introduction to volume 1. The liberal program is described on pp. 14–16 in *Harm to Others* and on pp. 3, 26, and 126 in *Harm to Self*.

2. *Harm to Others*, ch. 5, sec. 7; and *Harm to Self*, ch. 19, sec. 3.

3. Feinberg explains the concept of liberty-limiting principles in *Harm to Others* on pp. 9–10 and lists the ten possible principles on pp. 26–27 and the major categories on pp. 12 and 14–15.

4. See *Harm to Self* (pp. 61–62) and his references to "autonomy respecting rationales" for legislation (p. 26) and "honoring autonomy" when interfering with another person's life (p. 182).

5. See also the reference to the "underivative right of self-determination," *Harm to Self*, p. 61.

6. Feinberg discusses forms of coercion at length in *Harm to Self*, ch. 24, and their effect on validity of consent on pp. 261–262. He discusses forms of defective belief in ch. 25 and their effect on validity on pp. 300–305.

Chapter 14

1. I have analyzed the structure of professions and roots of professional power in *Ethics and Professionalism*.

2. See Magali Sarfati Larson, *Rise of Professionalism*.

3. See Wilbert E. Moore, *Professions: Roles and Rules*, pp. 25–33.

4. See Everett C. Hughes, *Sociological Eye*, p. 318.

5. Ibid., especially pp. 288 and 376.

6. This is essentially Alan H. Goldman's approach in *Moral Foundations of Professional Ethics*.

7. Bayles, *Professional Ethics*, p. 70.

8. Ibid., p. 74.

9. Quotes in the following discussion are from ibid., pp. 74–77.

10. Ibid., pp. 77–78.

Bibliography

Aristotle. *Nichomachean Ethics. A New Aristotle Reader*, edited by J.L. Ackrill. Princeton, NJ: Princeton University Press, 1987.

Arneson, Richard J. "Mill versus Paternalism." *Ethics* 90, 4 (1980): 470–489.

Arneson, Richard J. "Paternalism, Utility and Fairness." *Revue Internationale de Philosophie* 43 (1989): 409–437.

Barnet, Richard J. *Roots of War*. New York: Penguin, 1972.

Battin, Margaret Pabst. *Ethical Issues in Suicide*. Englewood Cliffs, NJ: Prentice-Hall, 1982.

Bayles, Michael D. "Criminal Paternalism," pp. 174–188 in Pennock and Chapman.

Bayles, Michael D. *Professional Ethics*, 2nd ed. Belmont, CA: Wadsworth, 1989.

Beauchamp, Tom L. "Paternalism and Biobehavioral Control." *Monist* 70, 1 (1977): 62–80.

Benn, S.I. "Freedom, Autonomy and the Concept of a Person." *Proceedings of the Aristotelian Society* 76 (1975–1976): 109–130.

Benn, S.I. and R.S. Peters. *The Principles of Political Thought*. New York: Free Press, 1959.

Bok, Sissela. *Lying: Moral Choice in Public and Private Life*. New York: Pantheon, 1978.

Brandt, Richard B. "Some Merits of One Form of Rule Utilitarianism," pp. 39–65 in *University of Colorado Studies*. Boulder: University of Colorado Press, 1966.

Brandt, Richard B. "Toward a Credible Form of Utilitarianism," pp. 107–143 in *Morality and the Language of Conduct*, edited by Hector Neri-Castañeda and George Naknikian. Detroit: Wayne State University Press, 1963.

Brock, Dan. "Paternalism and Promoting the Good," pp. 237–260 in Sartorius.

Buchanan, Allen E. "Medical Paternalism." *Philosophy and Public Affairs* 7, 4 (1978): 370–390.

Carter, Rosemary. "Justifying Paternalism." *Canadian Journal of Philosophy* 7, 1 (1977): 133–145.

Childress, James. "Paternalism and Health Care," pp. 21–32 in Robison and Pritchard.

Churchill, Robert Paul. "Nuclear Deterrence and Nuclear Paternalism," pp. 194–204 in Peden and Sterba.

D'Agostino, Fred. "Mill, Paternalism and Psychiatry." *Australasian Journal of Philosophy* 60, 4 (1982): 319–330.

Davis, A. J. and M. A. Aroskar. *Ethical Dilemmas and Nursing Practice*, 2nd ed. New York: Appleton-Century-Crofts, 1983.

Devlin, Patrick. *The Enforcement of Morals*. Oxford: Oxford University Press, 1959.

Douglas, Jack D. "Cooperative Paternalism versus Conflictful Paternalism," pp. 171–200 in Sartorius.

Dworkin, Gerald. "Paternalism," pp. 143–158 in *Morality and the Law*, edited by Richard Wasserstrom. Belmont, CA: Wadsworth, 1971.

Dworkin, Gerald. "Paternalism: Some Second Thoughts," pp. 105–112 in Sartorius.

Dworkin, Ronald. "Lord Devlin and the Enforcement of Morals." *Yale Law Journal* 75 (1966): 986–1005.

Farberow, Norman L. and Edwin S. Schneidman, eds. *The Cry for Help*. New York: McGraw Hill, 1961.

Feinberg, Joel. *Harm to Others. The Moral Limits of the Criminal Law*, volume 1. New York: Oxford University Press, 1983.

Feinberg, Joel. *Harm to Self. The Moral Limits of the Criminal Law*, volume 3. New York: Oxford University Press, 1986.

Feinberg, Joel. "Legal Paternalism." *Canadian Journal of Philosophy* 1, 1 (1971): 105–123.

Feinberg, Joel. *Rights, Justice, and the Bounds of Liberty*. Princeton, NJ: Princeton University Press, 1980.

Feinberg, Joel. *Social Philosophy*. Englewood Cliffs, NJ: Prentice-Hall, 1973.

Fotion, N. "Paternalism." *Ethics* 89, 2 (1979): 191–198.

Fromm, Erich. *The Art of Loving*. New York: Bantam, 1963.

Gert, Bernard. *The Moral Rules*. New York: Harper and Row, 1973.

Gert, Bernard and Charles M. Culver. "The Justification of Paternalism." *Ethics* 89, 2 (1979): 199–210.

Gert, Bernard and Charles M. Culver. "Paternalistic Behavior." *Philosophy and Public Affairs* 6, 1 (1976): 45–57.

Gewirth, Alan. *Reason and Morality*. Chicago: University of Chicago Press, 1978.

Gibson, Quentin. *The Logic of Social Enquiry*. London: Routledge and Kegan Paul, 1960.

Gilligan, Carol. *In a Different Voice*. Cambridge: Harvard University Press, 1982.

Gilligan, Carol, "Preface" and "Remapping the Moral Domain," pp. i–vi and 3–20 in *Mapping the Moral Domain*, edited by Carol Gilligan, Janie Victoria Ward, and Jill McLean. Cambridge: Harvard University Press, 1988.

Glass, Marvin. "Not Going to Hell on One's Own." *Philosophy* 58 (1983): 471–480.

Goldman, Alan H. *The Moral Foundations of Professional Ethics*. Totowa, NJ: Rowman and Littlefield, 1980.

Gutmann, Amy. "Children, Paternalism and Education: A Liberal Argument." *Philosophy and Public Affairs* 9, 4 (1980): 338–358.

Hart, H.L.A. *Law, Liberty and Morality*. Stanford, CA: Stanford University Press, 1963.

Hart, H.L.A. "Social Solidarity and the Enforcement of Morality." *University of Chicago Law Review* 35, 1 (1967): 1–13.

Heidegger, Martin. *Being and Time*, translated by John Macquarrie and Edward Robinson. New York: Harper, 1962.

Heidegger, Martin. "Letter on Humanism." *Martin Heidegger: Basic Writings*, edited by David Farrell Krell. New York: Harper and Row, 1977.

Hobson, Peter. "Another Look at Paternalism." *Journal of Applied Philosophy*, 1, 2 (1984): 293–304.

Hodson, John D. "The Principle of Paternalism." *American Philosophical Quarterly* 14, 1 (1977): 61–69.

Hughes, Everett C. *The Sociological Eye: Selected Papers*. Chicago: Aldine-Atherton, 1971.

Husak, Douglas. "Paternalism and Autonomy." *Philosophy and Public Affairs* 10, 1 (1980): 27–46.

Illich, Ivan, et al. *Disabling Professions*. London: Marion Boyars, 1977.

Kant, Immanuel. *Foundations of the Metaphysics of Morals*, edited by Lewis White Beck. New York: Macmillan, 1988.

Kasachoff, Tziporah. "Paternalistic Solicitude and Paternalistic Behavior: Appropriate Contexts and Moral Justifications," pp. 79–93 in Peden and Sterba.

Kleinig, John. *Paternalism*. Totowa, NJ: Rowman and Allanheld, 1984.

Kohlberg, Lawrence. "The Claim to Moral Adequacy of a Highest Stage of Moral Judgment." *Journal of Philosophy* 70, 18 (1973): 630–646.

Kohlberg, Lawrence. *The Philosophy of Moral Development. Essays on Moral Development*, vol. 1. San Francisco: Harper and Row, 1981.

Kohlberg, Lawrence, Charles Levine, and Alexandra Hewer. *Moral Stages: A Current Formulation and a Response to Critics. Contributions to Human Development*, vol. 10, edited by John A. Meacham. Basil: S. Karger, 1983.

Larson, Magali Sarfatti. *The Rise of Professionalism*. Berkeley: University of California Press, 1977.

Lieberman, Jethro K. *The Tyranny of the Experts*. New York: Walker, 1970.

Locke, John. *Two Treatises of Government*, edited by Peter Laslett. Cambridge: Cambridge University Press, 1963.

Lucretius. *The Nature of the Universe*, translated by R. E. Lathan. Baltimore, MD: Penguin, 1951.

MacIntyre, Alisdair. *After Virtue*, 2nd ed. Notre Dame, IN: University of Notre Dame Press, 1984.

McDonald, Michael. "Autarchy and Interest." *Australasian Journal of Philosophy* 56, 2 (1978): 109–125.

Mill, John Stuart. *On Liberty. Collected Works*, vol. 18. Toronto: University of Toronto Press, 1963.

Mill, John Stuart. *Principles of Political Economy. Collected Works*, vols. 1–2. Toronto: University of Toronto Press, 1963.

Mill, John Stuart. *Utilitarianism. Collected Works*, vol. 10. Toronto: University of Toronto Press, 1963.

Moore, Wilbert E. *The Professions: Roles and Rules*. New York: Russell Sage Foundation, 1970.

Morris, Herbert. "A Paternalistic Theory of Punishment," pp. 139–152 in Sartorius.

Munson, Ronald. *Intervention and Reflection*. Belmont, CA: Wadsworth, 1979.

Murphy, Jeffrie G. "Incompetence and Paternalism," *Archiv für Rechts- und Sozialphilosophie* 60 (1974): 465–486.

The New English Bible. New York: Oxford University Press, 1961.

Nielsen, Kai. "Problems of Ethics," pp. 118–119 in *The Encyclopedia of Philosophy*, vol. 3. New York: Macmillan, 1967.

Nygren, Anders. *Agape and Eros*, translated by Philip S. Watson. Philadelphia: Westminster Press, 1953.

Peden, Creighton and James P. Sterba. *Freedom, Equality, and Social Change. Studies in Social and Political Theory Today. Social Philosophy*, vol. 3, no. 2. Lewiston, NY: Edwin Mellen Press, 1989.

Pennock, J. Roland and John W. Chapman, eds. *The Limits of the Law. Nomos XV*. Yearbook of the American Society for Political and Legal Philosophy. New York: Lieber-Atherton, 1974.

Plato. *The Republic*, translated by G.M.A. Grube. Indianapolis, IN: Hackett, 1974.

Plato. *The Symposium*, translated by Alexander Nehamas and Paul Woodruff. Indianapolis, IN: Hackett, 1989.

Pollock, Lansing. *The Freedom Principle*. Buffalo, NY: Prometheus, 1981.

Rawls, John. "A Decision Procedure for Ethics." *Philosophical Review* 60 (1951): 177–197.

Rawls, John. *A Theory of Justice*. Cambridge MA: Harvard University Press, 1971.

Rees, J.C. "A Re-reading of Mill on Liberty." *Political Studies*, vol. 7. Oxford: Clarendon, 1960.

Regan, Donald H. "Justifications for Paternalism," pp. 189–210 in Pennock and Chapman.

Regan, Donald H. "Paternalism, Freedom, Identity, and Commitment," pp. 113–138 in Sartorius.

Robison, Wade and Michael Pritchard, Eds. *Medical Responsibility*. Clifton, NJ: Humana Press, 1979.

Sankowski, Edward. " 'Paternalism' and Social Policy." *American Philosophical Quarterly* 22, 1 (1985): 1–12.

Sartorius, Rolf, ed. *Paternalism*. Minneapolis: University of Minnesota Press, 1983.

Sartre, Jean-Paul. *Being and Nothingness*, translated by Hazel E. Barnes. New York: Philosophical Library, 1956.

Scarre, Geoffrey. "Children and Paternalism." *Philosophy* 55 (1980): 117–124.

Schrag, Francis. "The Child in the Moral Order." *Philosophy* 52 (1977): 167–177.

Smiley, Marion. "Paternalism and Democracy." *Journal of Value Inquiry* 23 (1989): 299–318.

Soble, Alan. "Paternalism, Liberal Theory, and Suicide." *Canadian Journal of Philosophy* 12, 2 (1982): 335–352.

Stephen, James Fitzjames. *Liberty, Equality, Fraternity*, 2nd ed., edited by R. J. White. Cambridge: Cambridge University Press, 1967.

Taylor, Susan G. "Rights and Responsibilities: Nurse-Patient Relationships." *Image* 17, 1 (1985): 9–13.

Ten, C. L. "Paternalism and Morality." *Ratio* 13 (1971): 56–66.

Thompson, J. B. and H. O. Thompson. *Ethics in Nursing*. New York: Macmillan, 1981.

VanDeVeer, Donald. "Paternalism and Subsequent Consent." *Canadian Journal of Philosophy* 9, 4 (1979): 631–642.

VanDeVeer, Donald. *Paternalistic Intervention*. Princeton, NJ: Princeton University Press, 1986.

Weirich, Paul. "Utility Tempered with Equality." *Nous* 17 (1983): 371–381.

Wikler, Daniel. "Paternalism and the Mildly Retarded." *Philosophy and Public Affairs* 8, 4 (1979): 377–392.

Index